Pain Management:
Principles and Practice

First Edition

**WESTERN®
SCHOOLS**

By
Cas Cahill, MS, CNS, ARNP

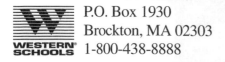

P.O. Box 1930
Brockton, MA 02303
1-800-438-8888

ABOUT THE AUTHOR

Cas Cahill, MS, CNS, ARNP, has specialized in Pain and Headache Management for close to twenty years. She's a longstanding member of the American Pain Society and its' Pediatric Pain subcommittee, the International Association for the Study of Pain and The American Academy of Pain Management. Cas has an extensive expertise in all areas of pain management, including but not limited to cancer, pediatric and burn pain. Ms. Cahill, an Advanced Registered Nurse Practitioner and Clinical Nurse Specialist in Pain Management, is self-employed as a Pain Management Consultant and is a member of the Clinical Faculty of the University of South Florida College of Nursing.

Ms. Cahill is also active in the area of headache management and has been both clinical trial coordinator and co-investigator in numerous nation-wide pharmacological studies. Ms. Cahill also specializes in the development of paradigms for the evaluation of outcomes related to Pain & Headache Management Programs. A paper Ms. Cahill co-authored, "A Paradigm for the Quantitative Evaluation of Headache Treatment Outcomes," was an invited part of the prestigious International Headache Research Symposium in Denmark and was selected for publication as a chapter in the textbook *Frontiers in Migraine Research.*

As an educator and national consultant, Ms. Cahill assists in the development and establishment of pain management and headache programs and services in hospitals and physician practices. Cas has been proactive in educating nurses by developing curriculum on pain and headache management for graduate level nursing programs. She also serves as an expert witness in medical/legal cases involving pain management and related pharmacology.

Copy Editor: Jackie Bonham, MSN, RN

Indexer: Sylvia Coates

Typesetter: Kathy Johnson

ISBN: 978-1-57801-076-9

IMPORTANT: Read these instructions *BEFORE* proceeding!

Enclosed with your course book you will find the FasTrax® answer sheet. Use this form to answer all the final exam questions that appear in this course book. If you are completing more than one course, be sure to write your answers on the appropriate answer sheet. Full instructions and complete grading details are printed on the FasTrax instruction sheet, also enclosed with your order. Please review them before starting. *If you are mailing your answer sheet(s) to Western Schools, we recommend you make a copy as a backup.*

ABOUT THIS COURSE

A "Pretest" is provided with each course to test your current knowledge base regarding the subject matter contained within this course. Your "Final Exam" is a multiple choice examination. **You will find the exam questions at the end of each chapter.** Some smaller hour courses include the exam at the end of the book.

In the event the course has less than 100 questions, leave the remaining answer boxes on the FasTrax answer sheet blank. **Use a <u>black pen</u> to fill in your answer sheet.**

A PASSING SCORE

You must score 70% or better in order to pass this course and receive your Certificate of Completion. Should you fail to achieve the required score, we will send you an additional FasTrax answer sheet so that you may make a second attempt to pass the course. Western Schools will allow you three chances to pass the same course…*at no extra charge!* After three failed attempts to pass the same course, your file will be closed.

RECORDING YOUR HOURS

Please monitor the time it takes to complete this course using the handy log sheet on the other side of this page. See below for transferring study hours to the course evaluation.

COURSE EVALUATIONS

In this course book you will find a short evaluation about the course you are soon to complete. This information is vital to providing the school with feedback on this course. The course evaluation answer section is in the lower right hand corner of the FasTrax answer sheet marked "Evaluation" with answers marked 1–25. Your answers are important to us, please take five minutes to complete the evaluation.

On the back of the FasTrax instruction sheet there is additional space to make any comments about the course, the school, and suggested new curriculum. Please mail the FasTrax instruction sheet, with your comments, back to Western Schools in the envelope provided with your course order.

TRANSFERRING STUDY TIME

Upon completion of the course, transfer the total study time from your log sheet to question #25 in the Course Evaluation. The answers will be in ranges, please choose the proper hour range that best represents your study time. You MUST log your study time under question #25 on the course evaluation.

EXTENSIONS

You have 2 years from the date of enrollment to complete this course. A six (6) month extension may be purchased. If after 30 months from the original enrollment date you do not complete the course, *your file will be closed and no certificate can be issued.*

CHANGE OF ADDRESS?

In the event you have moved during the completion of this course please call our student services department at 1-800-618-1670 and we will update your file.

A GUARANTEE TO WHICH YOU'LL GIVE HIGH HONORS

If any continuing education course fails to meet your expectations or if you are not satisfied in any manner, for any reason, you may return it for an exchange or a refund (less shipping and handling) within 30 days. Software, video and audio courses must be returned unopened.

Thank you for enrolling at Western Schools!

WESTERN SCHOOLS
P.O. Box 1930
Brockton, MA 02303
(800) 438-8888
www.westernschools.com

Pain Management: Principles and Practice

WESTERN® SCHOOLS
P.O. Box 1930
Brockton, MA 02303

Please use this log to total the number of hours you spend reading the text and taking the final examination (use 50-min hours).

Date	Hours Spent
_____	_____
_____	_____
_____	_____
_____	_____
_____	_____
_____	_____
_____	_____
_____	_____
_____	_____
_____	_____
_____	_____
_____	_____
_____	_____

TOTAL [   ]

Please log your study hours with submission of your final exam. To log your study time, fill in the appropriate circle under question 25 of the FasTrax® answer sheet under the "Evaluation" section.

PLEASE LOG YOUR STUDY HOURS WITH SUBMISSION OF YOUR FINAL EXAM. Please choose which best represents the total study hours it took to complete this 30 hour course.

A. less than 25 hours

B. 25–28 hours

C. 29–32 hours

D. greater than 32 hours

Pain Management: Principles and Practice

WESTERN SCHOOLS' NURSING CONTINUING EDUCATION EVALUATION

Instructions: Mark your answers to the following questions with a black pen on the "Evaluation" section of your FasTrax® answer sheet provided with this course. You should not return this sheet. Please use the scale below to rate the following statements:

A Agree Strongly	**C Disagree Somewhat**
B Agree Somewhat	**D Disagree Strongly**

The course content met the following education objectives:

1. Cited statistics related to chronic pain in the United States, identified diseases that place the patient at risk for pain and differentiated between chronic and acute pain.

2. Described the impact patient and professional variables have on pain its treatment and identified the role that regulatory issues and fear of addiction have on the treatment of pain.

3. Specified how myths and misconceptions can impact pain and described two types of pain assessment tools.

4. Identified the primary elements of the peripheral and central nervous system related to pain, described the primary pain mechanisms, and cited the primary pain neurotransmitter.

5. Described the pharmacologic options for the management of pain and identified non-opioid analgesics, the potential organ effects of NSAID's, and three adjuvant's that may be used for pain management.

6. Described the mechanism of action of and receptors for opioids and differentiated between addiction, tolerance and dependence.

7. Listed the opioids indicated for management of mild to severe acute and chronic pain, described the differences between the sustained and immediate release preparations and identified the nursing interventions for managing the patient receiving opioids.

8. Cited non-pharmacological and psychological interventions for pain management and identified indications for therapeutic exercise is indicated and noted the role of biofeedback in pain management.

9. Differentiated between chronic and acute pain and described the treatment paradigm and interventions for chronic pain.

10. Discussed the role of nerve blocks in acute and chronic pain, as well as, nursing interventions for patients receiving nerve blocks and differentiated between sympathetic and non-sympathetic nerve blocks.

11. Identified populations at high risk for inadequate pain management and/or severe or chronic/re-current pain and described a treatment approach unique to each population.

12. Described the scope of pain from cancer pain syndromes resulting from cancer and nursing interventions directed at care of the patient with cancer pain.

13. Described a paradigm for the treatment of cancer pain and both pharmacologic and non-pharmacologic interventions for cancer pain management.

14. Described acute and recurrent pain states, with related nursing interventions.

15. Described the origin of the JCAHO Pain Management Standards, the focus of each of the six pain management chapters and analyzed applications of the standards to clinical practice situations with delineation of various nursing roles within practice settings.

16. This offering met my professional education needs.

17. The objectives met the overall purpose/goal of the course.

18. The course was generally well written and the subject matter explained thoroughly. (If no, please explain on the back of the FasTrax instruction sheet.)

19. The content of this course was appropriate for home study.

20. The final examination was well written and at an appropriate level for the content of the course.

Please complete the following research questions in order to help us better meet your educational needs. Pick the ONE answer which is most appropriate.

21. What was the SINGLE most important reason you chose this course?
   A. Low price
   B. New or newly revised course
   C. High interest/Required course topic
   D. Number of contact hours needed

22. Where do you work? (If your place of employment is not listed below, please leave this question blank.)
   A. Hospital
   B. Medical clinic/Group practice/ HMO/Office setting
   C. Long term care/Rehabilitation facility/Nursing home
   D. Home health care agency

23. Which field do you specialize in?
   A. Medical/Surgical
   B. Geriatrics
   C. Pediatrics/Neonatal
   D. Other

24. For your last renewal, how many months BEFORE your license expiration date did you order your course materials?
   A. 1–3 months
   B. 4–6 months
   C. 7–12 months
   D. Greater than 12 months

25. **PLEASE LOG YOUR STUDY HOURS WITH SUBMISSION OF YOUR FINAL EXAM.** Please choose which best represents the total study hours it took to complete this 30 hour course.
   A. less than 25 hours
   B. 25–28 hours
   C. 29–32 hours
   D. greater than 32 hours

CONTENTS

Evaluation v

Pretest xix

Introduction xxiii

Chapter 1 **Overview: The Problem of Pain: An Overview** 1

    Introduction 1

    The Problem 1

        Prevalence of Non-Cancer Pain in America 2

        Disease States Associated with Pain 2

        Prevalence of Pain in Malignant Disease 2

    Barriers to Pain Management 3

        The Cost of Chronic Pain 3

        Litigation 3

        Definitions 4

    Nursing Approach 4

        Pain Through a Sensory-Reactive Paradigm 4

    Exam Questions 7

Chapter 2 **Pain as a Subjective Phenomenon** 9

    Introduction 9

    Variables 10

        Patient Variables 10

            Ethnicity 10

            Age 11

            Gender 12

            Meaning of the Pain 12

            Compliance 13

        Health Professional Variables 13

            Knowledge Deficit 14

            Regulatory Barriers to Adequate Pain Management 14

                Synopsis of Regulatory Impact 15

            Fear of Addiction 15

                Supportive Studies 15

            Clarification of Terms 16

        Summary 16

        Exam Questions 17

Chapter 3 **Pain Assessment** 21

    Introduction 21

        Pain Management Myths 21

    Pain Assessment 21

Three Truths of Pain Assessment 22

Process of the Pain Assessment 22

Pain Assessment Instruments 23

Pain Scales 23

Numeric Scale 23

Variables 23

Choosing a Pain Scale 24

Pain Assessment Tools/Instruments 24

The McGill Pain Questionnaire (MPQ) 24

The Acute and Chronic Pain Form 24

Special Populations 24

Unresponsive Patients 27

Summary 27

Exam Questions 29

Chapter 4 **The Physiology of Pain** **31**

Introduction 31

Major Structures 31

Neurons 31

Spinal Cord 32

Brain 32

Anatomy and Physiology of Pain 33

Transduction 33

Transmission 33

WIND-UP 35

Neurotransmitters 35

Modulation 35

Gate Control Theory 35

Summary 36

Exam Questions 37

Chapter 5 **Non-Opioid Analgesics and Adjuvants** **39**

Introduction 39

Non-steroidal Anti-Inflammatory Drugs (NSAIDs) 39

Mechanism of Action 40

Side Effects of NSAIDs 40

Gastrointestinal 40

Coagulation 41

Hepatotoxicity 41

Central Nervous System (CNS) Effects 41

Bronchial Effects 42

Indications for Use 42

Cancer Pain 42

Post-operative Pain 42

Back Pain 42

Analgesic Adjuvant Agents 42

   Antidepressants 44

      Mechanism of Action 44

      Indications 44

      Primary Effects 44

      Side Effects 44

      Administration 45

   Anti-Epileptic Drugs 45

      Mechanism of Action 45

      Indications 46

   Benzodiazepines 46

   Psychostimulants 47

   Lidocaine 47

   Capsaicin 47

   Steroids 47

   Antispasmodics 47

   Botulinum Toxin 48

      Pharmacology of Botulinum Toxin 48

      Indications 48

      Serendipitous Discovery of Botulinum Toxin Type A for Migraines 48

      Botulinum Toxin Type A for Headaches 48

      Botulinum Toxin Type A for Chronic Facial Pain 48

      Documentation 49

   Herbal Agents 49

Nursing Implications 49

   TCAs and AEDs 49

   Botulinum Toxin 51

   Antispasmodics 51

Exam Questions 53

Chapter 6 **Managing Pain With Opioids: Part One** **55**

Introduction 55

Mechanism of Action 55

   Opioid Receptors 56

   Metabolism 56

   Tolerance 57

   Incomplete Cross-Tolerance 57

   Pseudotolerance 57

   Diversion 58

   Dependence 58

   Addiction 58

   Role of the Nurse 59

Exam Questions 61

Chapter 7 **Managing Pain With Opioids: Part Two** **63**

Introduction 63

Opioid Dosing 63

Routes of Administration 63

Oral 64

Rectal 64

Parenteral 64

Absorption 66

Ceiling Effect 66

Intraspinal 66

Delivery Systems 66

Patient Controlled Epidural Analgesia (PCEA) 66

Medications 66

Nursing Implications 66

Pain Cocktails 68

Nursing Implications 68

Organ System Effects 69

Central Nervous System 69

Opioid Analgesics 70

Legal Requirements 70

Most Commonly Used Opioids 70

Opioid Data 70

Nursing Interventions for Patients Receiving Opioids 73

General Nursing Guidelines 74

Exam Questions 75

Chapter 8 **Non-Pharmacological Approaches to Pain Management** **77**

Introduction 77

Physical Therapy 78

TENS Unit 78

Mechanism of Action 78

Heat/Cold 79

Orthoses/Assistive Devices 79

Case Example 79

Diathermy/Cryotherapy 79

Exercise 80

Biofeedback and Relaxation Therapy 81

The Procedure 81

Techniques 81

Imagery 81

Progressive Muscle Relaxation 82

Deep Breathing 82

Distraction 82

Elements of Biofeedback 82

Muscle Re-Education 82

Headache Program 83

Pain Management Muscle Education 83

Psychological Therapy 83

Introduction 83

Psychology and Pain 83

Cognitive-Behavioral Techniques 84

Psycho-Educational Groups 84

Selected Psychological and Biofeedback Interventions 84

Psychometric Instruments 84

Summary 85

Acupuncture 85

Nursing Interventions 85

Summary 86

Exam Questions 87

Chapter 9 **Chronic Pain and Related Syndromes** **89**

Overview 89

Philosophy of Chronic Pain Treatment 90

Outcomes 90

Pathogenesis of Chronic Pain 90

Treatment Approaches to Chronic Pain 90

Types of Pain Programs 91

Multidisciplinary Program 91

Modality Oriented Clinic 91

Syndrome Oriented Clinic 91

Treatment Components 91

Physical Therapy 92

Psychological Therapy 92

Occupational Therapy (OT) 92

Biofeedback and Relaxation Therapy 92

Intensity of Treatment 92

Pharmacotherapeutics 93

Chronic Pain Syndromes 95

Chronic Back Pain 95

Types of Chronic Low Back Pain 95

Facet Disease 95

Degenerative Disc Disease (DDD) 95

Herniated Disc 95

Spinal Stenosis 97

Treatment 97

Case Study 97

   History 97

   Treatment Course 97

   Surgery 97

   Outcome 98

   Psychosocial Data 98

   Treatment 98

   Pain Management Treatment Plan 98

   Occupational Therapy 99

   Outcomes 99

Reflex Sympathetic Dystrophy Syndrome (RSD/CRPS) 99

   Pathogenesis 99

   Stages of RSD/CRPS 100

      Stage I 100

      Stage II 100

      Stage III 101

   Signs and Symptoms 101

   Treatment 101

   Summary 101

Neuropathic Pain 102

   Mechanisms 102

      Etiology 102

      Characteristics of the Pain 102

Trigeminal and Post-Herpetic Neuralgias 102

   Treatment 103

      Phantom Limb Pain 103

Summary 106

Exam Questions 107

Chapter 10 **Nerve Blocks** **109**

Introduction 109

Non-Sympathetic Nerve Blocks 110

   Trigger Point Injections 110

      Nursing Interventions 110

   Greater Occipital Nerve Blocks 110

      Nursing Interventions 110

   Epidural Nerve Blocks/Analgesia 110

   Patient Candidacy 111

   Environment 111

   The Procedure 111

   Agents 111

      Nursing Interventions 111

      Infusion Systems 112

        Therapeutic Effects 113

        Side-Effects 113

    Sympathetic Nerve Blocks 114

        Stellate Ganglion Block 114

        Lumbar Sympathetic Block 114

        Celiac Plexus Blocks 114

            Nursing Interventions 115

    Spinal Cord Stimulation (SCS) 115

        Procedure 116

            Nursing Interventions 117

    Summary 117

    Exam Questions 119

Chapter 11 **Management of Pain In Specialized Populations** **121**

    Introduction 121

    Pain From Burns 121

        Pain Mechanisms 122

        Causes of Pain 122

        Factors Impacting Burn Injury Pain 122

            Challenges of Burn Pain Management 123

    Case Presentation 123

        Extent of Injuries 124

        Treatment 124

        Psychosocial Data 124

        Coping Mechanisms 124

        Characteristics/Location of Pain 124

        Analysis of Treatment Plan 124

        New Treatment Plan 125

        Course of Treatment 125

        General Treatment Principles 125

    Pain in Geriatric Patients 125

        Barriers to Pain Management 126

        Supportive Research 126

        Pain Assessment in the Elderly 127

        Pharmacological Considerations 127

        General Nursing Principles 128

    Pain in Pediatric Patients 128

        Barriers to Pain Management 128

        Pain Assessment in Children 129

            Faces Pain Scale 129

            Study Design 130

            Study Results 130

        Procedure-Related Pain 130

Selected Interventions 131

TENS Unit 131

Neonates 131

Children and Adolescents 131

Pain-Related Research 132

Nursing Guidelines 132

Developmental Approach 132

Family Role 132

General Treatment Principles 132

Pain in Patients with AIDS and HIV 133

Incidence and Prevalence of Pain 133

Barriers to Pain Management 134

General Treatment Principles 134

Summary 134

Exam Questions 135

Chapter 12 **Patients with Pain from Cancer** **137**

Scope of Cancer Pain 137

Barriers to Cancer Pain Management 138

Healthcare Barriers 138

Patient Barriers to Effective Pain Management 139

Mechanisms of Cancer Pain 139

Types/Causes of Pain With Cancer 139

Etiology of Cancer Pain 140

Characteristics of Pain in Cancer Pain Syndromes 140

Pain Due to Tumor Involvement 140

Vertebral Body 140

Peripheral Nerve Syndromes 142

Plexopathies 142

Leptomeningeal Metastases 143

Pancreatic Cancer Pain 143

Pain Due to Cancer Treatment 143

Chemotherapy 143

Radiation Therapy 143

Postsurgical Pain Syndromes 143

Assessment of Cancer Pain 144

Pain and Suffering 144

Psychological State 144

Depression 144

Anxiety 144

Fatigue and Sleeplessness 144

Pain 145

Acute Versus Chronic 145

        Constant or Intermittent 145
        Location 145
        Intensity 145
        Characteristics 145
        Ameliorating/Intensifying Factors 145
    Establish Goals 145
  Types of Patients with Pain From Cancer 146
  Nursing Interventions and Treatment Considerations 146
    Patients with Acute Cancer-Related Pain 146
    Patients with Chronic Cancer-Related Pain 148
    Patients with Pre-Existing Chronic Pain and Cancer-Related Pain 148
    Patients with a History of Drug Abuse and Cancer-Related Pain 148
    Dying Patients with Cancer-Related Pain 149
  Summary 149
  Exam Questions 151
Chapter 13 **Cancer Pain Management** **153**
  Managing Cancer Pain 153
    Pain Management Team 154
  WHO Analgesic Ladder 154
  Pharmacological Therapy 155
    Analgesics 155
      Introduction 155
    Non-Steroidal Anti-inflammatory Agents 155
    Opioids 156
      Selecting the Agent 156
      Side Effects 156
      Constipation 157
      Opioids to Avoid 157
    Delivery Options 157
      Oral 157
      Conversions 157
      Transdermal 158
      Rectal 158
      Parenteral 158
      Spinal Route 159
  Adjuvants 160
    Antidepressants 160
    Anti-Epileptic Drugs 160
    Benzodiazepines 161
    Psychostimulants 161
    Lidocaine 161
    Steroids 161

Invasive Techniques 161

Non-Pharmacological Approaches to Cancer Pain 162

   Physiatric 162

   Psychologic 162

      Meaning of the Pain 163

Summary 163

Exam Questions 165

Chapter 14 **Acute and Recurrent Pain** **167**

Introduction 167

Post-Operative Pain 167

   Factors Influencing Post-Operative Pain 168

   Physiology and Pathophysiology of Post-Operative Pain 168

   Ambulatory Surgery 168

   Preemptive Analgesia 169

   Effective Management of Post-Operative Pain 169

      Pharmacological Agents 169

      Non-Pharmacologic Interventions 170

   Nursing Interventions 172

   Summary 172

Pain from Sickle Cell Disease 172

   Incidence and Characteristics of Pain 173

   Treatment 173

   Nursing Interventions 173

Headaches 173

   International Headache Society (IHS) Criteria 174

      Migraine Without Aura 174

   Incidence and Prevalence 174

   Pathogenesis 174

      Menstrual Migraine 175

      Treating Menstrual Migraine 175

   Phases of Migraine 176

   Evaluating Migraine Headaches 177

   Treating Migraine Headaches 177

   Stratified Approach 178

   Treatment Options 178

      Prophylactic Treatment 178

      Abortive Treatment 178

   Rebound Headache 179

   Treatment of Rebound Headache 179

   Nursing Role 179

      IV Protocols 179

   Outcomes in Headache Management 179

Summary 181

Exam Questions 183

Chapter 15 **Organizational and Professional Issues** **185**

Introduction 185

Organizations Respond to the Problem of Undertreated Pain 185

Joint Commission of the Accreditation of Health Organizations (JCAHO) Responds 186

JCAHO Standards 186

Settings 186

Documents 186

Implementation 187

Overview 187

Expectations 187

Providers 187

Patients 187

Organizations 188

Examples of Implementation 188

Rights and Ethics 188

Assessment of Persons with Pain 189

Care of Persons With Pain 189

Education of Persons With Pain 189

Continuum of Care 189

Improving Organizational Performance 189

Organizational Guidelines 190

Nursing Practice in Pain Management 190

Professional Roles in Pain Management 190

Primary Care Setting 190

Secondary Care Setting 190

Tertiary Care Settings 191

Case Managers 191

Hospice/Home Care Nurse 191

Exam Questions 193

Appendices **195**

Glossary **205**

Bibliography **209**

Index **227**

Pretest Key **236**

PRETEST

Begin by taking the pretest. Compare your answers on the pretest to the answer key (located in the back of the book). Circle those test items that you missed. The pretest answer key indicates the course chapters where the content of that question is discussed. Circle the answers to the pretest questions. Do not log pretest questions on the FasTrax answer sheet.

Next, read each chapter. Focus special attention on the chapters where you made incorrect answer choices. Exam questions are provided at the end of each chapter so that you can assess your progress and understanding of the material.

1. The percentage of cancer patients who could have their pain effectively managed is

    a. 90%.

    b. 80%.

    c. 60%.

    d. 40%.

2. According to the American Migraine Study II, the direct and indirect cost of migraine has been estimated at

    a. 7 billion dollars per year.

    b. 10 billion dollars per year.

    c. 13 billion dollars per year.

    d. 15 billion dollars per year.

3. Addiction

    a. is synonymous with dependence.

    b. will be present to side effects concomitant to analgesic effects.

    c. does not occur in cancer pain.

    d. is rare in patients on opioids.

4. Special populations, with respect to pain assessment, are

    a. elderly, professionals and children.

    b. children, elderly and professionals.

    c. elderly, sedated and children.

    d. children, professionals and sedated.

5. A function of the nurse in the assessment of pain is to

    a. know and share facts.

    b. demonstrate bias.

    c. control the process.

    d. defer to the physician.

6. 5HT is

    a. a neurotransmitter.

    b. an enkephalin.

    c. an opioid.

    d. a dendrite.

7. Opioids have the side effect of constipation through binding with

    a. receptors in the CNS.

    b. metabolites in the CNS.

    c. receptors in the periphery.

    d. receptors in the intestines.

8. Meperidine is indicated for

    a. cancer pain.

    b. chronic pain.

    c. acute pain of greater than seven days duration.

    d. acute pain of seven days or less duration.

9. Your peer is caring for a comatose patient and notes an area of lumbar spasm. A suggestion is made to place a heating pad on the area. You respond by informing the nurse that

   a. the use of heat or cold may be harmful in a non-responsive patient.

   b. ice would be better.

   c. a combination of heat followed by ice would be better.

   d. a combination of ice followed by heat would be better.

10. Differences in anesthesia and analgesia are primarily related to

    a. site of action and agent used.

    b. epidural space utilization.

    c. diagnosis of the patient.

    d. whether an anesthesiologist performs the procedure.

11. The administration of an anesthetic into the epidural space is

    a. within the scope of RN practice.

    b. within the scope of RN practice in a pain clinic.

    c. outside the scope of RN practice.

    d. within the scope of an RN credentialed by the hospital.

12. When assisting with a painful procedure in a child, the nurse should

    a. advise the parents not to be present.

    b. set up for the procedure in the patient's room.

    c. plan to use distraction techniques.

    d. tell the parents that as the procedure is brief, no analgesia is needed.

13. The best approach to opioid induced constipation is to

    a. have the patient use daily enemas.

    b. avoid the use of opioids.

    c. control for it.

    d. use daily suppositories.

14. What side effect of tricyclic antidepressants makes them contraindicated in a patient with prostatic hypertrophy?

    a. decreased B/P

    b. urinary retention

    c. dizziness

    d. dry mouth

15. The route of choice for opioid administration is

    a. parenteral.

    b. oral.

    c. transdermal.

    d. rectal.

16. Patient controlled analgesia (PCA) can be beneficial for the patient in pain who

    a. is scheduled for physical therapy.

    b. has chronic non-malignant pain.

    c. who is comatose.

    d. who is paralyzed.

17. Chronic pain is

    a. time limited.

    b. always associated with a clear etiology.

    c. a disease.

    d. a symptom.

18. In using opioids for cancer-related pain, the nurse should know that

    a. higher doses should be reserved for end stage pain.

    b. escalating doses can rapidly lead to addiction.

    c. the agent and dosage needed to effect analgesia should be used.

    d. opioids are the last resort.

19. Triptans as a class are effective in the management of

    a. just the pain from migraine.

    b. the pain and associated symptoms of migraine.

    c. just the nausea and vomiting from migraine.

    d. just the aura of migraine.

20. The Joint Commission for the Accreditation of Healthcare Organizations (JCAHO) has mandated that pain will be addressed in

    a. all patient care settings.

    b. post operative settings.

    c. cancer care settings.

    d. inpatient settings alone.

INTRODUCTION

Over the past several decades significant gains have been made in the field of pain management. There is a better understanding of its neurophysiological mechanisms along with an appreciation of the systems involved in pain states that historically have been disabling. This understanding has led to both the development of new pharmacotherapeutic agents and new indications for the use of existing agents.

An appreciation of the relevance of psychosocial factors in pain management and the advent of pain management as a specialty have made pain management a realistic goal in healthcare. Yet, effective pain management doesn't happen. The truth is, patients continue to suffer, often at the expense of their dignity, with drawers full of narcotics on hand.

It is the nurse who assesses the patient's pain and serves as an information conduit between the patient and others involved in prescribing and providing interventions designed to ameliorate the problem. As a profession, nursing has the potential to make the greatest difference in the management of pain. Unfortunately, pain-related myths and misconceptions pervade the nursing profession with a deleterious impact on nursing practice. In order to effect change, nursing practice must change.

This state-of-the-art publication is written by a nurse for nurses. The curriculum is designed to take the learner from basic pain management principles to the application of said principles in a variety of settings for a variety of diagnoses.

Over a thousand years ago, the philosopher St. Augustine declared, "The greatest evil is physical pain." The nurse who has cared for a burn victim; endeavored to make a dying patient's last days comfortable; or watched a child suffer through a sickle cell crisis would be hard pressed to dispute this declaration. In this publication, nurses now have a valuable adjunct to their clinical practice; nurses can make a difference!

CHAPTER 1

THE PROBLEM OF PAIN:
AN OVERVIEW

CHAPTER OBJECTIVE

Upon completion of this chapter, the reader will be able to cite statistics related to chronic pain in the United States, identify diseases that place the patient at risk for pain and differentiate between chronic and acute pain.

LEARNING OBJECTIVES

After studying this chapter, the learner will be able to

1. recognize the incidence and prevalence of pain in the general population.

2. recall the percentage of patients with unmanaged pain from cancer.

3. cite the incidence of pain in patients with AIDS.

4. identify one organization that is addressing the problem of under-treated pain.

5. list two possible contributing factors to the problem of under-treated pain.

INTRODUCTION

An age old problem—written of by poets, analyzed by philosophers, challenged by physicians and now litigated by lawyers—pain continues to be a controversial healthcare concern. Healthcare professionals know how to treat pain, are equipped to assess pain but by and large, pain is ignored. This chapter will address the incidence and prevalence of some common pain states but does not by any means hope to cover the myriad elements of this challenging, complex, sensory-reactive phenomena called PAIN.

THE PROBLEM

Despite technological advances made in medicine during the latter half of the 20th century, little has been done to address pain.

- At any given point in time, one-half of all Americans have experienced some kind of pain within the previous two weeks.

- Some 50 million people have disabling chronic pain.

- 16% of U.S. households have someone who suffers from severe chronic pain.

- One in five patients with cancer has uncontrolled pain.

- Although pain can be relieved in up to 90% of cancer patients, fewer than 50% receive adequate treatment (American Pain Foundation, 1999; Bonica, 1990; Ahmedzai, 1997).

Prevalence of Non-Cancer Pain in America

Despite astounding advances in medical research leading to a host of new pain medications over the past few decades, too much pain goes unrelieved. The American Pain Society (APS), the American Academy of Pain Management (AAPM) and Janssen Pharmaceutica commissioned a survey to evaluate the prevalence of chronic pain in America (American Pain Society, 2002). The results of the survey were interesting, with 805 individuals responding. The study disclosed that:

- Despite the millions of dollars spent annually to treat pain, four out of every ten persons with moderate to severe pain report their pain relief is inadequate.

- Four out of ten respondents with moderate to severe chronic pain reported that their pain was out of control.

- More than 50% of these patients had been experiencing pain for at least five years.

Birse and Landers (1998) revealed interesting findings in their clinical study of randomized chronic pain patients. They found that people in chronic pain were more likely to rate their general health as poor than people not in pain.

While these studies were specific to patients with chronic pain, unmanaged pain is present in the general public. The Mayday Fund Survey on public attitudes about pain and analgesics reported that 71% of more than 1,000 respondents avoided calling the doctor when in pain; 46% of respondents avoided any analgesic medication until the pain "got bad," while 35% avoided medication until the pain was unbearable (Bostrom, 1996).

Disease States Associated with Pain

A number of non-malignant disease states are also associated with significant pain. These include but are not limited to the following:

- **Back pain** has a general yearly prevalence of 15–20% of the American population. Back pain is the second most common reason for visits to primary care physicians and the most common cause of disability for people under the age of 45 (Andersson, 1991).

- **Arthritis** afflicts nearly 43 million Americans (Arthritis Foundation, 1999) with approximately 2.5 million people suffering from rheumatoid arthritis (Arthritis Foundation, 1998) and 2 million people suffering from fibromyalgia (Arthritis Foundation, 1999).

- The **American Migraine Study II** estimated that 28 million Americans have severe migraine headaches. The impact of headaches on the economy in terms of direct and indirect costs is staggering, with an estimated 13 billion dollars lost per year as a result (Silberstein, Lipton & Goadsby, 2002b).

- **Osteoporosis and diabetes,** conditions that affect a considerable proportion of the population, are associated with painful sequelae:

  — Osteoporosis is responsible for more than 1.5 million painful bone fractures each year (Arthritis Foundation, 1998).

  — 60–70% of diabetics experience mild to severe forms of diabetic nerve damage which, in severe forms, can lead to significant disability (American Diabetes Association, 1999).

Prevalence of Pain in Malignant Disease

Pain treatment is inadequate in 84% of patients with AIDS and in 73% of advanced cancer patients admitted for palliative care (Field & Cassel, 1997; Brietbart, Rosenfeld, Passik, McDonald, Thaler & Portnoy 1996; Brescia, Portenoy, Ryan, Krasnoff & Gray, 1992). Thirty percent of cancer patients present with pain at the time of diagnosis (Levy, 1996); with chronic pain prevalent in 30–50% of patients undergoing active cancer therapy; and in

70–90% of patients with advanced disease (Portenoy & Lesage, 1999). Among cancer patients in pain, 40-50% rate their pain as moderate to severe, while 25–30% rate their pain as very severe (Bonica, 1990).

In the mid-1980s the World Health Organization (WHO) published clinical guidelines for cancer pain relief. The efficacy of the WHO guidelines was demonstrated in field tests in several different countries. Implementation of the guidelines has been shown to relieve pain for up to 90% of cancer patients (WHO, 1996). Despite the availability of the WHO guidelines and other high quality clinical guidelines for cancer pain relief, such as those issued by the American Pain Society (APS, 1999), pain from malignant disease remains a widespread problem.

BARRIERS TO PAIN MANAGEMENT

Despite dissemination of information regarding the importance of effective cancer pain management, along with published guidelines and standards, conclusions reached by the Outpatient Pain Needs Assessment Survey conducted by the Eastern Cooperative Oncology Group (ECOG) are as follows:

- Among cancer sub-specialists, significant variability exists in the quality of pain treatment of cancer patients, suggesting an even greater variance among physicians with specialized training (Cleeland et al., 1994).

- Minorities being treated at centers where their numbers were greatest were more likely to receive inadequate pain management than non-minorities at centers where their numbers were greatest (Cleeland et al., 1994).

- Published guidelines and standards have not had a positive impact on cancer pain management—many patients continue to experience

pain and/or receive inadequate analgesia (Cleeland et al., 1994).

State medical boards and state/federal legislation can impact pain management. Diversion of controlled substances designed for pain management is a real problem. Consequently, legal and regulatory policies have been adopted—primarily triplicate prescriptions and limits on the number of medication dosages that may be prescribed at one time (Field & Cassel, 1997).

The Cost of Chronic Pain

Pain accounts for a significant portion of the U.S. healthcare annual expenditure. Some of the direct costs associated with pain are listed below:

- At least 40 million patient visits are made to doctors each year for chronic pain treatment (Hendricks, 1999).

- At least 40 million Americans spend $4 billion for medication for chronic, recurrent headaches.

- More than $4 billion in lost income, productivity, and healthcare has been attributed to arthritis pain.

- Over $5 billion is spent annually in costs associated with low back pain.

Pain is also associated with significant indirect costs for the patient and the patient's family. Chronic pain can impair function, mood, and overall quality of life.

Litigation

In what has been viewed as a precedent-setting case in regard to changing perspectives in pain management, the Oregon Board of Medical Examiners disciplined a physician for under-treatment of pain in six patients (Barnett, 1999). This case was the first in the nation to take a stand against pain under-treatment instead of pain over-treatment. The outcome of the case was somewhat of a paradox in that the Oregon Board had been strict on physicians in the 1980s who were felt to be giving too much medication.

Definitions

Pain is defined as "an unpleasant sensory and emotional experience associated with actual or potential tissue damage or described in terms of such damage" (Federation of State Medical Boards of the United States, Inc., 1998).

"Acute pain is the normal, predicted physiological response to an adverse chemical, thermal, or mechanical stimulus and is associated with surgery, trauma, and acute illness. It is generally time-limited and is responsive to opioid therapy, among other therapies" (Federation of State Medical Boards of the United States, Inc., 1998).

Acute pain is of short duration, typically resulting from an accident, trauma, surgery, or other injury (Curtis, 1997).

- Acute pain usually resolves on its own as healing occurs.

- The patient experiencing acute pain may experience variations in vital signs and may exhibit signs of discomfort.

Chronic pain is not time-limited and may be associated with a long-term intractable medical condition or disease.

- Chronic pain may be associated with cancer or a chronic nonmalignant illness (i.e., arthritis, back pain, pain from nerve damage).

- Patients typically do not demonstrate clinical or physical signs of pain.

- Chronic pain rarely resolves spontaneously.

Pain management is:

- The systematic study of clinical and basic science and its application for the reduction of pain and suffering (American Academy of Pain Management [AAPM], 2002).

- A newly emerging discipline emphasizing an interdisciplinary approach with a goal of reduction of pain and suffering (AAPM, 2002).

- A team approach that includes patient and family (Joint Commission of the Accreditation of Health Organizations [JCAHO], 1999a).

Perhaps the most important component of the definition of pain management is the concept of a team approach to pain relief. In addition to healthcare professionals, the team must include the patient and, when appropriate, the patient's family. This tenet is supported in the recently developed revised Joint Commission of the Accreditation of Healthcare Organizations (JCAHO) Standards for Pain Management (Joint Commission of the Accreditation of Health Organizations [JCAHO], 1999b).

NURSING APPROACH

Each patient brings to the pain experience their history, gender, age, culture and socioeconomic status. As noted in this overview, pain continues to be a problem despite the advances in the basic science and pharmacology directed at solutions. How the nurse approaches the assessment and management of pain is an important factor. Irregardless of the practice setting, nurses can make a difference. Training has improved, but more must be done in order for nursing to make a difference in pain and its management.

Pain Through a Sensory-Reactive Paradigm

For too long nurses have been trained to approach pain in a stimulus-response paradigm or model, which infers that once the stimulus is removed the response will cease. For example, a patient has surgery and complains of pain. Nurses look to the physician's order for the prescribed analgesic and administer it. Now, the patient should have pain relief once the analgesic takes effect. The response (medication administration) has taken care of the stimulus (the pain).

When attempting to manage the patient's pain with such an approach, the nurse is not attempting to treat the **patient** in pain but attempting to treat the pain itself. Moreover, this approach limits the experience of pain to its sensory dimension and ignores the evaluative and temporal dimensions of pain.

The evaluative dimension of pain refers to the overall magnitude of the pain: Mild, moderate or severe. The temporal dimension of pain reflects the non-physical/sensory attributes of the patient, referring more to attributes of suffering, loss and the like.

A nurse who has been in practice for a long time knows that effective pain management is much more complex than this stimulus-response approach wherein a dose of medication always provides relief for the patient in pain. When pain is approached through a **sensory-reactive paradigm,** not only is the pain itself looked at but assessment of the patient in pain, as well.

If nurses are to be effective at managing the patient in pain, they must understand what makes each patient unique. When nurses approach the management of pain in a patient, they look past the pain, incorporating that sensory data into the assessment and then get to the reactive phenomenon of the pain. This is why every patient brings to the pain experience their unique history, perspective and reaction.

EXAM QUESTIONS

CHAPTER 1
Questions 1–5

1. The percentage of American households where someone is in severe, chronic pain is

   a. 10%.

   b. 12%.

   c. 14%.

   d. 16%.

2. What listed sequelae of osteoporosis place the patients at risk for pain?

   a. fractures

   b. bone spurs

   c. facet disease

   d. stenosis

3. The percentage of patients with AIDS who have unrelieved pain is

   a. 54%

   b. 64%.

   c. 84%.

   d. 94%.

4. The Oregon Medical Board has mandated that

   a. narcotics be used for cancer pain only.

   b. physicians must manage their patients' pain.

   c. medical marijuana may be used.

   d. methadone be used for opioid withdrawal management only.

5. According to the Levy study, the percentage of patients with cancer who presented with pain at the time of their diagnosis was

   a. 30%.

   b. 35%.

   c. 40%.

   d. 45%.

CHAPTER 2

PAIN AS A
SUBJECTIVE PHENOMENON

CHAPTER OBJECTIVE

Upon completion of this chapter, the reader will be able to recall the impact patient and professional variables have on pain and its treatment and identify the role that regulatory issues and fear of addiction have on the treatment of pain.

LEARNING OBJECTIVES

After studying this chapter, the learner will be able to

1. list three variables that put patients at risk for poor pain management.

2. identify two variables that impact pain and its treatment by professionals.

3. differentiate between addiction, tolerance and pseudoaddiction.

INTRODUCTION

When assessing pain and formulating a plan for its management, the nurse should have an understanding of the definition of pain put forth by the International Association for the Study of Pain (IASP) (Mersky & Bogwik, 1994). Why? In its definition, the IASP uses terms like "subjective," and "personal experience." Inherent in the IASP definition of pain is the cornerstone of the effective pain management; that pain is a personal, private and subjective event with complex reactions unique to the person experiencing it.

Persons in pain do not always know what to do with or how to respond to their pain. Patients may not understand their role in the management of their pain or that they even have a role, relying instead on the healthcare professional to handle it all. For example, patients may not request as needed (prn) pain medication believing that if they are to have medication it will be brought to them without their having to request it. At the point that the person in pain decides to involve another person in the experience, a social transaction between the patient and caregiver occurs. Therefore, in order for that transaction to be therapeutic, a positive relationship must exist between the patient and the healthcare provider(s) (Agency for Health Care Policy and Research, 1992). Few transactions have this truth in operation as does the transaction focused on the assessment and management of pain. The nurse, as the healthcare provider with the most patient contact, engages in social transactions with patients on a regular basis. As such, the nurse has the role of patient advocate, communication conduit and information source.

The challenge of affording quality care in the area of pain management is daunting enough in the face of the lack of knowledge, but when this knowledge deficit is coupled with attitudes that bias the practitioner against certain groups of patients, change can appear hopeless. A positive therapeutic relationship is not feasible in the presence of bias, inadequate or inaccurate knowledge and ineffective communication. There is a vast difference between knowledge and attitude. Knowledge can be impacted in a positive fashion and still not re-shape attitudes.

VARIABLES

Variables or elements of the person that make them unique, impact their reaction to pain. There are many patient variables that come into play when the nurse attempts pain management.

It is interesting to note that variables impact both the patient in pain as well as the healthcare professional charged with managing the patient in pain. Confusion surrounding inadequate or ineffective pain management may therefore result from patients' underreporting pain, having an inordinate fear of addiction or having the belief that pain is inevitable. The most common patient variables, elements that make each person unique within the context of pain, and variables that impact the health professional charged with managing pain in the patient, will be examined.

Patient Variables

For the purpose of this publication selected *patient variables* reported in the literature will be discussed. These include but are not limited to:

- Culture/Ethnicity
- Age
- Gender
- Meaning of the pain
- Compliance

It is important to note that ethnicity/gender, while out of the patient's control, are variables that place certain patients at higher risk for under-treatment or less than adequate management of their

pain than other patients. As noted in the following studies, minority patients in pain are treated differently than non-minority patients. It is important that this data be used by nurses to identify patients at risk for inadequate pain management and to be cognizant of what are often subconscious behaviors on the part of treating professionals.

Ethnicity

Each culture has its own perceptions, beliefs, and ways of defining and managing pain. It is known that ethnic and racial differences may cause variations in responses to treatment (Kudzma, 1992).

Researchers have examined the role of culture and ethnicity in pain and its management. An interesting study was conducted looking at how elderly Caucasian and African American patients handled pain. The researcher used the McGill Pain Questionnaire and found similarities and differences in pain perception between both groups. Pain descriptors, or words used to describe pain, were different in both groups with the term "nagging" as the only one used by both. Another finding was that African American patients used a larger variety of words to describe their pain (Johnson-Umezulike, 1999). Researchers in another study have documented that the more affective-motivational dimension of thermal pain may be more greatly influenced by ethnicity than the sensory component. In other words, a study of responses to thermal pain in African Americans and Whites found that the two groups did not differ in their ratings of heat pain intensity or threshold, but the African Americans found the heat pain more unpleasant than the Whites (Purdue Pharma, 2002b).

Another study evaluated the effects of temporal summation in 62 African American and 58 non-Hispanic Whites. In this study, a brief repetitive heat pulse in the pain range was delivered at an interval of less than three seconds. While the temperature of the stimulus is the same, it is perceived as hotter due to increasing responses of second order neurons in the spinal cord. Overall, the pain and unpleasantness ratings were higher in the African Americans than the Whites (Purdue Pharma, 2002b).

Studies have not been limited to Whites, Hispanics and African Americans. Koreans value emotional self-control. This can translate to stoicism. In these patients, the nurse should not assume that they will demonstrate pain behaviors (Abbott et al., 2002). They may hurt but not show it. Explain that pain is an expected symptom, and medication is available to help manage the pain. Analgesics, as well as other pain management interventions, should be offered.

What are the implications of studies of this sort for nursing practice? In addition to the interventions noted, nurses caring for patients with similar ethno-cultural backgrounds may want to use multi-dimensional pain assessment tools and provide a wide variety of pain descriptors in assisting patients in reporting their pain. It is important that patients using dramatic descriptors or complaining about the pain not be perceived as exaggerating to get more medication. This also underscores the important role that culture plays in the assessment of pain.

The Eastern Cooperative Oncology Group Minority Outpatient Pain Study (ECOG) was a large, prospective study with a two-fold aim: It evaluated the severity of cancer-related pain and the adequacy of prescribed analgesics.

The sample consisted of 281 minority outpatients with recurrent or metastatic cancer. Of the first group, there were 168 respondents and of the latter group, there were 180 respondents (Cleeland et al., 1997).

The results of this study were at the least alarming, demonstrating that:

- Patients receiving care at university centers that treat minorities were more likely to receive less than adequate pain relief (77%) than patients at centers that treated non-minority patients (52%).

- There was a trend toward under-medication in women, with 57% of the men under-treated versus 71% of the women.

- At least 50%, and in some centers almost 75%, of minority patients were not receiving quality care in the area of pain management.

Another study found evidence of the presence of a hierarchy in the amounts of medication prescribed for patient controlled analgesia (PCA) (Ng, Dimsdale, Rollnik & Shapiro, 1996). The hierarchy was as follows:

- Whites were ordered more opioids than Hispanics; and

- Blacks were ordered more than Hispanic or Asian patients.

An interesting outcome of this same study demonstrated that the amount of medication taken via PCA did not appear to be influenced upon by gender or culture. In other words, when the amounts of medication used were calculated, there was no significant difference between races or gender. This finding did not support the prescribing pattern of the physicians.

Age

Perception and expression of pain are influenced by a person's age, with patients in both ends of the age continuum at risk for inadequate pain management. Studies have shown that elderly patients are at risk for inadequate pain management, while infants and children have their pain poorly managed due to misconceptions regarding their perceptions of pain and the inability to communicate pain and needs for analgesia. One misconception is that infants and children do not feel pain as adults do. Stevens and Johnston (1994) documented physiological pain responses such as changes in heart rate and oxygen saturation levels, in premature infants receiving a heel-stick procedure. Term infants demonstrated the same responses.

Gender

The issue of women and pain is somewhat dualistic: Women respond to pain differently than men, and women with pain are treated differently than men. Women are at higher risk for the development of certain chronic pain disorders. Temporomandibular disorders (TMD), fibromyalgia and migraine headache predominantly affect women. These disorders are characterized by enhanced sensitivity to experimental pain stimuli (Symposium Spotlight, 2002a).

Yet another basic science study found that men are less sensitive to some modalities of experimental pain than women. Interestingly, the gender differences were detected for thermal (heat) pain only (Bragdon et al., 2002).

Contributing Variables to Gender Differences

Sex-related hormones may influence differences noted in responses to painful stimuli between men and women. Most studies have found that sensitivity to experimental pain stimuli is greater in women during the luteal or premenstrual phase of the menstrual cycle, compared to the follicular or postmenstrual phase.

Moreover, certain pain disorders exacerbate during the menstrual cycle, and it has been suggested that exogenous hormone use may be associated with increased pain severity (Symposium Spotlight, 2002a). This was borne out in another experimental pain study analyzing group differences in pain modulation. Researchers identified oral contraceptive use as a variable that contributed to pain (Bragdon et al., 2002).

Pain coping strategies may also play a role with respect to gender and pain responses. A study of patients with osteoarthritis disclosed that women

reported higher levels of disability and exhibited increased pain behavior compared to men (Symposium Spotlight, 2002a). Another study analyzed relationships between pain processing and gender. Data were collected and analyzed from a sample size of 967 women and 680 men with chronic pain. The researchers discovered that women reported higher pain-related frustration and fear. Women related pain to frustration more highly than men, who related pain more highly with depression and anxiety. An interesting and surprising finding was that pain-related emotions were more strongly related to pain in men than in women (Riley, Robinson, Wade, Myers & Price, 2001).

Interventions and Gender

The Eastern Cooperative Oncology Group Minority Outpatient Pain Study demonstrated a trend toward under-medication in women, with 71% of the women under-treated versus 57% of the men (P = 0.068) (Cleeland et al., 1997). In evaluating PCA prescription practices, Ng, Dimsdale, Rollnik and Shapiro (1996), noted that men were ordered to receive more pain medication than women.

Meaning of the Pain

Studies have shown that the meaning of pain has powerful implications on some patients. One researcher studied the meaning of pain in patients with low back pain. Patients with low back pain continually searched for causal explanations, and the pain altered their lifestyles and quality of life (Bowman, 1991).

Barkwell (1991) found that in patients with cancer, the perception of the pain impacted specific outcomes. In the groups studied, pain meant either a challenge, punishment or was perceived as the enemy. Subjects who perceived pain as a challenge had significantly lower pain and depression scores than those who perceived pain as punishment or as the enemy. Furthermore, the patients in the group who perceived pain as a challenge had higher coping scores than those who saw the pain as punishment or the enemy.

How the patient perceives their pain can have a dramatic impact on the pain. For example, to the patient with pain from cancer the pain may mean that death is near or that the cancer is spreading. The person with pain from a work-related injury may associate loss with the pain. In the injured worker who cannot return to their previous job, the pain may alter their self-concept.

Compliance

Several factors influence patient compliance to a medication regimen and any one, or a combination of these factors, may result in a lack of treatment efficacy or treatment failure. One factor is the presence of side effects. In fact, 80% of the patients in the following oncology study had difficulty with side effects. Another is a misconception regarding addiction, with patients fearing addiction if they take analgesics as prescribed.

Miakowski described a study that examined 'real-life problems" faced by 60 cancer patients and their families when attempting to implement a prescribed treatment regimen at home (Purdue Pharma, 2002a). A six-week program was implemented wherein nurses educated and supported the patients, all of whom had pain from bone metastasis, in putting the plan into effect. Out of this study, seven problems faced by patients in the implementation of the pain management program were identified. They included misunderstanding with respect to the medications ordered. In order for a treatment regimen to have its desired effects, the patient must adhere to or comply with the prescribed or recommended regimen. There are several basic nursing interventions that can have a positive impact on treatment outcomes. *Patient education* is one, *simplifying the treatment regimen* is another, and *assisting patients in accessing educational resources is yet a third.*

Facilitating the implementation of treatment programs that are congruent with the patient's financial resources is another intervention that the nurse can provide. For example, patients without insurance benefits who do not qualify for federal programs can be covered under certain local or county health care plans, subsidized by local sales tax. These types of plans pay for prescriptions but require that medications be in the plan's formulary. If the only sustained-release opioid that the plan will pay for is methadone, and a patient has been given a prescription for a month's supply of 20 mg Oxycontin® to be taken BID, that patient will have to pay over $200.00 out of pocket to have that prescription filled.

By reviewing written prescriptions or formalizing discharges with planning conferences, the nurse can monitor resources and control for situations before they become problematic. These efforts must be collaborative among healthcare systems, departments, teaching institutions, care providers, payors and patients and their families (Berg, Dischler, Wagner, Raia & Palmer-Shevlin, 1993).

Communicating in a manner that is relevant to the patient's background, educational level and comprehension along with identifying and addressing patient resources and concerns, also serves to enhance patient compliance. If they are to be executed, pain management treatment plans must be realistic, appropriate and feasible.

HEALTH PROFESSIONAL VARIABLES

If pain is to be managed, then pain management must be done intelligently and without bias, so an understanding of these variables and how they impact pain assessment and management is imperative. There are many variables that impact the healthcare professional with consequences on their pain management practices. The Agency for Health Care Policy and Research (AHCPR), (1994) and the American Academy of Pain Management (AAPM), (2002) and American Pain Society (APS), (1997), have identified the following healthcare professional variables:

• Low priority given to pain treatment.

• Inadequate reimbursement.

• Restrictive regulation of controlled substances.

• Problems with availability of or access to treatment.

For the purpose of this course, the three variables with the broadest reaching impact on the healthcare provider: Knowledge deficit, regulatory barriers and the fear of addiction/diversion will be addressed.

Knowledge Deficit

Healthcare professionals often have inadequate knowledge of pain management. Recently, one study reported that 48% of new graduates from accredited nursing programs spend four hours or less learning about pain and its management techniques (Ferrell, McCaffery & Ropchan, 1992). Another study of fourth semester baccalaureate nursing students demonstrated inadequate knowledge of pain management mechanisms, principles and pharmacology. The provision of an educational intervention had a positive impact on the knowledge base of the same students (Cahill, 1991). Knowledge deficit is not exclusive to the nursing profession as demonstrated by the following studies.

The results from the Eastern Cooperative Oncology Group (ECOG) study demonstrated physician barriers to adequate pain management (Von Roenn, Cleeland, Gonin, Hatfield & Pandya, 1993). Findings from the ECOG study demonstrated that:

• Only 51% of physicians stated that pain control in their own practices was good or very good.

• Approximately 31% of physicians indicated they would wait until the patient's estimated survival was six months or less before beginning maximal analgesic treatment.

• 76% of physicians pointed to poor pain assessment as the most important barrier to effective pain management.

A survey of 805 individuals, released by the APS, the AAPM, and Janssen Pharmaceutica revealed the following (American Pain Society, 1999):

• Four out of every ten persons with moderate-to-severe pain report their pain relief is inadequate—more than 50% of these patients had been experiencing pain for at least five years.

• Nearly one-half of patients had switched physicians at least once.

In this same study, patients perceived a knowledge deficit regarding pain management in their treating physicians. This led to problems with continuity of care in that among those with very severe pain, *29% had switched physicians three or more times. Of the 29%:*

• 42% changed because of too much pain.

• 31% switched because they felt their physician did not know enough about pain treatment.

• 29% changed because they thought their doctor was not taking their pain seriously.

• 27% switched because of their physician's unwillingness to treat their pain aggressively.

Yet, only 22% of the patients had been referred to a specialized pain treatment program or clinic.

Regulatory Barriers to Adequate Pain Management

State medical boards and state and federal legislation can affect how pain is managed. For example, concern regarding possible diversion of pain relief medications has resulted in adoption of legal and regulatory policies; primarily triplicate prescriptions and limits on the number of medication dosages that may be prescribed at one time. (Field & Cassel, 1997). Although these policies may limit drug diversion, they can also deter legitimate prescribing of opioids (Cooper, Czechowicz, Peterson & Molinari, 1992).

Physicians whose prescribed medications are diverted or misused may be held liable for deaths that result from their use. In the state of Florida, a physician was charged with manslaughter in four patient deaths (*Tampa Tribune,* 2002).

Synopsis of Regulatory Impact

- Anti-diversion policies
  - triplicate prescriptions
  - limits on the number of medication dosages that may be prescribed at one time
- Anti-addiction policies
  - laws, regulations, and medical board disciplinary policies based on a general antipathy toward drug use
- Fear of punitive action
  - regulatory scrutiny
  - disciplinary action
  - criminal prosecution

  (Field & Cassel, 1997)

Fear of Addiction

Unfortunately, diversion and drug abuse are real problems faced by each prescriber. Many physicians have cited concerns about adverse effects of and tolerance to analgesics as limiting factors in providing adequate pain relief (Von Roenn et al., 1993). Consequently, pain is treated conservatively by many physicians; in fact, 14% reported they would not provide a morphine-class opioid for a patient with severe pain, even following unsuccessful palliative therapy (Von Roenn et al., 1993). Fear of addiction can impede the appropriate management of pain through the use of controlled substances designed for this purpose.

Clinical experience shows that addiction is rare in patients treated for pain with opioids (Porter & Jick, 1980) and supports that the risk of addiction is extremely low in the typical patient with no prior history of drug abuse who is prescribed an opioid for a painful medical condition (Portenoy & Kanner, 1996).

Supportive Studies

- In 11,882 hospitalized patients who received at least one narcotic preparation, addiction was documented in less than 1% of patients who had no history of addiction (Porter & Jick, 1980).

- A study conducted in a bone marrow transplant unit documented that self-administration of opioids in a medical setting does not put patients at risk for addiction (Chapman & Hill, 1989).

It is important to note that addiction is a psychological and behavioral disorder. When pain relief is inadequate, a patient may become intensely focused on finding relief for pain (pseudoaddiction). In the presence of effective pain treatment, this behavior will resolve (American Society of Addiction Medicine, 1997). Patients who have been labeled as "drug seeking" are in reality "relief seeking."

Addiction, tolerance and physical dependence are terms that have come to be misconstrued by both the healthcare and patient populations. What has been termed addiction is often physical dependence or tolerance, both expected physiological consequences of opioid use. In addition to addiction, tolerance and dependence, there is also psuedotolerance as a term to be understood within the context of ethical pain management. Pseudotolerance may occur in the presence of disease progression as in the diagnosis of cancer.

Clarification of Terms

Addiction is a behavior associated with the compulsion to use opioids in a manner other than what they have been prescribed for.

Physical dependence is an expected result of opioid use and by itself, does not equate with addiction.

Tolerance is a physiologic state resulting from regular use of a drug in which an increased dosage is needed to produce the same effect.

There are a variety of factors other than addiction that might be impacting the patient's analgesic requirements. These are often excluded as possible reasons for patient behaviors, with addiction or diversion the "knee-jerk" explanation for patient behavior.

SUMMARY

Pain as a subjective experience poses unique challenges to the nurse who is charged with its assessment and treatment. Each patient brings with them their unique perceptions, explanations and means by which pain is expressed. Using this data can make the task of assessing and managing pain easier for the nurse. Developing a knowledge base related to culture and its impact on pain can assist in exemplifying nursing practice. The nurse in turn can use image objective, scientific approaches to the humanity that is experiencing pain and searching for its meaning and relief.

Variables that impact pain and its expression are numerous, but the nurse must recognize that some of those same variables operate within those charged with the assessment and treatment of pain. Knowledge is the key to meeting these unique challenges. Much has yet to be done if nurses are to understand this often perplexing phenomenon called pain.

EXAM QUESTIONS

CHAPTER 2
Questions 6–10

Please read the following case presentation and select the best answer to questions 6–8.

M.S. was a middle-aged female with a chief complaint of persistent left upper quadrant abdominal pain. She was employed in the housekeeping department of a large hospital and had been seen in Employee Health on numerous occasions over a period of years for work-related injuries. There were strong indications that secondary gain, time off with pay and a lighter work load played a role in her numerous complaints. There had never been any objective findings for her complaints of pain. M.S. was perceived as a problem employee and a problem patient.

For this new complaint of abdominal pain, she had been exhaustively and extensively worked up with blood work, CT imaging and a variety of gastrointestinal procedures prior to her referral to the pain clinic.

In her history, she reported a 70 pound weight loss but still weighed over 300 pounds with a height of 5'3". Review of systems was negative, apart from the weight loss and pain. She had a cholecystectomy in the distant past. Her surgical history was otherwise negative. Apart from non-referred tenderness on mild to moderate palpation of the abdomen under the ribs on the left, there were no significant findings on physical examination. Her short-acting narcotics were discontinued; she was placed on sustained-release morphine and adjuvants; referred to physical therapist for a trial of a TENS unit; and released to work. The goal was to begin a narcotic wean and maximize the adjuvants.

The pain was under satisfactory control for several months, but her narcotics could not be decreased. The patient returned for a follow-up visit reporting that her pain had increased, and she had lost 30 additional pounds. She requested "stronger pain pills."

Because of the increase in pain and continued unexplained weight loss, she was referred back to GI for another evaluation. The re-evaluation did not disclose an etiology to her pain or weight loss. In light of her morbid obesity, the weight loss was felt to be therapeutic.

Several months passed, and she presented with another 30–40 pound weight loss and stated that her pain was worse than ever. On this visit, she exhibited exaggerated pain behaviors of rocking and holding her stomach. She had a depressed affect. She requested "stronger pain pills" and to be placed on temporary total disability. An employee who lived near the patient shared that the patient lived nearby and was observed rocking on her porch, crying and holding her stomach in obvious pain. The woman stated that the patient's sister told her that the patient was up most nights, walking the house in agonizing abdominal pain.

The Nurse Practitioner conferred with the physician she worked with and discussed the case, sharing the opinion that something was being missed in this woman. This physician also examined the patient. She agreed to put the patient out of work and changed her analgesics to methadone at a higher than equivalent dose to the morphine.

Following the "gut feeling" that there was something very wrong that was not being picked up in this patient, the Nurse Practitioner ordered a repeat CT of the abdomen, a surgical consult for a diagnostic laproscopic evaluation and an anesthesia pain consultation for a celiac plexus block for added relief.

The pain clinic office telephoned the surgeon who had treated the patient in the past for her numerous work-related complaints, but he refused to see her again. The patient's sister called the next day and reported the patient was vomiting bile. The Nurse Practitioner instructed her to call an ambulance and have the patient brought to the emergency room and ask for the surgeon who had treated her in the past. The Nurse Practitioner then personally walked over to the surgeon's office and asked if she could see him about this patient.

The surgeon was convinced that this was just her typical "behavior" which over the years had not resulted in any pathology but did result in time off from work and job adjustments requested by the patient. He insisted that this was just more manipulation for time off from work and suggested that there may be a psychological component that was missed.

The Nurse Practitioner argued with the surgeon and insisted that the weight loss in the presence of the increasing pain warranted a laproscopic evaluation. He said that they did not do these procedures with negative workups very much any more, but the Nurse Practitioner refused to take no for an answer and insisted that the surgeon at least evaluate the patient, stressing the unexplained weight loss and reports by uninvolved observers of her pain behaviors.

He finally agreed to see her in the ER and did admit her for laporoscopic evaluation. The Nurse Practitioner went to see the woman the next day in her room. She was tearful and hugged and thanked the Nurse Practitioner for finally getting someone to investigate her complaints. She was receiving IV analgesics and was comfortable.

Unfortunately, the Nurse Practitioner's instincts were correct and the laproscopic evaluation revealed diffuse cancer throughout the entire abdominal cavity. It was in the form of very small tumors that were not detectable by CT and other imaging. The patient died within days of the surgery.

Select the best answer to each question.

6. What patient variable caused her concerns to be ignored?

   a. age

   b. use of opioids

   c. meaning of the pain

   d. employment situation

7. A primary issue from the MD's perspective was the

   a. patient's occupation.

   b. patient's age.

   c. previous pain history with the same patient.

   d. patient's insurance.

8. In requesting more pain medication, what was in operation?

   a. addiction

   b. physical dependence

   c. pseudoaddiction

   d. drug seeking behavior

9. In the Porter and Jick study, what was the incidence of addiction?

   a. 5%

   b. 3%

   c. less than 1%

   d. 8%

10. Tolerance

   a. is synonymous with dependence.

   b. can be confused with addiction.

   c. does not occur in cancer pain.

   d. is a predictor of addiction.

CHAPTER 3

PAIN ASSESSMENT

CHAPTER OBJECTIVE

Upon completion of this chapter, the reader will be able to specify how myths and misconceptions can impact pain and recall two types of pain assessment tools.

LEARNING OBJECTIVES

After studying this chapter, the learner will be able to

1. list three elements to consider in the assessment of pain.

2. identify one assessment tool that may be used in children.

3. identify one assessment tool that may be used in adults.

4. cite a pain assessment tool that may be used with unconscious patients.

INTRODUCTION

It is incredible that the myths and misconceptions related to pain and its management continues to be perpetuated by the very health professionals charged with its management, as well as members of the general public.

If nurses are going to manage pain, then they must be able to assess pain. The information in the preceding chapters should equip nurses in the assessment of pain. In addition, the dispelling of myths is important if nurses are to be the best advocates for patients. Toward that end, some of the most common myths surrounding pain management are as follows:

Pain Management Myths

• Prolonged use of narcotic analgesics for pain will lead to addiction.

• If Abstinence Syndrome is experienced, then the person is an addict.

• Pain is inevitable.

• Pain cannot kill.

• Taking pain medication early—when the pain appears to be most bearable—leads to the development of tolerance, making agents less effective when the pain becomes severe.

• Opioids should not be used in the absence of malignancy.

• Potent opioids for use in pain with cancer should be used only when death is imminent.

• Third degree burns do not hurt.

PAIN ASSESSMENT

Now that the factors that can impact pain and its management have been covered, what should be done with the information? The information is utilized in the assessment of the patient's pain, toward the development of an effective, realistic treatment plan and the evaluation of treatment outcomes. To do this, nurses must start with the pain assessment, the most important element in the development of the pain management plan.

When assessing the patient's pain the nurse looks first and foremost to the patient. The nurse accepts that the patient owns his/her pain and that pain is a subjective experience, which the nurse then tries to quantify or measure so as to better evaluate the efficacy of the prescribed interventions. The nurse needs to remember that an individual in pain is being assessed; the pain does not exist apart from the person in whom it is present. This common mistake factors the patient out of the equation. It is the pain experience that the nurse is attempting to quantify and that experience does not exist apart from the patient, who must be at the center of its treatment.

Three Truths of Pain Assessment

1. Assessment is the most important component of effective pain management.

    • All patients should be assessed for pain during the initial evaluation.

    • When pain is present, it should be quantified and qualified with an appropriate measurement tool.

    • When pain is present, a pain management goal, individualized to meet the patient's needs, should be established.

2. All patients have a right to effective pain management.

    • Interventions should be designed to meet the pain management goal.

    • Patients should receive appropriate educational materials regarding pain and its management.

    • Selection of treatment for pain management should include consideration of the severity and type of pain.

    • Side effects of treatment should be anticipated, monitored and managed appropriately.

3. Outcomes should be measured, and this measurement must be ongoing. Outcomes serve to:

    • Validate the pain management intervention/program.

    • Identify areas of need.

    • Ensures participation of multiple disciplines in the Pain Management Plan.

    • Standardize documentation of pain assessment, treatment and re-assessment.

Process of the Pain Assessment

When approaching the assessment of pain, the nurse must be methodical and concise and at the same time, thorough. The assessment starts with the temporal dimension and progresses from there.

Its intensity and character:

• Onset and temporal pattern

    — How often does the pain occur?

    — Has pain intensity changed?

    — If so, how?

• Location

    — Where is the pain?

    — Is there more than one site of pain?

    — Does the pain radiate?

• Description

    — What does the pain feel like?

    — What are the pain's characteristics; is it aching, stabbing, shooting?

• Aggravating and ameliorating factors

    — What makes the pain better?

    — What makes the pain worse?

• Effect

    — How does the pain affect physical function?

    — How does the pain make you feel?

- Intensity

  — Using an appropriate pain assessment scale, rate the intensity of the pain.

The patient and nurse begin to form a relationship during the initial pain assessment. By asking the patient specific questions about the nature of their pain, the nurse elicits important information that will guide treatment and assures the patient that the pain is being taken seriously.

Pain assessment scales can be used to determine the intensity of pain when it is at its worst and its best. Other assessments include how the pain affects the patient's function and quality of life, and what pain relief measures have or have not alleviated the pain.

Pain Assessment Instruments

There is a difference in a pain scale and a pain tool. A pain scale typically provides information about the sensory dimension of the pain. The scale is a tool of sorts but a pain assessment tool provides multi-dimensional data related to the pain. An example of a pain scale is the Visual Analogue Scale (VAS) (see *Figure 3-1*). On a linear continuum, the patient marks in proximity to a 0 or a 10 where on the continuum their pain falls. zero (0) means "NO PAIN" and ten (10) means "THE WORST PAIN POSSIBLE." This provides data relative to the intensity of the pain, the sensory dimension. This can be included in a pain data base, questionnaire or tool to provide sensory/intensity data but is insufficient in and of itself to provide meaningful data about the pain, as it is uni-dimensional—limiting the assessment to the sensory dimension of the pain experience.

PAIN SCALES

Numeric Scale

In addition to the VAS, there is the numeric scale (see *Figure 3-1*). A numeric scale works in quite the same fashion; it provides a numerical pain score, the verbal report by the patient of a number on a continuum of 0 to 10, and reflects the sensory dimension of the pain experience.

The numeric scale is pragmatic and functional for use by nurses on busy units. It is similar to the VAS in that patients factor within a horizontal continuum with fixed end-points, but in order to be documented, the VAS must have numerical values assigned, with interpretation made using a 10cm ruler. This is more time consuming than the provision of a score which is easily documented.

The American Pain Society (APS) has stated that the pain score should be the "fifth vital sign" (APS, 1999). When the initial intake of the patient is performed, be it in a medical office, clinic or on a nursing unit, the vital sign assessment is generally the first assessment to be performed. The APS has stated that the pain score or a verbal numerical descriptor of pain intensity must be documented as well.

Variables

It is important to understand that some of the same variables that impact pain management may impact its assessment. Kondamuri (2001) reviewed 1,000 consecutive charts to determine whether culture impacted the choice of a numerical value in rating the pain sensation. The researcher found that persons with certain racial and cultural background tend to report more extreme scores; while patients from other races and backgrounds under-reported pain, reluctant to report high scores in the presence of extreme pain.

Another finding in the Kondamuri study (2001) was the impact of education of the responders. Patients who were poorly educated had difficulty

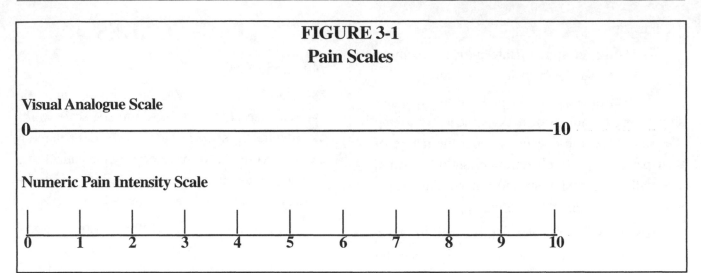

FIGURE 3-1
Pain Scales

Visual Analogue Scale

0 ————————————————————————————————————— 10

Numeric Pain Intensity Scale

0 1 2 3 4 5 6 7 8 9 10

factoring along a continuum. Persons from Eastern Europe were unfamiliar with the use of scales, and the Faces Pain Scale (see *Figure 3-3*), which has utility in the United States, does not work in Africa (Kundamuri, 2001).

CHOOSING A PAIN SCALE

Selection of a tool to measure pain intensity should take into account the patient's:

- Developmental stage;

- Chronological age;

- Functional status;

- Cognitive abilities; and

- Emotional status (JCAHO, 1999a).

For example, younger children cannot factor along a horizontal continuum, so a visual analogue scale that factors on a horizontal continuum would not be appropriate for a child. If the patient cannot read or has physical limitations that preclude writing, then a verbal scale would be used.

Pain Assessment Tools/Instruments

Tools in addition to scales, serve to assess other dimensions, along with the sensory dimension. These tools assess the perceptions of the pain, the quality of the pain and the temporal and overall magnitude of the pain. Examples are the McGill Pain Questionnaire (see *Figure 3-2)* and the Acute

and Chronic Pain Form (see *Figure 3-3).* These tools can be used in a variety of settings.

The McGill Pain Questionnaire (MPQ)

The McGill Pain Questionnaire (MPQ) is the most widely used pain questionnaire (Melzack, 1975). It is a 78 item instrument that uses verbal descriptors to report pain in the sensory, evaluative and affective dimensions. It is available as a short form, which has been demonstrated to have more utility in the cancer pain setting, as the long form has been found to be too tiring for patients with pain from neoplastic disease (Melzack, 1997).

The Acute and Chronic Pain Form

The Acute and Chronic Pain Form may be used in an acute care setting, as it takes into account acute events in the presence of a chronic pain history (see *Figure 3-3).* It can also be used in an outpatient surgery facility or in a procedural setting, as it is concise and easy to use. It can be used as a screening instrument. It uses two different pain tools, the Faces Pain Scale and the numerical scale, and it incorporates the evaluative dimension as it measures the overall intensity of the pain.

SPECIAL POPULATIONS

Special consideration should be given to certain patients, including the elderly, the very young, the non-English-speaking patient,

FIGURE 3-2
The McGill Pain Questionnaire (MPQ)

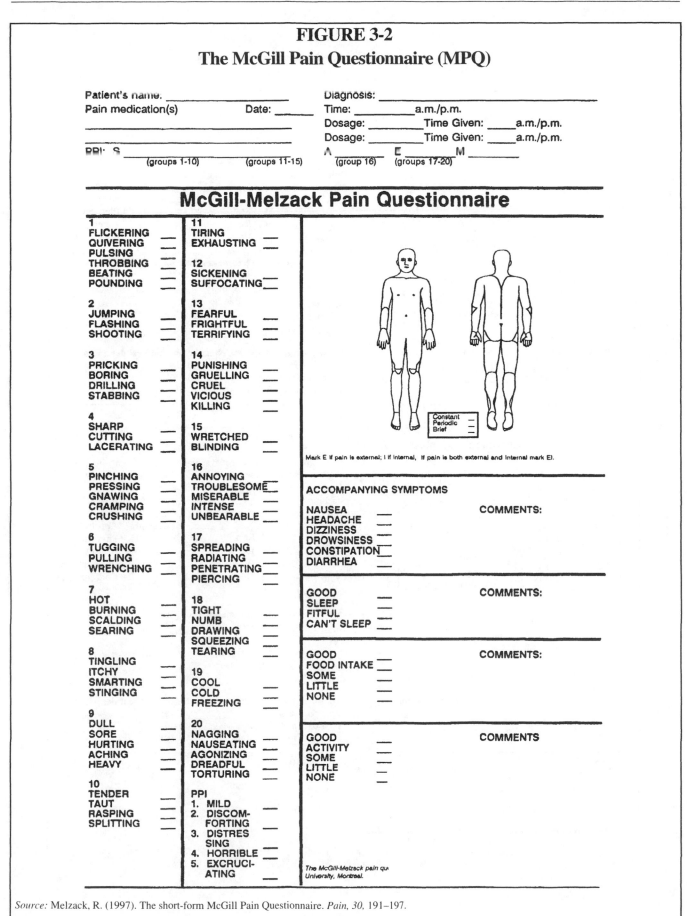

Patient's name. _____   Diagnosis: _____

Pain medication(s)   Date: _____   Time: _____ a.m./p.m.

_____   Dosage: _____ Time Given: _____ a.m./p.m.

_____   Dosage: _____ Time Given: _____ a.m./p.m.

PRI: S _____ A _____ E _____ M _____
(groups 1-10) (groups 11-15) (group 16) (groups 17-20)

McGill-Melzack Pain Questionnaire

1 FLICKERING ___ QUIVERING ___ PULSING ___ THROBBING ___ BEATING ___ POUNDING ___

2 JUMPING ___ FLASHING ___ SHOOTING ___

3 PRICKING ___ BORING ___ DRILLING ___ STABBING ___

4 SHARP ___ CUTTING ___ LACERATING ___

5 PINCHING ___ PRESSING ___ GNAWING ___ CRAMPING ___ CRUSHING ___

6 TUGGING ___ PULLING ___ WRENCHING ___

7 HOT ___ BURNING ___ SCALDING ___ SEARING ___

8 TINGLING ___ ITCHY ___ SMARTING ___ STINGING ___

9 DULL ___ SORE ___ HURTING ___ ACHING ___ HEAVY ___

10 TENDER ___ TAUT ___ RASPING ___ SPLITTING ___

11 TIRING ___ EXHAUSTING ___

12 SICKENING ___ SUFFOCATING ___

13 FEARFUL ___ FRIGHTFUL ___ TERRIFYING ___

14 PUNISHING ___ GRUELLING ___ CRUEL ___ VICIOUS ___ KILLING ___

15 WRETCHED ___ BLINDING ___

16 ANNOYING ___ TROUBLESOME ___ MISERABLE ___ INTENSE ___ UNBEARABLE ___

17 SPREADING ___ RADIATING ___ PENETRATING ___ PIERCING ___

18 TIGHT ___ NUMB ___ DRAWING ___ SQUEEZING ___ TEARING ___

19 COOL ___ COLD ___ FREEZING ___

20 NAGGING ___ NAUSEATING ___ AGONIZING ___ DREADFUL ___ TORTURING ___

PPI
1. MILD ___
2. DISCOMFORTING ___
3. DISTRESSING ___
4. HORRIBLE ___
5. EXCRUCIATING ___

Constant ___
Periodic ___
Brief ___

Mark E if pain is external; I if internal. If pain is both external and internal mark EI.

ACCOMPANYING SYMPTOMS

NAUSEA ___
HEADACHE ___
DIZZINESS ___
DROWSINESS ___
CONSTIPATION ___
DIARRHEA ___

COMMENTS:

GOOD SLEEP ___
FITFUL ___
CAN'T SLEEP ___

COMMENTS:

GOOD FOOD INTAKE ___
SOME ___
LITTLE ___
NONE ___

COMMENTS:

GOOD ACTIVITY ___
SOME ___
LITTLE ___
NONE ___

COMMENTS

The McGill-Melzack pain qu
University, Montreal.

Source: Melzack, R. (1997). The short-form McGill Pain Questionnaire. *Pain, 30,* 191–197.

FIGURE 3-3
Acute & Chronic Pain Assessment Form

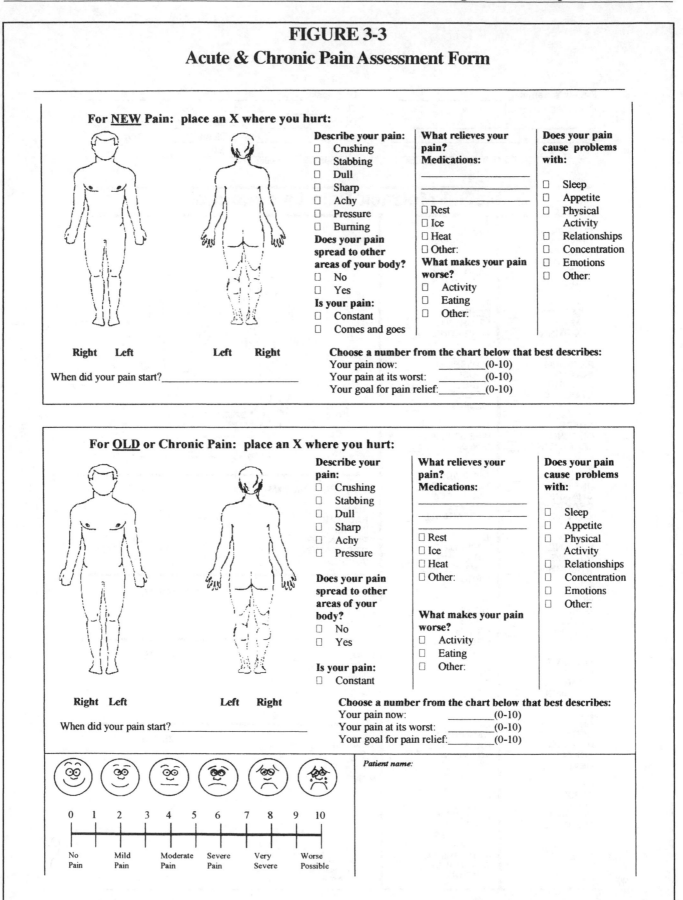

For **NEW** Pain: place an X where you hurt:

Right   Left   Left   Right

When did your pain start?_____

Describe your pain:
☐ Crushing
☐ Stabbing
☐ Dull
☐ Sharp
☐ Achy
☐ Pressure
☐ Burning

Does your pain spread to other areas of your body?
☐ No
☐ Yes

Is your pain:
☐ Constant
☐ Comes and goes

What relieves your pain?
Medications:
_____
_____
_____
☐ Rest
☐ Ice
☐ Heat
☐ Other:

What makes your pain worse?
☐ Activity
☐ Eating
☐ Other:

Does your pain cause problems with:
☐ Sleep
☐ Appetite
☐ Physical Activity
☐ Relationships
☐ Concentration
☐ Emotions
☐ Other:

Choose a number from the chart below that best describes:
Your pain now: _____(0-10)
Your pain at its worst: _____(0-10)
Your goal for pain relief:_____(0-10)

For **OLD** or Chronic Pain: place an X where you hurt:

Right   Left   Left   Right

When did your pain start?_____

Describe your pain:
☐ Crushing
☐ Stabbing
☐ Dull
☐ Sharp
☐ Achy
☐ Pressure

Does your pain spread to other areas of your body?
☐ No
☐ Yes

Is your pain:
☐ Constant

What relieves your pain?
Medications:
_____
_____
_____
☐ Rest
☐ Ice
☐ Heat
☐ Other:

What makes your pain worse?
☐ Activity
☐ Eating
☐ Other:

Does your pain cause problems with:
☐ Sleep
☐ Appetite
☐ Physical Activity
☐ Relationships
☐ Concentration
☐ Emotions
☐ Other:

Choose a number from the chart below that best describes:
Your pain now: _____(0-10)
Your pain at its worst: _____(0-10)
Your goal for pain relief:_____(0-10)

Patient name:

0	1	2	3	4	5	6	7	8	9	10
No Pain		Mild Pain		Moderate Pain		Severe Pain		Very Severe		Worse Possible

the seriously ill patient and the unconscious/non-responsive patient. Assessment tools for pediatric and geriatric pain are discussed at length in the chapter dealing with specialized populations.

Having alternative scales available and a translator or a close family member at hand (when needed) for patients who may not be able to respond to questions, facilitates information gathering during the process of pain assessment (AHCRP, 1994).

The scales/tools most commonly used in pain assessment are the numerical scale, the Visual Analogue Scale, the Faces Pain Scale and the Mcgill Pain Questionnaire. The numerical scale can be used in conjunction with the Faces Pain Scale, where a number is consigned to a face for ease of documentation.

The numerical scale uses 0 to 10 as a continuum with 0 meaning no pain and 10 the worst pain imaginable. The patient is cued to remember the worst pain they have ever felt or the worst that the current pain level has been and to rate it from 0 to 10. They then verbalize the pain score that reflects their current pain level.

Unresponsive Patients

Patients who cannot respond, either because of sedation or mechanical ventilation, pose challenges in the quantification of their pain experience. Objective indicators such as facial grimacing, changes in blood pressure or pulse values are what nurses rely on in assessing pain. Payen et al. (2002) developed a scale for use in patients such as these and evaluated the tool in a prospective study conducted over six months in a ten bed trauma and postoperative intensive care unit (ICU). The tool is the Behavioral Pain Scale (BPS), and it provided a sum score for facial expression, upper limb movement, and compliance with mechanical ventilation. A four point scale was used. Inter-rater reliability was also evaluated. While recommending further studies for validity and reliability, the authors

reported satisfaction with the utility of the BPS in 24 of 28 cases, reporting the BPS as safe and reliable for pain assessment in sedated patients on mechanical ventilation.

SUMMARY

When assessing pain, the nurse should treat it as the multidimensional event that it truly is. While tremendous gains are being made in understanding pain and modest gains are accomplished in nurses' attempts to appropriately assess it, patients still report inadequate pain management. The onus of pain assessment and its management is still primarily on the nurse. Nurses assess and treat pain in a variety of healthcare settings. With the often heavy patient assignments that nurses manage, it is not always practical for nurses to perform a multidimensional evaluation of a patient's pain, but nurses do the best that they can with what they have at their disposal.

What nurses can do, is increase their knowledge of the variables that impact pain, validate patient complaints, be cognizant of biases and identify the patients at risk for inadequate pain assessment. Nurses can be proactive by sitting on pain committees and offering recommendations for the development and utilization of pain assessment tools. Nurses can also negotiate with the physician managing the patient on their behalf.

Nurses need to use appropriate pain assessment tools and scales assessing and re-assessing, considering each patient's unique needs and issues, revising as needed and measuring outcomes. Nurses must communicate with the patient, family and other members of the healthcare team, and should be certain that myths and misconceptions about pain, medications and addiction are clarified. When developing a treatment plan directed at the management of pain it is important for nurses to:

• Know and share facts;

- Be alert to unresolved pain;

- Be alert to biases in themselves and others; and

- Educate their peers and patients.

EXAM QUESTIONS

CHAPTER 3
Questions 11–16

11. The most important element in the development of a pain management plan is

    a. pain assessment.

    b. use of narcotics.

    c. pain treatment.

    d. the use of pain scales.

12. A difference in a *pain scale* and *pain tool* is a

    a. scale is limited to the temporal dimension.

    b. tool is limited to the sensory dimension.

    c. scale is limited to the sensory dimension.

    d. tool is limited to the temporal dimension.

13. Which of the following should be taken into account when selecting a pain scale?

    a. patient's developmental level

    b. patient's perception of the pain

    c. nurse's perception of the pain

    d. patient's use of opioids

14. Based on this chapter, which are considered special populations with respect to pain assessment?

    a. elderly, professionals and children

    b. children, elderly and professionals

    c. elderly, unconscious/non-responsive patients and children

    d. children, professionals and non-English speaking patients

15. In patients who are mechanically ventilated, what objective measures of pain can be used?

    a. intracranial pressure values

    b. verbal pain scores

    c. family member reports

    d. facial expression, vital signs

16. Which of the following was identified as a variable in pain assessment in this chapter?

    a. culture

    b. income

    c. gender

    d. eye color

CHAPTER 4

THE PHYSIOLOGY OF PAIN

CHAPTER OBJECTIVE

Upon completion of this chapter, the reader will be able to identify the primary elements of the peripheral and central nervous system related to pain, recall the primary pain mechanisms and cite the primary pain neurotransmitter.

LEARNING OBJECTIVES

After studying this chapter, the learner will be able to

1. list the three basic stages involved in pain.

2. identify the response to pain as a reflex.

3. identify a pain neurotransmitter.

4. define transduction.

5. recognize the three primary algogenic substances.

6. select the structures involved in modulation.

7. cite one opioid receptor in the brain and one in the spinal cord.

8. recall a mechanism for the pain of Reflex Sympathetic Dystrophy Syndrome (RSD) (CRPS).

INTRODUCTION

In order to evaluate the efficacy of pain treatment and to properly assess pain, it is important for the nurse to have an understanding of its basic neurophysiological processes. While there is an abundance of data available regarding the physiology of pain, this chapter will explore the structures involved with pain, the three stages of the pain impulse and related mechanisms. These are some of the basic processes and mechanisms. An understanding of these processes also aids the nurse in understanding the mechanisms of action of various analgesics and adjuvants.

MAJOR STRUCTURES

Neurons

Pain is a reflex. When something hot is touched, the reflex arc in the spinal cord has already caused a withdrawal from the thermal stimuli before the cotex perceives the stimulus.

Neurons or nerve cells carry sensory information through the peripheral, central and sympathetic nervous systems. In order for a neuron to fire, electricity is needed. One primary way that electricity or energy is generated is by the sodium pump. Dendrites pick up the sensory information, in this case pain, and the sodium pump provides the energy required to transmit the information from the dendrites to the terminal bulb of the neuron.

This same electricity then provokes the release of neurotransmitters from nissl bodies in the terminal bulb, which carry or transmit the information to the next neuron and so on. Neurons are the basic structural units of the nervous system and are functionally categorized into primary afferent and second order nociceptive neurons (Sinatra & Aratimos, 2001).

The primary afferent neurons are located in the dorsal root ganglion. They may release one or more excitatory amino-acids or peptide neurotranmitters, such as substance P.

Second order nociceptive neurons either respond exclusively to A-delta and C fibers or wide-dynamic range neurons. The wide-dynamic range neurons respond to both noxious and benign stimuli.

With *nerve blocks,* local anesthetics decrease the membrane permeability of the nerve cell to sodium, and the cell is depolarized. Opioids bind with specific receptors located at the terminal bulb of the neuron. The primary receptor in the brain for morphine is mu and the primary receptor in the spinal cord is kappa. Once the binding occurs, energy is sufficiently depleted to inhibit the release of the excitatory neurotransmitter in the terminal bulb.

With *botulinum toxin,* the toxin inhibits the release of acetylcholine so that energy is not transmitted to the next nerve cell. This is the primary effect of the botulinum toxin, but there are also nociceptive effects that appear to contribute to the toxin's mechanism of action.

Spinal Cord

Nerve fibers enter into the spinal cord through the dorsal horn nucleus (DHN). It has always been accepted that most of the pain fibers enter through this dorsal aspect of the cord, but it is now thought that as much as 40% of the sensory fibers enter in the ventral root (Worldwide Intensivist, 2001).

There are ten laminae, or divisions of the grey matter of the spinal cord. The dorsal part is divided into five laminae (I–V), dealing primarily with incoming pain fibers. Laminae VII is between these and the more ventral laminae, VIII–X. Laminae VI is discernable in the bulges of the cord wherein limb innervation originates (Sinatra & Aratimos, 2001).

Once the spinal nerves terminate into these laminae, sensation is carried via interneurones in the spinal cord. The stimulus then travels through the substantia gelatinosa (SG) and up the anterolateral spinothalamic tract of the spinal cord.

Brain

Pain becomes pain once it is perceived as such by the cerebral cortex. Once it is perceived, the interpretation and response to pain is a result of motivational-affective and sensory-discriminative functions. Culture, ethnicity, socialization and previous pain experiences are some of the factors involved with the motivational-affective response and the ability to perceive the location of the pain. This is a function of the sensory-discriminate functions (Worldwide Intensivist, 2001).

Thalamus: Sometimes referred to as the "central relay station" of the brain. The thalamus is a complex structure. Several of its many nuclei are primarily involved with pain. The lateral nuclei deal with the sensory/discriminative aspects such as location and radiation pattern of the pain. The medial nuclei deal with affective pain.

Midbrain: Has circuitry primarily involved with pain. The periaqueductal grey matter (PAG) site of opioid receptors in the brain, is located in the midbrain which has connections to the reticular system of the brainstem

Pons: The most important pain-related nuclei in the pons is full of noradrenaline neurons. This is important in the modulation of pain.

Medulla: Is also involved in the motivational-affective aspects of pain.

ANATOMY AND PHYSIOLOGY OF PAIN

Basically the pain system has been presented as one in which afferent or sensory impulses are encoded peripherally, propagated and processed centrally and then perceived (see *Figure 4-1*). This is a basic explanation which helps us understand pain but does not begin to address the complicated molecular, chemical and neural mechanisms involved in this complex phenomenon.

The three primary processes involved with pain providing the framework for this discussion are transduction, transmission and modulation.

- *Transduction* is the conversion of peripheral nociceptor stimulation into a neural impulse. This stimulation may be thermal, mechanical or chemical.

- *Transmission* involves the passage of the impulse from the periphery into and through the central nervous system.

- *Modulation* influences and manages pain signals by means of descending or efferent nerve pathways, including inhibitory and excitatory neurotransmitters and opioid receptors. Psychodynamic mechanisms are involved as well.

Transduction

Transduction occurs at peripheral nociceptors which are stimulated when injury liberates cell interiors. Nociceptors exist as free nerve endings and are found in all tissues of the body. The largest numbers of nociceptors are present in the skin, joint synovium and arterial walls, with less dense concentrations in most of the internal organs.

This disruption of cell membranes through surgical injury or trauma sets into motion a biochemical set of events termed the **arachidonic acid cascade,** which generates pain producing or algogenic substances. An element of the arachidoinc acid cascade is a primary enzymatic precursor for prostaglandin, cyclo-oxygenase. This is the enzyme whose production is inhibited by aspirin (ASA) and traditional non-steroidal anti-inflammatory drugs (NSAIDs).

These algogenic substances include **bradykinin, histamine** and **prostaglandin.** Bradykinin produces pain by local release; prostaglandin exists as PGE-1 or PGE-2. PGE-1 is a precursor to thromboxane and is involved in the maintenance of the protective lining of the stomach and bronchial tubes. This is why when NSAIDs or ASA are given, they decrease platelet aggregation, precipitate gastric distress and can provoke broncho-spasm in severe asthmatics. PGE-2 provokes the pain response by sensitizing bradykinan and histamine. The newer NSAIDs termed COX-2 agents are specific for PGE2, sparing PGE1, thereby producing fewer side effects. Histamine release occurs with injury and hypersensitivity responses, effecting vasodilation and enhancing blood vessel permeability and bronchial constriction.

These substances in turn stimulate nociceptors. This stimulation is converted into a neural impulse, which is then carried or transmitted via specialized peripheral nerve fibers.

Transmission

At this point, the stage of transmission has occurred. The nerve fibers responsible for the transmission of pain are the smallest of the sensory fibers and are divided into **A-delta** or **C fibers.** The A-delta fibers are myelinated, involved in discrimination and responsible for what is termed **first order pain.** This first order pain lasts as long as the original painful stimulus persists (Sinatra & Aratimos, 2001). The C fibers are un-myelinated,

FIGURE 4-1
Physiology of Pain

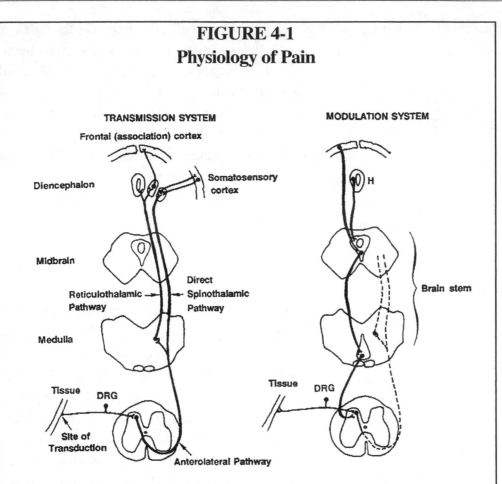

Diagrammatic outline of the major neural structures relevant to pain. The sequence of events leading to pain perception begins in the transmission system with transduction (lower left), in which a noxious stimulus produces nerve impulses in the primary afferent nociceptor. These impulses are conducted to the spinal cord, where the primary afferent nociceptors contact the central pain-transmission cells. The central pain-transmission cells relay the message to the thalamus either directly via the spinothalamic tract or indirectly via the reticular formation and the reticulothalamic pathway. From the thalamus, the message is relayed to the cerebral cortex. (DRG: dorsal root ganglion.) The pain-modulation system has inputs from the frontal association cortex and the hypothalamus (H). The outflow is through the midbrain and medulla to the dorsal horn of the spinal cord, where it inhibits pain-transmission cells, thereby reducing the intensity of perceived pain.

This transmission has been carried into the spinal cord, wherein the nerve fibers synapse into superficial layers of the Rexed laminae. The A-delta neurons synapse in laminae I, II, and V and the C fibers in laminae I and II (Ahmad, Ackerman, Munir & Saleem, 2001). A variety of neurotransmitters are released by the first-order nociceptive neurons.

The pain signals are relayed via the spinothalamic tract, but the sensation carried by the A-delta fibers terminate in different laminae than the C fibers. The sensory information is carried up the anterolateral spinothalamic tract into the brain stem and thalamus to areas of the cerebral cortex, especially the somatosensory area. This portion of the cortex can discriminate the area from which the original message was sent.

Pain signals from the C fibers are also transmitted through the spinothalamic tracts, but the C fibers terminate in fewer laminae than the A-delta fibers, so transmission is slower. These slower pain signals terminate over a wider area of the brain stem and thalamus, making discrimination and localization of pain difficult. It is believed that C fiber mediated thereby effecting a slower rate of conduction, and responsible for **second order pain,** which persists once the stimulus has been removed.

sensations are responsible for chronic pain and suffering, and the A-delta are responsible for acute pain.

An example of first and second order pain is when a person stubs their toe. The first pain sensation is deep and acute, and the person knows exactly where the pain is located. Thus, first order pain is transmitted by the A-delta fibers. (The person almost instinctively massages or rubs the area). After a few seconds, there is a dull, diffuse, aching pain, which is C fiber mediated.

WIND-UP

WIND-UP is a process that occurs in a sequence of component stages. A primary neurotransmitter in the spinal cord is substance P, which induces the release of excitatory amino acids such as glutamate and aspartate. These amino acids have their effect at the N-methyl-D-aspartate (NMDA) receptor and this receptor has been felt to have a possible role in chronic pain syndromes.

Enhanced synaptic transmission caused by substance P release can induce a prolonged enhancement of responses by dorsal horn neurons to glutamate or aspartate. This enhanced depolarization causes calcium influx into postsynaptic neurons, which induces persistent changes in the excitability of the cell. The term WIND-UP has been used to describe this enhanced excitability and sensitization of the dorsal horn cells. In addition to causing WIND-UP, repeated noxious stimulation of the dorsal horn may increase the number of neurons in laminae I and II. The nuclei of these neurons express a protein called c-fos, thought to be involved in the memory of pain (Ahmad et al., 2001).

WIND-UP explains some of the findings associated with chronic pain and the spread of chronic pain from neuropathic and sympathetically mediated pain such as RSD. WIND-UP has impacted the understanding of other chronic pain states and the direction of their management. An example involves patients who have chronic radiculopathy. This is pain in an extremity that may be from a herniated disc in the spine. If, on EMG and Nerve Conduction Studies the nerve pain is termed as chronic, the pain will persist even if the disc is removed.

Neurotransmitters

While substance P is an excitatory neurotransmitter, gamma-aminobutyric acid (GABA) and glycine are important inhibitory or pain inhibiting neurotransmitters. Some of the agents used as adjuvants are referred to as GABAergic, as they enhance the amount of GABA and/or its effects at receptors.

Modulation

Modulation involves efferent pathways while transduction and transmission are afferent processes. Modulation occurs in the midbrain, medulla and spinal cord. There are two inhibitory descending pathways modulating responses at the dorsal horn.

Modulation is effected through activation of these pathways and processes and is mediated through inhibitory neurotransmitters, opioid receptors, endogenous peptides called endorphins and enkephalins (natural inherent painkillers) which bind on opioid receptors. Studies of cerebrospinal fluid have shown that use of exogenous opioids (narcotics) will decrease production of these "endogenous opioids," or natural painkillers, as a function of homeostasis by the organism.

The psychodynamic mechanism is also involved with modulation related to pain. This mechanism is impacted by sensory input and psychological factors, which can activate mechanisms of modulation.

Gate Control Theory

Justice cannot be done to the concept of modulation without involving the Gate Control Theory of Melzack and Wall (1965). The Gate Control

Theory proposes that descending pathways in the midbrain and brain stem act to suppress pain. Since its inception in 1965, this theory has been debated.

Massage and TENS units are examples of the Gate Control Theory in practice. The SG in the spinal cord and PAG in the brain are sites of the "gates" and sites of opioid receptors. When larger diameter sensory fibers, such as those which transmit vibration and touch, are stimulated, they will override the smaller diameter pain fibers and close the gate to their transmission. This is why a person instinctively rubs a sore or painful area, and it works! TENS units stimulate the larger fibers with low electrical currents.

Unfortunately, the pain fibers will eventually override or bypass the larger fibers. That is why TENS units are to be used for brief periods of time, and massage eventually wears off.

SUMMARY

The neurobiology and neurophysiology of mechanisms that cause and perpetuate pain are complex and fascinating. Understanding of how the psychodynamic mechanisms interface with the physiological mechanisms is evolving. A tremendous amount of ongoing basic science and clinical research is being conducted so that someday a more complete understanding of these complexities might be arrived at.

Understanding the use of certain medications for pain can also be understood in the context of the neurobiology and pathophysiology of pain. Algogenic substances are inhibited with NSAIDs, and nerves do not fire with Botox. If the nurse is to promote compliance with pharmacotherapeutic regimens, a basic understanding of these processes is warranted.

The content of this chapter has been presented as a basic overview of these intriguing mechanisms and has not been intended to provide all of the data that has been and is forthcoming with respect to pain.

EXAM QUESTIONS

CHAPTER 4
Questions 17–23

Read the following case and question 17 and choose the best response.

A pediatric rehabilitation hospital received admission of two brothers aged three and five. They had sustained severe scald burns of their hands. Their mother's boyfriend had gotten angry with them and as punishment, took them to the basement and opened the hot water heater onto their little hands. When the mother came home she took the boys to an ER. She told the ER physician that they were playing with hot water in the bathtub and "were so shocked by the hot water they couldn't pull their hands out." He informed her that this was impossible, but he did not tell her why. Unfortunately, the physician did not post a guard on the mother and children, and she promptly fled the hospital with them. She treated them at home with butter, ice and alcohol until they were septic. She took them several days later to another ER and gave the physician there the same story. This time the physician led her to believe that he accepted her explanation and discretely called the police and child protective services. The children underwent years of reconstructive surgeries.

17. Based on what you know about pain and the reflex arc, why did the first physician tell the mother that her explanation was impossible?

    a. The boys' hands would have been removed as a spinal reflex in response to the hot water.

    b. Boys that age cannot turn on bathwater.

    c. Hot water would not cause such severe burns.

    d. He had an inadequate knowledge base in pain.

18. Neurons are

    a. the basic functional unit of the nervous system.

    b. not involved in the transmission of pain.

    c. the basic structural unit of the nervous system.

    d. not naturally permeable to sodium.

19. Substance P is

    a. a neurotransmitter.

    b. an enkephalin.

    c. an opioid.

    d. a dendrite.

20. Which of the following is a site for modulation?

    a. nociceptors

    b. C fibers

    c. opioid receptors

    d. substance P

21. WIND-UP has helped to explain

    a. RSD.

    b. postop pain.

    c. tumor cell activity.

    d. opioid mechanism.

22. Dull aching pain after an injury is likely to be mediated by

    a. A-delta fibers.

    b. opioids.

    c. PAG.

    d. C fibers.

23. The three stages in sequential order for pain are

    a. transmission, transduction and modulation.

    b. transduction, modulation and transmission.

    c. modulation, transduction and transmission.

    d. transduction, transmission and modulation.

CHAPTER 5

NON-OPIOID ANALGESICS AND ADJUVANTS

CHAPTER OBJECTIVE

Upon completion of this chapter, the reader will be able to recall the pharmacologic options for the management of pain and recognize non-opioid analgesics, the potential organ effects of NSAIDs, and three adjuvants that may be used for pain management.

LEARNING OBJECTIVES

After studying this chapter, the learner will be able to

1. cite two contraindications and two indications in the use of NSAIDs for pain management.

2. identify an indication for the use of antidepressants for pain management.

3. identify two side effects of tricyclic anti-depressants (TCAs).

4. choose a nursing intervention with botulinum toxin administration.

INTRODUCTION

An optimally efficacious approach to the pharmacologic management of pain typically involves "prudent poly-pharmacy." In other words, combinations of medications directed at the management of pain by impacting its underlying mechanisms. This involves the use of both analgesic and non-analgesic classes of medications for the management of pain. Several classes of agents serve as adjuvants in pain management, with antiepileptic and antidepressant drugs the primary agents for this purpose. Some anti-emetics have also been found to be efficacious in the management of pain and headache.

For the purpose of this chapter, the agents to be discussed in detail will be the non-steroidal anti-inflammatory drugs (NSAIDs), COX-2 NSAIDs, tricyclic anti-depressants (TCAs), selective serotonin re-uptake inhibitiors (SSRIs), botulinum toxin and anti-epileptic drugs (AEDs). Other classes of drugs will also be addressed. It is important to note that some of the agents, while common in research and in the literature, are used in an "off-label" manner, which means that there is not an indication for pain management in the legend of the agent.

NON-STEROIDAL ANTI-INFLAMMATORY DRUGS (NSAIDS)

At the forefront of non-opioid analgesics are the non-steroidal anti-inflammatory agents (see *Tables 5-1* and *5-2*). Over one hundred years have passed since Felix Hoffman, while working at Bayer Laboratories, reported success with the synthesis of acetylsalicylic acid. The compound, called aspirin, was purported to represent a convenient mechanism for the delivery of salicylic acid in the treatment of pain from arthritis, menstrual cramps and fever (Wolfe, Lichtenstein & Singh, 1999).

In the seventies, new NSAIDs were developed, and these agents constitute one of the most widely used classes of drugs with more than 70 million prescriptions and 30 billion over-the-counter tablets sold annually in the United States (see *Tables 5-1* and *5-2*). It is estimated that 13 million Americans regularly use NSAIDs for various types of pain (Wolfe et al., 1999).

There is no doubt that this class has been the mainstay of non-opioid management of pain, but as a class, the NSAIDs are not benign, having been associated with toxicities involving several organ systems. While associated with pathologies involving the kidneys, liver, platelets, and central nervous system, the gastrointestinal effects of this class of medication has proven the most common toxic effect of the class.

Mechanism of Action

This class of medication has its effect on the inflammation that results from trauma to cells in the periphery, where the first step in the pain process occurs. This initiation of the pain impulse is referred to as transduction and is detailed in Chapter 4.

When cells are disrupted, a series of biochemical events ensues. This biochemical event and its elements are termed the arachidonic acid cascade. This cascade occurs at the site of peripheral nociceptors; releasing algogenic or pain producing substances, the most important of which is prostaglandin.

An enzyme, cyclo-oxygenase is necessary for the conversion of arachidonic acid to prostaglandin. Prostaglandin is the primary nociceptive substance involved in transduction, the first step in the genesis of pain. From the arachidonic pathway, the enzyme cyclo-oxygenase drives the progression to prostaglandin.

The mechanism of action of NSAIDs is the inhibition of cyclo-oxygenase. Originally thought to exist as one enzyme, cyclo-oxygenase exists as two different isoenzymes: Cyclo-oxygenase-1 (COX-1) and Cyclo-oxygenase-2 (COX-2). NSAIDs as a class target both COX-1 and COX-2, but much excitement has been generated with the development of a class of NSAIDs that target COX-2, which diminishes the incidence of side effects typically associated with this class of medications (Kelly & Small, 2001). NSAIDS do not have an effect on burning or sharp shooting pain, they do help aching pain.

Side Effects of NSAIDs

Gastrointestinal

All NSAIDs exhibit anti-inflammatory, analgesic and anti-pyretic properties. This is primarily through the inhibition of the production of prostaglandin, which is synthesized by cyclo-oxygenase. Prostaglandin exists as PGE 1 and PGE 2. PGE 2 is an algogenic substance, while PGE 1 provides the protective lining of the stomach and bronchial tubes. With inhibition of the cyclo-oxygenase enzyme, "good prostaglandin" is inhibited along with the "bad prostaglandin." A lack of prostaglandin can increase the vulnerability of the stomach mucosa.

Consequently, traditional NSAIDs have been shown to be associated with an increased risk of gastropathy and upper GI bleeding. Increased risk is associated with age, higher dosages, concurrent use of more than one NSAID, use of anticoagulants, and a pre-existing history of GI disease. A principle difference in the use of NSAIDs and COX-2 agents is fewer adverse GI events associated with the COX-2 agents (Wolfe et al., 1999).

Irrespective of the differences in these two classes of NSAIDs, patients receiving treatment with both of these classes of medication should be

TABLE 5-1
Non-Steroidal Anti-Inflammatory Drugs (NSAIDs)

Ibuprofen	200–800 mg every 6 hours po
Choline Magnesium Trisalicylate (Trilisate)	1000–1500 every 8 hours or TID
Diclofenac Sodium (Voltaren)	50–75 mg every 8–12 hours
Diflunisal (Dolobid)	500 every 12 hours
Etodolac (Lodine)	200–400 every 8–12 hours
Flurbiprofen (Ansaid)	200–300 mg every 4–8 hours
Naproxen (Naprosyn)	250–275 mg every 12 hours
Naproxen Sodium (Anaprox, Aleve)	275 mg every 12 hours; 550 mg every 12 hours
Oxaprozin (Daypro)	600–1200 mg/daily
Piroxicam (Feldene)	10–20 mg/daily
Nabumetone (Relafen)	1000–2000 mg/daily in one or two divided doses
Ketoprofen (Orudis)	500 mg every 6 hours
Ketorolac (Toradol)	10 mg. First dose, two 10 mg then 10 mg every 4/6 hours limit 5/days LIMIT 10 days/60 mg IM initial 30 mg every 6 hours IM (limit 5 days)

Source: American Pain Society. (1999). *Principles of analgesic use in the treatment of acute pain and cancer pain* (4th ed.). Glenview, IL: Author.

advised to take their medication with food or milk. Nurses should instruct patients to report any GI symptoms to a healthcare professional.

Coagulation

NSAIDs can also impact coagulation through inhibition of the enzymatic precursor to thromboxane. The COX-1 isoenzyme has a platelet presence, and as a result, all NSAIDs have the ability to inhibit platelet aggregation. On the other hand, Prostacyclin synthesis is dependent on the COX-2 isoenzyme; prostacyclin has an important role in platelet aggregation. Treatment of a patient wherein coagulation is a concern or issue must be handled individually on a case by case basis. The concurrent use of anticoagulants and NSAIDs is contraindicated. Observation for petechiae, bruising, and purpura is a nursing intervention for all patients receiving NSAIDs and COX-2 agents.

Hepatotoxicity

Mild elevations of liver enzymes have been associated with the chronic use of this class of medication. It is believed that there exists a dose-dependant response to the liver with respect to the NSAIDs. Once the dose is lowered, liver enzymes typically revert to normal. Hepatotoxic events are rare, and patients with hepatotoxicity are generally asymptomatic. Enzymes should be monitored bi-annually in the presence of chronic use of the NSAIDs and COX-2 agents.

Central Nervous System (CNS) Effects

The most common effect associated with the CNS and the use of NSAIDs is tinnitus. A patient with pre-existing tinnitus should be informed that they are to call the prescribing party if tinnitus worsens.

Patients will occasionally experience headaches with the use of NSAIDs, but this class of medication is widely used in the prophylactic and abortive regimen of headache management. There appears to be a relationship between patient age and NSAID induced headaches. Headaches have been seen more with the use of indomethicin and tolmetin (Rappaport, Sheftell & Tepper, 2001a). Interestingly, indomethicin is the agent of choice for the use of a headache called *paroxysmal hemicrania.*

Bronchial Effects

Patients with severe asthma can suffer bronchspasom and constriction when treated with NSAIDs and COX-2 agents. Both prostaglandin and leukotrienes play a role in the tone of bronchial airways. Because of this, people who have a hypersensitivity to NSAIDs and/or aspirin should not use NSAIDs or the COX-2 agents.

Indications for Use

Both acute and chronic pain are managed with NSAIDs, which is why they are widely used. Pain associated with inflammation is particularly responsive to this class of medication. Pain from osteoarthritis and rheumatoid arthritis are two conditions for which NSAIDs are a first line treatment agent.

Cancer Pain

Many of the bony metastases produce a prostaglandin which results in osteolysis, producing further destruction of the bone and resulting in pain. Therefore, cancer pain from bony metastases is very responsive to NSAIDs.

Post-operative Pain

Ketorolac (Torodol®), an NSAID with potent analgesic effects, comes in parenteral as well as oral forms. Several studies have been conducted evaluating its use intramuscularly for the management of post-operative pain. The studies have demonstrated analgesic efficacy comparable to

meperidine and morphine (Twersky, Lebovitz, Williams & Sexton, 1995).

Another study compared the analgesic efficacy of intravenous ketorolac with intravenous fentanyl for moderate to severe post-operative pain. The study examined 69 patients undergoing elective laproscopies, inguinal hernia repairs and knee arthroscopies. The study was randomized, double-blind in design and documented superior efficacy of ketorolac over fentanyl in the later post-operative period. Fentanyl was demonstrated superior in analgesic efficacy in early post-operative pain (Twersky et al., 1995).

While an effective analgesic in both parenteral and oral forms, ketorolac has been associated with GI bleeding with prolonged use. It is indicated for abortive treatment of severe periodic pain on a very limited basis. It is utilized for painful emergencies such as migraine headaches in emergent care and physician offices.

Back Pain

At the annual meeting of the American Pain Society, findings of two 4-week, double-blind, placebo-controlled studies for the investigational use of rofecoxib (Vioxx®) for chronic low back pain were presented. The studies included 690 patients with chronic back pain for a minimum of three months and for an average of 12 years, who had regularly used analgesics. Patients were randomized into three groups; placebo, Vioxx 25 mg and 50 mg. The studies documented statistically significant efficacy of the Vioxx over placebo with no differences in the dosage strength (Vioxx significantly reduced…, 2001).

ANALGESIC ADJUVANT AGENTS

While opioids are the cornerstone of therapy, they are not a panacea for all pain. Not all types of pain respond to

TABLE 5-2
Selected Non-Opioid Analgesics

Drug	Average Analgesic DOSE (mg)*	Dose Interval (hours)	Pediatric Dose (mg/kg)
Acetaminophen	500–1000	4–6	10–15 q4–6hr
Salicilates			
Aspirin	500–1,000	4–6	10–15 q4–6hr
Diflunisal (Dolobid®)	1,000 initial 500 subsequent	8–12	
Choline magnesium trisalicylate (Trilisate®)	1000–1500	12	25 bid
NSAIDs			
Propionic Acids			
Ibuprofen (Motrin®, Rufen®, Nuprin®, Advil®, Medipren®)	200–400	4–6	q6–8 hr
Naproxen	500 initial		
Naprosyn	250 subsequent	6–8	5 bid
Naproxen sodium (Anaprox®)	500 initial 250 subsequent	6–8	5 bid
Naproxen Sodium OTC (Aleve®)	220 mg	8–12	
Orudis®	25–50	6–8	
(Actron®, Orudis-K+®)	12.5–25	4–6	
Indolacetic Acids (Indomethacin) (Indocin®)	25–50–75	8–12	
Pyrrolacetic Acids Ketorolac (Toradol®)	30 or 60 mg IM or 30 mg IV initial, 15 or 30 IV or IM subsequent	6	
Phenylacetic Acids Diclofenac potassium (Cataflam®)	50 mg	8–12	

*All doses are oral unless otherwise specified

Source: American Pain Society. (1999). *Principles of analgesic use in the treatment of acute pain and cancer pain* (4th ed.). Glenview, IL: Author.

opioids, and opioids are not always indicated for chronic pain. In such instances, adjuvants (helper drugs) should be utilized. This is especially true of patients with neuralgic and/or neuropathic features to their pain. The adjuvants are more specific for certain types of pain; so they do not have the broad utility of the opioids and to a lesser extent, NSAIDs. Some adjuvants do not have a dose-response mechanism, meaning when a dose of an antiepileptic drug or an antidepressant is administered, relief does not appear shortly after the dose.

When choosing an adjuvant, it is important to maximize the benefits of the agent by selecting the appropriate one. It is also important to minimize the amount of medication the patient should take. If the patient has a concurrent medical problem, it should be considered when choosing an adjuvant. For instance, the incidence of reactive depression is high in patients with chronic pain. If a patient is felt to be suffering from depression, an antidepressant should be utilized over an anti-epileptic drug (AED) in order to treat both the depression and the pain. Another example is in the case of a patient with a seizure disorder and migraine headaches. Instead of introducing a second AED, the prescriber should maximize the one currently in use for the seizure disorder. This prudent poly-pharmacy does not always work out, but whenever possible, it should be tried.

Antidepressants

Antidepressants come in two primary classes, tricyclics (TCAs) and selective serotonin reuptake inhibitors (SSRIs) (*Table 5-4*). By inhibiting the re-uptake of serotonin and norepinephrine, the anti-depressants make more of the agent available. Serotonin has an inhibitory effect on pain impulses. Most of the research has been focused on amitriptyline and imipramine (TCAs) and their use in chronic non-cancer pain (Patt & Burton, 1999). For the purpose of this course, the TCAs will be discussed.

Mechanism of Action

TCAs inhibit the re-uptake of serotonin and noradrenaline, central neurotransmitters with inhibitory effects on pain impulses. The tricyclics have their greatest impact on burning, dysethetic pain. It appears that their analgesic effects are independent of their antidepressant effects (Saberski & Romero, 2000) and are realized within 3–7 days (Patt & Burton, 1999).

Amitriptyline (Elavil®) is the prototype. Nortriptyline (Pamelor®), amitriptyline's metabolite, imimpramine, and desipramine are used as well. Most of the research has focused on amitriptyline and imipramine In animal studies, the effects of opioids are potentitated by the TCAs (APS, 1999).

Indications

Antidepressants are particularly beneficial in the presence of neuropathic pain and for neuralgic pain when combined with an AED. They have been frequently used for neuropathic pain from trauma, radiation therapy, chemotherapy or malignant nerve infiltration, but reports have been anecdotal with no controlled studies performed (APS, 1999). Most studies have documented efficacy in post-herpetic neuralgia and diabetic peripheral neuropathy. They are not recommended for abortive use in acute pain, as they do not have a "dose-response" profile of action; in other words, they do not work within 30–45 minutes of the dose. The analgesic benefits are realized with therapeutic blood levels for prophylaxis.

Primary Effects

Patients will report a decrease in the "burning" characteristics of the pain. The added benefits of the antidepressants are improved sleep, enhanced mood and analgesia. The analgesic effects are usually seen within 3–7 days (Patt & Burton, 1999)

Side Effects

The main side effects that are most commonly associated with TCAs are dry mouth, sedation and

TABLE 5-3
Selected AEDs Used in Pain Management

Name	Schedule	Side Effects
Topamax Topiramate	Dosed BID	Weight loss; personality changes
Depakote Valproic acid	Dosed BID	Weight gain; hair loss; >LFT's changes in platelets; labs must be checked periodically
Neurontin Gabapentin	Dosed TID	Mild dizziness or sedation
Zonegran Zonisamide	Dosed at HS	Weight loss; cannot use if allergic to sulfa

weight gain. Desipramine has the lowest incidence of these and anticholinergic effects than the other agents. Urinary retention may also occur, and for this reason, patients with a history of urinary retention or prostatic hypertrophy are not candidates for the TCAs. This class of medication is relatively contraindicated for coronary disease, as they can worsen ventricular arrthymias. Conduction disorders may worsen with their use.

Administration

Dosages are best started low and incrementally increased. They are to be taken at bedtime because of their sedative effects. The APS (1999) recommends starting at 10–20 mg for patients weighing more than 50 kg and 0.3 mg/kg in others. They should be used with caution in the elderly and at lower doses.

Anti-Epileptic Drugs

This class (AEDs) has been utilized as first-line agents for **neuralgic pain** and **neuropathic pain,** when used in conjunction with the antidepressants (see *Table 5-3*). In the United States, of all the AEDs prescribed, approximately 5% are prescribed for analgesia (APS, 1999).

One of the newer agents, gabapentin (Neurontin®), has a low side effect profile and does not warrant regular laboratory studies. The most prevalent side effects with this agent are weight gain and dizziness, although weight loss has been seen with topiramate (Topamax®) and zonisamide (Zonegran™).

Mechanism of Action

It is thought that some forms of neuropathic pain result from autonomous, abnormal firing of neurons in unstable membranes. (This instability is similar to that seen with epilepsy.) These medications stablilize abnormal electrical patterns via effects on nerve membranes—specifically, the sodium and calcium channels. Other mechanisms involve their effect on GABAergic inhibitory systems and NMDA-receptors.

Examples of AEDs used for pain management are gabapentin, topiramate, zonisamide, and valproic acid (Depakote®). Of these agents, gabapentin

TABLE 5-4
Selected Antidepressants Used in Pain Management

Name	Class	Schedule	Side Effects
Desipramine	TCA	Dosed HS	Weight gain; somnolence; dry mouth
Elavil Amitripyline	TCA	Dosed HS	Weight gain; somnolence; dry mouth; increased appetite
Zoloft® Sertraline	TCA	Dosed AM or BID	Sleeplessness; visual changes

appears to have the lowest side effect profile with efficacy and does not require monitoring of lab values.

Indications

The AEDs are indicated for sharp, shooting, lancinating pain (termed neuralgia) seen with damage to nerves. The pain is shock-like and always at its greatest intensity on an analogue scale. The pain follows a nerve pathway and is not as widely distributed as neuropathic pain. Pain involving nerve entrapment, radiation fibrosis, and other nerve damage, such as that from certain chemotherapeutic agents, responds to this class of medications.

Typically with neuropathic pain there will be concomitant neuralgic pain as well. Most of the research involving AEDs has been for trigeminal and post-herpetic neuralgias. There have also been studies and clinical evidence that document and demonstrate the effectiveness of AEDs in the prophylaxis of migraine and post-traumatic headaches. Topiramate is currently being evaluated in national, placebo-controlled, double-blind studies, and valproate has long been an on-label agent for these types of headaches.

These agents have several mechanisms of action. They primarily involve an impact on GABA, which is an inhibitory neurotransmitter for pain impulses and alteration of neuronal membrane permeability in the sodium and calcium channels. Thus, the mechanism of action is two-fold: It stabilizes neurons and activates pain inhibitors.

Benzodiazepines

Clonazepam, a benzodiazepine with anticonvulsant action is thought to decrease neuronal firing. It is well absorbed, has a low potential for toxicity and no blood level requirements. These factors have made it extensively utilized for home care hospice patients (Cole, 2002). One drawback is that it is somewhat sedating. Usual daily dosage ranges are from 1–4 mg per day (Cole, 2002).

There are some drawbacks to the use of agents from this class. Patt and Burton (1999) state that, "a careful review of the literature reveals insufficient evidence to support the contention that benzodiazepines have meaningful analgesic properties in most circumstances" (page 359). The authors go on to state that they should not be considered first-line agents due to the potential for cognitive impairment, physical and psychological dependence, worsening depression and other side effects associated with their use (Patt & Burton, 1999). The AHCPR (1994) recommends their use for procedures only, as their analgesic efficacy has not been documented, and the American Pain Society (APS, 1999) lists them as adjuvants but recommends their use in cancer pain in the presence of "recurrent anxiety" and pain related to muscle spasm. The APS recommends that if they are to be used with opioids, there should be a downward titration of the opioids.

Psychostimulants

This class of medication is useful in offsetting the sedating side effects of opioids. Dextroamphetamine and methylphrenidate have been found to enhance the analgesic effects of opioids in patients with cancer pain, as well as improving the appetite, decreasing fatigue and relieving depression (Cole, 2002). Pemoline, another agent, comes in chewable form which can be absorbed through the buccal mucosa (Cole, 2002). The APS (1999) recommends psychostimulant use to combat sedation from opioids. They are used in this fashion primarily for patients with pain from neoplastic disease.

Lidocaine

Lidocaine may be administered via the parenteral, transdermal or transmucosal routes. Neuralgic pain and pain from diabetic neuropathy is responsive to this local anesthetic. It has also been utilized in the differential diagnosis of organic nerve injury (Marchettini et al., 1992).

Recommended dosing with intravenous use for neuralgia is 5 mg/kg over 30 minutes. Effects of the intravenous administration have ranged from 5 to 21 days (Aronoff & Gallagher, 1999). Lidocaine has been used for continuous infusions for brachial plexus injuries and has also been used for epidural infusions. Patients receiving parenteral lidocaine should do so on telemetry.

The transdermal formula comes in a patch and in gel preparations. Topical application is thought to reduce ectopic charges in superficial somatic nerves as its mechanism of action. The patch is "Lidoderm" and has been used very successfully with analgesic onset noted within the first week of treatment. Nurses should instruct patients that the patch is to be worn for 12 hours and removed for 12 hours. This is easily confused with changing the patch every 12 hours, and the distinction should be made. Up to three patches can be worn at one time. There have been no systemic side effects reported.

Capsaicin

Capsaicin derives its mechanism of action through its depletion of substance P, the pain neurotransmitter. It was very popular and promising when it was initially released. Unfortunately, before the substance P is depleted, it is stimulated, and most patients have difficulty with continued use due to the burning it causes on administration. Because of the burning caused on application, double-blind or placebo studies have not been done as the burning un-blinds the agent immediately. Patient should be instructed to wear latex gloves when applying the agent. Outcome studies have been mixed in terms of efficacy.

Steroids

Steroids have specific indications for chronic cancer pain. They are indicated for suspected malignant cord compression and for shrinkage of tumors, especially those associated with lymphoma (APS, 1999). The Medrol Dose Pak has also been found to be effective in certain headaches and inflammatory and arthritic conditions.

Antispasmodics

Baclofen is a GABA agonist that has been extensively studied for its use in spasticity. While typical muscle relaxants are not indicated for long-term use in spasm from muscle strain, baclofen has been found to be very effective in the management of pain from spasticity, reflex sympathetic dystrophy syndrome (RSD) and a variety of myofascial pain disorders. It has also been used for the pain associated with trigeminal neuralgia.

Baclofen is usually administered on a TID, or every eight hour dosing schedule, at 10 mg per dose. Usual daily doses for myofascial pain are 30

TABLE 5-5
Major Differences in Botulinum Toxin Serotypes

• Biochemical structure and molecular weight

• Potency (ED50)

• Intracellular target

---

to 40 mg. Higher doses are usually required for trigeminal neuralgia at 60 to 80 mg per day.

Botulinum Toxin

Pharmacology of Botulinum Toxin

Botulinum toxin is produced by the bacterium *Clostridium botulinum*. Its basic mechanism of action is believed to be through its interference with neuromuscular transmission via its impact on acetylcholine. It binds to the presynaptic nerve terminal preventing the release of acetylcholine and preventing neurotransmission (Swope, 2002).

It appears that botulilinum toxin A may possess some antinociceptive properties in addition to its anticholinergic effects, as evidenced by unanticipated reductions in pain. Case reports and double-blind studies suggest an antincocoeptive effect, the mechanism for which is unknown (Aoki, 2000).

There are seven distinct antigenic types or neurotoxins (serotypes) each with unique differences (see *Table 5-5*). These serotypes have been given the letters A, B, C, D, E, F, and G. Three—A, B, and F—have been tested for clinical efficacy, and A is the best studied of all the serotypes (Aoki, 2001). The twin demand for Botox® (Type A) used in cosmetic and analgesic arenas, has caused enhanced sales.

Indications

Botox has been used for cosmetic purposes for more than a decade. For years, the toxin has been used for spasmodic torticollis, cervical pain from spasm, back pain from spasm, muscle stiffness from Cerebral Vascular Accidents and facial tics in patients diagnosed with Tourette's syndrome. It has also been used for spasticity in cerebral palsy. Most of Botox's uses have been off label, in that they are not approved by the FDA as diagnostic categories for the agent.

Serendipitous Discovery of Botulinum Toxin Type A for Migraines

In 1992, Dr. William Binder, a plastic surgeon, injected botulinum toxin type A into patients' foreheads to treat wrinkles. Several months later, these same patients reported a lessening of their migraine symptoms. This was the first correlation between use of botulinum toxin and a reduction in the severity of headaches.

Botulinum Toxin Type A for Headache

Since Dr. Binder's report on the therapeutic use of botulinum toxin for migraines, additional clinical trials have supported his findings and have expanded knowledge on how best to utilitize this new treatment option. These subsequent trials range from small case studies to larger, double-blind, placebo-controlled trials. Furthermore, the safety and efficacy of botulinum toxin in tension-type headaches and chronic daily headaches have also been studied. Thus, the treatment of headache with botulinum toxin evolves with each new clinical experience reported.

Botulinum Toxin Type A for Chronic Facial Pain

Borodic and Acquardo (2002) conducted an open label pilot study of 44 facial pain patients with diagnoses of temporomandibular disorder, postsurgical pain syndromes, essential headaches and idiopathic trigeminal neuralgia. The study evaluated the safety and efficacy of botulinum toxin type A.

Desired outcomes were: A reduction of frequency and intensity of pain by at least 50% and reduction in use of analgesic medications or requests for more injections. Outcomes were positive in 75% of the patients evaluated at two and six weeks post-injection.

There are currently two brands of botulinum toxin on the market at present. The most popular is **Botox,** which is serotype A and **Myobloc®,** which is serotype B. Undoubtedly, with continued research and broader on-label indications, there will be many more brands on the market.

Documentation

Prior to administration of the agent, an informed consent should be obtained. Patients should be informed of the therapeutic benefits and possible side effects prior to signing the informed consent. The person performing the procedure should provide this information. These steps and the procedure should be documented in the patient record. *Figure 5-1* is a sample format for documenting the injection.

Herbal Agents

Sometimes, in desperation, patients will use herbal agents to aid in their pain management. Patients should be instructed to discuss these agents with their physician and pharmacist when they are taking concomitant prescription drugs.

Research does not substantiate the use of many of these agents as analgesics. The most popular ones are cayenne (Capsaicin), the only agent approved for use by the FDA, and feverfew, also known as St. John's Wort. A recent study of the use of feverfew for pain from polyneuropathy found that it had no effect (Sindrup, Madsen, Bach, Gram & Jensen, 2000).

Glucosamine and chrondroitin combinations have been studied and appear to facilitate the regeneration of new cartilage.

Case Presentation: An 85-year-old male patient presented with diffuse osteoarthritis which had not significantly impacted his function. His primary complaint was severe pain with decreased mobility and strength of the thumb of his dominant hand due to severe osteoarthritis. He was placed on daily supplements of chondroitin and glucosamine and within a few months he had full use of the thumb and little to no pain. While this is anecdotal data involving only one case, there have been other anecdotal reports of the efficacy of this supplement for pain from osteoarthritis.

NURSING IMPLICATIONS

TCAs and AEDs

When utilizing adjuvants and non-opioid analgesics for pain patients, education is imperative. There are many indications and contra-indications for the use of these agents, and patient selection is critical. Once candidacy for management with these agents has been established, there are many questions to be answered and fears to be allayed. For example, many patients have expressed trepidation regarding the use of AEDs fearing the onset of "seizures" with their use.

On more than one occasion, frantic patients have wondered if they had epilepsy because their pharmacist commented on the indications for the use of the AED prescribed by their physician. Another misconception centers on the use of TCAs for pain with patients misconstruing their use with the perception that "the pain is in my head" or that they may have a "psychological problem."

Much of the pre-printed literature that is available for the AEDs and TCAs focuses on

---

FIGURE 5-1
Injection of Botulinum Toxin

PROCEDURE: Botulinum Toxin Injection   **PROCEDURE CODE**_____   **DATE**_____

CLINICAL INDICATION: _____ Spasms of muscle
          _____ Idiopathic torsion dystonia
          _____ Symptomatic torsion dystonia
          _____ Other:_____

Under aseptic technique, a total _____ units of Botulinum Toxin Type_____ were injected in the following muscles:

Procerus: _____ units

Corrugators   right   _____ units   left   _____ units

Frontalis: _____ units

Temporalis   right   _____ units   left   _____ units

Splenius capiti: right   _____ units   left   _____ units

Trapezius   right   _____ units   left   _____ units

Other:_____units

Response to treatment:_____

_____
          (Signature of person performing procedure)

BOTULINUM TOXIN PROCEDURE	ADDRESSOGRAPH

---

their indications for use in epilepsy, bi-polar disease and depression. It behooves the nurse to have customized handouts relating their use for pain management.

Concomitant use of many of these agents with MAO inhibitors and other classes of medications are contra-indicated. A thorough history and pharmacological profile is essential for the protection of the patient. For example, a patient with prostatic hypertrophy is not a candidate for a TCA because urinary retention is a potential side effect.

Side effects can be controlled for through conservative dosing with small incremental increases over time. However, this method does not guarantee that the patient will not experience side effects. Once patients experience side effects, it is difficult to convince them to try the agent again.

Table 5-6 provides some aids for the common side effects of the TCAs. These have proven helpful. If these tips do not help and the side effects are intolerable or interfering with the patient's activities of daily living for quality of life, other pharma-

---

TABLE 5-6
Tips for Common Side Effects of TCAs

- **Dry mouth:** Sugarless hard candies; frozen grapes; synthetic saliva.

- **"Hungover" in the morning:** Take the dose one hour earlier; slow down on the increases by staying on the same dose for three to five extra days.

- **Sedation:** This will resolve in time; slow down on the increases by staying on the same dose for three to five extra days.

- **Weight gain:** Keep non-fattening snacks on hand; avoid night-time eating, when the cravings increase, by drinking a lot of water.

---

cological options should be discussed with the prescriber.

While the analgesic benefits are appreciable with these agents, patients with chronic pain already have problems with increased weight due to a sedentary lifestyle. Extra weight can worsen certain pain problems like back pain by adding stress to structures. Weight gain can also worsen depression if self-esteem is impacted. Switching to or adding an agent like topiramate, which has weight loss as a side effect, may provide some benefit.

Botulinum Toxin

When botulinum toxin is administered, patient education about ptosis or facial drooping should be provided. An informed consent should be signed prior to its administration. While patients are familiar with its use in cosmetic procedures, its use for headache and pain management is less well known. Its use in headaches is considered "off label," so many insurers will not pay for the drug or reimburse professional fees. Nurses in pain or headache clinics can resource with area pharmacies to negotiate rates for patients. An RN case manager did just that, and a pharmacist working in the pharmacy of a local store of a national grocery chain agreed to provide the medication to patients at his cost. This success was due in part to the fact that pharmacies in this particular chain are there as a service to their shoppers and not to make a profit.

Botox must be used upon reconstitution, as it is unstable thereafter. It must be refrigerated until use. When reconstituting the agent, and drawing up the syringes, the nurse should wear gloves to keep the toxin off the hands. Tuberculin syringes and 26 gauge needles are used.

Antispasmodics

Baclofen is the antispasmodic presented in this course, as it has been the most studied. There are two important facts the nurse should tell patients. The first is avoidance of abrupt cessation with chronic use. Convulsions have been reported in cases of abrupt cessation. The other is to make sure that patients have periodic liver enzymes drawn and to educate patients in this regard. Baclofen can elevate liver enzymes. Baclofen can also cause sedation when used initially, so patients should also be cautioned in this respect.

Another antispasmodic that warrants mention is Soma. This agent has a high abuse potential in that it is metabolized into meprobamate. Florida attempted to make Soma® a scheduled agent in June of 2002 for this reason, but the legislation did not pass. Patients have been known to mix Soma with alcohol for its potentiating effects, and it has a street value.

EXAM QUESTIONS

CHAPTER 5
Questions 24–29

Please read the following case presentation and select the best answer to questions 24–29.

Mr. W. has a long-standing history of low back pain, aching in character, which becomes sharp, shooting and burning as it radiates into his legs. He has been depressed because he cannot work, and the pain has kept him awake at night. His physician placed him on a combination of an NSAID, a TCA and an AED.

24. A direct potential benefit related to the use of a TCA for this patient is

   a. urinary retention.
   b. improved sleep.
   c. dry mouth.
   d. he can return to work.

25. The NSAID is primarily for the

   a. depression.
   b. sharp shooting pain.
   c. burning pain.
   d. aching pain.

26. Mr. W. reports that he has been diagnosed with benign prostatic hypertrophy. You inform the physician because he may need to discontinue the

   a. AED.
   b. NSAID.
   c. TCA.
   d. NSAID and the AED.

27. Referencing question #26, what side effect of this medication makes it contraindicated in a patient with prostatic hypertrophy?

   a. decreased B/P
   b. urinary retention
   c. dizziness
   d. dry mouth

28. Mr. W. reports a new onset of heartburn and stomach pain. This is likely due to the

   a. NSAID.
   b. AED.
   c. TCA.
   d. combination of the TCA and AED.

29. The physician has decided to use injections of Botox for Mr. W.'s spasm in the low back. You are instructing a new nurse on the procedure. An important step in setting up for the procedure is to

   a. shake the vial vigorously.
   b. use 22 gauge needles for injection.
   c. keep the Botox at room temperature for 60 minutes prior to injection.
   d. wear gloves.

CHAPTER 6

MANAGING PAIN WITH OPIOIDS: PART ONE

CHAPTER OBJECTIVE

Upon completion of this chapter, the reader will be able to recall the mechanism of action of and receptors for opioids and differentiate between addiction, tolerance and dependence.

LEARNING OBJECTIVES

After studying this chapter, the learner will be able to

1. differentiate between opioid agonists and agonist-antagonists.

2. recognize tolerance.

3. differentiate between dependence and addiction.

4. recall the effect of the active metabolite of mepridine.

5. choose a common side effect of opioid use.

INTRODUCTION

"Opioids remain one of the most misunderstood and mischaracterized classes of medications," stated Arthur G. Lipton, PharmD, Professor, College of Pharmacy and Director of Clinical Pharmacology at the Pain Management Center at the University of Utah Health Sciences Center in Salt Lake City.

This statement was made while chairing a symposium on issues centering on the use of opioid therapy during the 19th Annual Scientific Meeting of the American Pain Society (APS) (Purdue Pharma, 2001c). Despite the controversy surrounding their use and the availability of new analgesics and new indications for the use of adjuvants, opioids continue to have an important role in the management of acute and chronic pain.

MECHANISM OF ACTION

Opioids realize their primary mechanism of action through their binding with specialized receptors within the central nervous system (CNS). These opioid receptors are located primarily within the brain and spinal cord but have also been identified in the periphery and intestines. In order to relieve pain, the opioid must reach and bind with the receptor designed for that purpose. This binding takes place in a stereo-specific fashion, or in other words, as a lock interfaces with a key.

When an opioid is introduced into the organism, the receptors express themselves on the nerve cells through a mechanism termed up-regulation. It is postulated that these receptors are present for binding with endogenous analgesic agents termed endorphins and enkephalins. These are the organism's own natural pain suppressers, with enkephalins smaller in size than the endorphins.

TABLE 6-1
Action of Opioids at Receptors

RECEPTOR SUBTYPE

Agent	Mu	Kappa
Methadone	Agonist	Agonist
Morphine	Agonist	Agonist
Meperidine	Agonist	Agonist
Fentanyl	Agonist	Agonist
Codeine	Agonist	Agonist
Naloxone (Narcan®)	Antagonist	Antagonist
Pentazocine (Talwin®)	Antagosist	Agonist
Butorphanol (Stadol®)	Minimal effect	Agonist
Nalbuphine (Nubain®)	Antagonist	Partial agonist
Buprenorphine	Partial agonist	Agonist

Binding of the opioid takes place on the terminal bulb of the nerve cell or neuron and prevents the pain impulse-carrying neurotransmitter (Substance P) from being released; thereby blocking the pain impulse from being transmitted.

Opioid Receptors

There several opioid receptors and receptor subtypes but the two primary receptors that mediate analgesia are Mu and Kappa. The Mu receptor sub-type is in greatest abundance in the peri-aqueductal gray matter of the brain. The Kappa receptor is located primarily in the spinal cord and produces spinal analgesia when bound with the opioid.

Opioids include any natural or synthetic agent with morphine-like activity and are classified according to the affinity they have with their specialized receptors within the central nervous system (see *Table 6-1*). There are also several other subsets of receptors that, when activated, are responsible for the side effects seen with opioids.

Opioids are further classified as agonists, mixed agonist-antagonists or partial agonists (see *Table 6-1*). The agonist has a greater affinity for binding with the receptor and the agonist-antagonist and mixed agonist will compete with the pure agonist for receptors. The agonist-antagonists and mixed agonists were developed as a solution to the potentially addictive properties of the agonists. It has been found that these agents have the same habit forming potential as the agonists. The concomitant use of agonists and mixed angonist-antagonists is not recommended as this can precipitate withdrawal in the opioid dependent patient, with the antagonist competing with the agonist for receptor sites and actually remove the agonist from the receptor site (Ellison, Lipman, Patt & Portnoy, 1998).

Metabolism

Opioids are metabolized through the liver. Caution should be used in patients with hepatic impairment, with liver enzymes monitored for increases on a regular basis. The metabolites of the various opioids are partially excreted in the urine.

Several opioids have active or toxic metabolites. For example, morphine has two metabolites: M3G, which has been found to be analgesically inactive but may play a role in tolerance, and M6G which is a potent analgesic (Carr, 2001). The M6G is considered with conversions in patients who have renal impairment, as it may not be cleared as completely or efficiently in these patients. There may be a need for less of the drug due to the metabolite's analgesic properties.

Likewise, meperidine also produces two metabolites: Meperidinic acid, an inert agent, and normeperidine, which has appreciable pharmacological activity. Normeperidine causes central nervous system excitability, resulting in tremors, myoclonus and grand mal seizures. A milder analgesic, propoxyphene, is transformed into norpropoxyphene, a potentially toxic agent.

It is important to take the patient's renal and hepatic functioning into consideration when selecting a narcotic analgesic for the treatment of pain. A patient with impaired renal functioning is not an appropriate candidate for an agent with a toxic metabolite such as normeperidine.

Tolerance

The longer the patient takes an opioid the more receptors are expressed, and a phenomenon called tolerance occurs. With tolerance, the need for a higher dose of opioid—in order to achieve the equivalent analgesic effect—takes place. Tolerance develops to some degree in cancer pain, acute pain and in street use of opioids. The rate, extent and true incidence of tolerance warrants further study. It is felt that while human tolerance is initially linear it eventually plateaus, particularly in non-malignant pain and in the absence of disease progression. When utilizing opioids for cancer pain management, it is important to differentiate between disease progression and true tolerance when increases in dosage requirements are needed.

As tolerance to the analgesic properties of an agent occurs, a concomitant tolerance to the respiratory depressant and sedative effects occurs as well. Tolerance to the sedative effects of the opioids often occurs after a week.

Unfortunately, tolerance to the constipating effects of these agents does not occur and management for this important and often overlooked side

effect must begin at the outset of opioid therapy. Concomitant use of a mild laxative with a stool softener is recommended.

Incomplete Cross-Tolerance

While the most commonly used opioid analgesics bind with the same receptors, their activities differ, and patients vary in the how sensitive they are to the analgesic. This is also true of the side effects that patients will sometimes experience. For example, patients who cannot tolerate morphine due to nausea may do quite well on methadone. In addition, when tolerance to the analgesic effects occurs, the practitioner can switch to another Mu sensitive agonist and realize the same level of analgesia with lower dosages. This is termed incomplete cross-tolerance.

Pseudotolerance

Pseudotolerance is the need to increase dosage that is not due to true physiologic tolerance but is due to factors other than tolerance. This phenomenon may occur as a result of either physiological or behavioral factors, including:

- Disease progression;
- Increased physical activity;
- Drug interaction;
- Diversion;
- Addiction;
- Lack of compliance;
- New disease; and
- Change in medication.

Pseudotolerance may be seen in patients with metastatic disease wherein the current dosage does not cover the new pathophysiological processes. Another situation is when mini-withdrawal symptoms manifest following a change in medication brand. This sometimes results from a decrease in analgesic blood levels with some generic sustained-release opioids due to diminished bio-availability. Certain drug interactions may interfere with intestinal absorption or plasma clearance. With diversion, patients may be selling their drugs and reporting tolerance to obtain additional units or stronger preparations.

Diversion

The prescribing healthcare provider must complete an in depth evaluation of the patient and contact pharmacies in the area to see if the patient has been receiving controlled substances from other practitioners (see *Table 6-4*). In addition to the history and physical examination, a psychological evaluation may be helpful.

If addiction is confirmed or strongly suspected, a referral for drug treatment should be made. If diversion is suspected, the patient must be quickly weaned from all controlled substances and the area pharmacies and emergency rooms notified. If diversion is confirmed, the same steps must be followed and a police report filed, as "doctor shopping" or subterfuge as it is termed, is a felony offense in many states.

Dependence

Dependence, when discussing opioids, must be divided into physical and psychological dependence. Physical dependence occurs in any person taking an opioid for a period of time. When the opioid is removed and the half life expires, a variety of physiological responses occur in varying degrees.

These responses are termed "withdrawals or abstinence syndrome."

Signs and symptoms of withdrawal or abstinence syndrome can include but are not limited to

- hypertension and tachycardia;
- nausea/vomiting;
- abdominal pain;
- excessive yawning;
- feeling as though "coming out of their skin;"
- tremors; and

- diaphoresis.

It is imperative to treat the withdrawals with an agent that has an immediate onset of action or biphasic properties (both long and immediate acting).

Psychological dependence has been classified by a consensus group comprised of the American Pain Society, the American Academy of Pain Medicine and the American Society of Addiction Medicine. Psychological dependence may manifest as a consequence of fear of uncontrolled pain or avoidance of abstinence syndrome. In contrast to physical dependence, psychological dependence is a purely emotional state. If this type of dependence is suspected or evident, a consultation with a psychologist or other mental health counselor is warranted.

Addiction

Conversely, addiction is behavioral with the compulsion to use controlled substances for reasons other than pain relief and is felt to be a rare phenomenon in most acute and chronic pain conditions (see *Table 6-2*) (Fox, 2002). True addiction, though feared, is rare in most chronic pain patients, but the presence of personality disorders and sociopathic traits make addiction and subsequent abuse more likely (Fox, 2002).

When the problem is primarily addiction and secondarily pain, then a referral to drug treatment is indicated before the pain can be properly managed. In most cases, pharmacological alternatives to opioids should be exhausted. The addicted patient with a true chronic pain problem is best managed by pain specialists and/or addictionologists.

The term "pseudoaddiction" has been used to describe individuals who have severe unrelieved pain and who become focused on finding relief to the point that they appear preoccupied with obtaining opioids. This behavioral preoccupation is not truly "drug-seeking" but is in fact, "relief-seeking."

TABLE 6-2

Some Key Behavioral Differences Between an Addict and a Pain Patient

Addict	**Pain Patient**
Medications decrease Quality of Life	Medications increase Quality of Life
Will not comply with a contract	Adheres to a contract
Never has medications left over	Often has medications left over

---

This phenomenon may occur when doses are prescribed that are too low or spaced too far apart to achieve adequate pain relief or when the prescriber does not consider the patient's previous opioid use, which can affect his/her response.

The consequences of inadequate prescription practices is severe, unrelieved pain causing the patient to become focused on obtaining opioids, not for its euphoric effects but for its analgesic effects. Pseudoaddiction can be distinguished from true addiction by the following characteristics:

- Patient behavior, which might have suggested addiction, resolves after adequate analgesia is obtained.

- Patient does not use opioids to persistently cause sedation or euphoria.

- Patient's level of function is increased not decreased.

- Patient medications are used as prescribed (American Society of Addiction Medicine, 1997).

Role of the Nurse

The nurse is the person who typically has the greatest amount of contact with the patient. Depending on the treatment setting, the role of the nurse can be quite diverse.

The med-surg nurse is likely to work with more of the shorter acting opioids and acute pain patients but may also have patients admitted for procedures or events associated with acute pain who have a concurrent chronic pain problem. An assessment tool like the Acute and Chronic Pain Assessment Tool (see *Figure 3-3*) may have some utility in this situation. It is important that the nurse realize that the opioids used for the chronic pain will not mitigate the acute pain. Orders for additional short acting opioids and adjuvants should be obtained. Physicians may not realize this, and the nurse may realize a new role as educator of the physician. Obtaining a thorough medication history is very important in this situation.

The oncology nurse may be used to working with very high dosages of narcotics in a variety of delivery systems. Monitoring for increasing pain and/or decreasing efficacy of the interventions is important in this setting. The nurse should be alert for signs of disease progression which may be altering the patient's analgesic requirements.

The pediatric nurse will be working with the developmental aspects of pain expression. Procedural pain management is important in this setting. Optimizing IV access for administration of opioids is desirous but physicians often order IM routes in the presence of IV access. The nurse may assume the position of negotiator and educator to get the patient what they need for pain management.

Assessment and re-assessment is essential in the management of the patient receiving opioids for acute and chronic pain (see *Table 6-3*).

The nurse in a primary care practice may only occasionally come across patients in pain while a nurse in a pain management practice may be called

TABLE 6-3
Primary Treatment Outcomes to be Assessed

OPIOID THERAPY: OUTCOMES

- **EFFICACY:** Is the pain relieved or reduced to patient satisfaction?

- **SIDE-EFFECTS:** Are they being managed? Is the patient responding?

- **DOSAGES:** Is tolerance developing?

- **FUNCTION:** Has function improved?

- **AFFECT:** Be responsive and empathetic

- **BEHAVIORS:** Is the patient drug-seeking?

upon to handle multiple prescriptions of controlled substances or to do "detective work" in contacting area pharmacies checking on patients for activities related to diversion (see *Table 6-4*).

Nurses in all practice settings should be aware of the side-effects of these agents and provide the apropriate intervention. For example, constipation is a common side-effect that should be prevented and orders obtained for a stool softener and mild laxative at the onset of therapy.

TABLE 6-4
Activities Related to Diversion

OPIOID THERAPY: NURSING ART AND SCIENCE

- **DATA:** Know your analgesic pharmacology and pain physiology.

- **PRINCIPLES:** Understand relevant concepts and standards.

- **COMMUNICATION:** Be thorough and objective in your documentation.

- **INTUITION:** Follow through on "gut feelings."

- **ADVOCACY:** Champion your patient's rights to pain management.

- **EDUCATION:** Share your information with peers and colleagues.

EXAM QUESTIONS

CHAPTER 6
Questions 30–37

30. Opioids have their primary analgesic effects through binding with

    a. receptors in the CNS.

    b. metabolites in the CNS.

    c. receptors in the periphery.

    d. receptors in the intestines.

31. The smallest endogenous analgesics are called

    a. ketones.

    b. endorphins.

    c. enkephalins.

    d. androgens.

32. Methadone is an opioid

    a. mixed agonist.

    b. antagonist.

    c. agonist-antagonist.

    d. agonist.

33. Meperidine

    a. produces two inert metabolites.

    b. produces one active and one inert metabolite.

    c. produces M_3G.

    d. produces two active metabolites.

34. Your patient has been switched from morphine to methadone and has the same pain relief with less narcotic. This is an example of

    a. physical dependence.

    b. incomplete cross-tolerance.

    c. addiction.

    d. pseudotolerance.

35. A patient who is a poor candidate for meperidine is a(n)

    a. dialysis patient.

    b. post-laminectomy patient.

    c. adolescent patient.

    d. post-op cholecystectomy patient.

36. Constipation secondary to opioid use should

    a. not be a concern.

    b. decrease after one week.

    c. warrant the discontinuance of the medication.

    d. be prevented with the use of a stool softener and mild laxative.

37. Pseudotolerance is a result of

    a. physiologic tolerance.

    b. disease progression.

    c. drug allergy.

    d. decreased physical activity.

CHAPTER 7

MANAGING PAIN WITH OPIOIDS: PART TWO

CHAPTER OBJECTIVE

Upon completion of this chapter, the reader will be able to list the opioids indicated for management of mild to severe acute and chronic pain, recall the differences between the sustained and immediate release preparations and identify the nursing interventions for managing the patient receiving opioids.

LEARNING OBJECTIVES

After studying this chapter, the learner will be able to

1. identify the prototypical opioid.

2. cite the three primary routes of administration of opioids.

3. recognize what is meant by the hepatic first-pass effect.

4. choose one containdication to the use of tramadol (Ultram).

5. identify a benefit of Patient Controlled Analagesia (PCA).

6. identify the optimum dosing schedule for methadone.

7. recognzie the relationship between spinal catheter placement and the action of epidural opioids.

8. cite one nursing intervention for each opioid side effect.

INTRODUCTION

"One hundred years ago, morphine would without question been considered the most important drug used in medicine" (Way & Way, 1989, p. 368–382). Back then, there were no antibiotics, anti-psychotic or hormonal agents. In addition to managing pain, morphine was used for coughs, anxiety, diarrhea and insomnia. The panacea of its time, morphine led Sir William Osler to describe it as "God's own medicine." Opioid analgesics include natural and semi-synthetic alkaloid derivatives from opium. Morphine, one of opium's purified constituents, remains the prototypical opioid against which all others are measured. It was discovered by a German pharmacist, Sertimer, who isolated it from opium in 1803 (Way & Way, 1989).

OPIOID DOSING

Routes of Administration

Opioids bind with receptors within the CNS, following enteral, parenteral, spinal, or transdermal administration. Enteral administration is accommodated via the nose, mouth or rectum. Parenteral administration is achieved via intravenous, subcutaneous or intramuscular routes. Spinal administration is accomplished through epidural, or intrathecal injections.

Oral

This is the preferred route, as it is most convenient and most cost-effective. Analgesics are to be maximized via the oral route. Oral opioids come in liquid, tablet, and capsule forms. They are also available in immediate and sustained release preparations. The sustained release are preferred for chronic administration as the "peak and trough" effect is eliminated, providing the patient with a more steady-state analgesia. The euphoria that is realized with the short acting agents is not appreciated with the longer acting ones, thereby reducing the risk for psychological dependence.

Patients with chronic malignant or nonmalignant pain should have their medications converted from short to long-acting drugs using an equianalgesic conversion (see *Table 7-3*). This conversion provides a dosage of the new opioid that is the analgesic equivalent to the dosage of the current opioid. Morphine is the standard when assessing equivalency in the analgesics.

Patients on sustained-release preparations may experience breakthrough pain: Pain that "breaks through" despite the duration of action of the analgesic. Shorter-acting agents should be prescribed in anticipation of this and, depending on the setting, the short-acting dosages for each 24-hour dosing period should be incorporated into the sustained-release preparation in equivalent doses (i.e., every 8 or every 12 hours). Management of breakthrough pain is indicated for chronic malignant pain. If opioid requirements increase in the absence of disease progression in chronic non-malignant pain, discontinuance of the opioids may be warranted.

Rectal

When the oral route is not feasible, rectal administration is an option. When administered correctly, rectal administration can avoid an hepatic first-pass effect. The uppermost region of the rectum is mediated by the superior rectal vein which returns blood to portal circulation. In order to avoid this effect, the medication must be administered in the middle or inferior vault of the rectum, less than 15 cm high (Lipman & Jackson, 2000). In the case of a colostomy, medications can also be placed in the stoma, provided the rate of flow of effluent is such to afford absorption (AHCPR, 1994).

Parenteral

A continuous intravenous infusion affords the patient steady-state analgesia. Usually, the parenteral delivery system is used if the patient is unable to take medications by mouth, has persistent nausea/vomiting, requires rapid incremental dosages of analgesia, and/or has a mental state that is incompatible with ingesting the medication. The patient may also be on high, frequent doses of oral medications that warrant parenteral administration. In chronic non-malignant pain, parenteral administration is rarely warranted or indicated.

Patient Controlled Analgesia (PCA) may be utilized for the continuous administration of opioids for acute or chronic malignant pain control. An infusion device is utilized providing a continuous administration of the medication, with the option of an additional self-administered bolus dose. At initiation of the infusion, a bolus is given and a basal or continuous rate of infusion may be programmed. When PCA was introduced in the 1980s, it was initially used without a concomitant continuous infusion. Unfortunately, once patients went to sleep and did not access the machine for doses, the analgesic blood levels would drop, and pain would once again break through. The patient would then have to wait until the levels increased for analgesia to be realized. This was resolved with the use of the basal, or continuous infusion, on top of which the patient could self-administer a needed dose of analgesic.

A lock-out period is also programmed into the device so that the patient can receive medication at selected intervals, varying anywhere from 6 to 30 minutes. This allows the patient to dose at times

TABLE 7-1
Systemic Opioids for Acute Pain Management

Analgesic (Agonist)	Route	Loading[a,b] Dose (mg/kg)	Maintenance[d] Dose (mg/kg)	Frequency[c] (hours)
Codeine	PO	1.5	0.75	3–4
	SC, IM	1.0	0.5	3–4
Morphine	PO	0.5–1.0	.05–1.0	4
	Sustained Release	1.0	1.0—2.0	8–12–24
	SC, IM	0.15	0.1–0.2	3–4
	IV	0.15	0.01–0.04/HR	Continuous
Hydrocodone (Vicodin®, Lortab®)	PO	.15	.07–.15	4–6
Oxycodone[e] (Percocet®, OxyIR®)	PO	.15	0.07–0.15	3–4
	Sustained Release			12
Meperidine[f] (Demerol®)	PO	2.5–3.5	1.5–3.0	3–4
	SC, IM	1.5–2.0	1.0–1.5	3–4
	IV	1.5–2.0	0.3–0.6/HR	Continuous
Hydromorphone (Dilaudid®)	PO	0.04–0.08	0.04–0.08	3
	SC, IM	0.02–0.04	0.03–0.06	3
	IV	0.02	0.01/HR	Continuous
Methadone[g]	PO	0.2–0.4	0.1–0.4	Q 6 hours
Fentanyl[h] (Duragesic, Actiq®)	Transmucosal	200 mcg	variable	Q15 minutes
	Transdermal		Q 72 hours	
Tramadol	PO		Q4-6 hours	

Analgesic (Mixed Agonist Antagonist)[i]	Route	Loading[a,b] Dose (mg/kg)	Maintenance[d] Dose (mg/kg)	Frequency[c] (hours)
Pentazocine (Talwin)	PO	1.5–2.5	1.0–1.5	6
	SC, IM	1.0	0.7–1.0	6
	IV	1.0	0.7–1.0/HR	6
Nalbuphine (Nubain)	SC, IM	0.05–0.1	0.5–0.1	3–4
	IV	0.05–0.1	0.05–0.1/HR	3–4
Butorphanol (Stadol)	SC, IM	0.03	0.02—0.04	3
	IV, intranasal	0.03	0.02–0.04	3

Partial agonist[t]	Route	Loading[a,b] Dose (mg/kg)	Maintenance[d] Dose (mg/kg)	Frequency[c] (hours)
Buprenorphine (Buprenex®)	Sublingual	0.006	0.004	6–8
	SC, IM	0.004	0.002	6
	IV	0.004	0.002/HR	6

a IV front loading dose should be titrated slowly to control for overdose.
b Apart from pediatrics, body weight is not an accurate prediction for opioid efficacy. Titration is individualized taking into account patient variables.
c Maintenance dose is usually 1/2 the effective loading dose.
d If breakthrough pain occurs prior to next scheduled maintenance dose, give one additional maintenance dose, continue schedule
e May be compounded with acetaminophen (Percocet) or ASA (Percodan®), which limits amount per24 hour period due to potential hepatotoxic effects. Available as a sustained release preparation (Oxycontin) and as plain oxycodone (OxyIR), not compounded.
f Metabolite of normeperidine is cumulative and provokes CNS excitability. Not indicated for prolonged infusions/administration or higher doses as seizures may result.
g Observe for accumulation especially after 48 hours. Not indicated for persons with pulmonary compromise or elderly.
h Due to short duration of action the transmucoasl form is available as lollipop which is to be placed in the side of the mouth Q15minutes.
Transdermal patches will not load, therefore short-acting opioids or Actiq should be given in equivalent doses for the first 12 hours.
i Can precipitate abstinence syndrome in opioid-dependent patients.

Adapted from Ready, B. & Edwards, W. (Eds.). (1992). *The management of acute pain: A practical guide.* Seattle: International Association for the Study of Pain.

when the pain is going to be worse (i.e., transfers, cough and breathing, physical therapy). While there is a place for PCA in chronic malignant pain management, it is best suited for instances of acute and/or post-operative pain. Patients with malignant pain typically warrant continuous infusions.

Absorption

Following oral or rectal administration, opioids are readily absorbed from the gastrointestinal tract. Prior to reaching systemic circulation, they must first pass through the liver. This is referred to as hepatic first-pass metabolism. As some of the analgesic is converted to a metabolite following this first pass metabolism, greater dosages are needed for oral versus parenteral administration.

In most patients, immediate-release oral opioids have an onset of action of about 20–40 minutes. Peak analgesia occurs in about 45 to 60 minutes. Agents do present with some variability in attaining this peak effect. For example, morphine is reported to reach peak plasma levels in 30–45 minutes while oxycodone may take 60–90 minutes to realize the same effect (Lipman & Jackson, 2000).

Ceiling Effect

A dose ceiling occurs when there is a lack of additional efficacy after a pre-determined dose is achieved. In other words, pain relief won't increase with dosage increases. Once this ceiling has been reached, toxicity occurs when upward titration is attempted. This is referred to as a true dose ceiling. The mixed agonist-antagonist and the partial agonist opioid have a true dose ceiling effect. A true ceiling dose does not exist for the pure Mu agonists.

Intraspinal

Delivery Systems

Analgesics may be administered intraspinally when pain is not adequately controlled via other routes. This is indicated for postoperative, labor or chronic malignant pain. Intraspinal opioids for chronic malignant pain are usually indicated for pain from sacral and pelvic metastasis of the disease to the sacrum and pelvis.

The catheter for the delivery of the medication is placed in either the epidural space or the subacrachnoid area specific to the dermatome that corresponds with the site of pain. For example, for a post-op thoracotomy, the catheter will be placed at the thoracic level.

Patient Controlled Epidural Analgesia (PCEA)

Patient controlled analgesia may also be utilized for epidural infusions of opioids or mixed concentrations of opioids with a local anesthetic, such as bupivicaine. Access to the epidural space is created with the physician utilizing an epidural needle to introduce a small catheter. Once the catheter is in place, the needle is removed and the catheter advanced and secured with a clear occlusive dressing. The catheter is then attached to an infuser which is programmed to deliver a continuous low dose infusion of the concentration on top of which the patient may choose to deliver bolus injections of the same concentration at pre-programmed intervals. There are well-documented advantages to the use of both PCA and PCEA systems, including decreases in analgesic level peaks and troughs, steady state analgesia, and shorter lengths of stay with earlier ambulation following surgery due to lower pain levels.

Medications

The concomitant use of an opioid with bupivacaine, a long acting local anesthetic, has proven to be more efficacious than the use of opioids alone (Raj & Rasz, 1998). Typically bupivacaine in concentrations of 0.03% to .125% in combination with either morphine or fentanyl is employed. A lower incidence of side effects has been reported in the fentanyl-bupivacaine combination (Raj & Racz, 1998).

Nursing Implications

Epidural analgesia may be delivered continuously or intermittently. Continuous infusions utilize

TABLE 7-2

The Most Important Problems and Nursing Interventions Specific to Caring for Patients Receiving Intraspinal Analgesics

Problem	Signs/Symptoms	Interventions
Respiratory depression from migration of opioid to the brain	Respiratory depression will be preceded by miosis and is usually gradual	Maintain IV access for administer naloxone as ordered
		Stop infusion & assess respiratory function including rate, quality of effort, & presence of apneic spells
		Continued vigilance
		Elevate HOB
		Have MD establish acceptable respiratory parameters
		Provide supportive measures until and after naloxone is administered and has taken effect
Urinary retention related to effect of opioid on spinal nerves	Decreased output, distention, discomfort	Catheterization as ordered
		Naloxone infusion as ordered
Spinal headache as result of puncture of dura	Usually develops 24 hours after catheter insertion	Do not place patient in upright position for 24 hours (HOB may be raised) Stop infusion Notify MD who may elect to perform a blood patch to seal the leak
Infection due to poor sterile technique or systemic bacteremia	Swelling/redness at site of insertion	Adhere to hospital policy for catheter care
	Signs of meningitis	Use occlusive transparent dressings at site
	Elevated temperature and pulse	Stop infusion, notify MD
		When catheter is discontinued in the presence of elevated temperature, send tip for C&S

Source: American Pain Society. (1999). *Principles of analgesic use in the treatment of acute pain and cancer pain,* 4th ed. Glenview, IL: Author.

an infusion device. Only specially trained personnel should manage intraspinal infusion systems (see *Table 7-2*). Ideally, the hospital should have a credentialing program for nurses caring for these patients. Institutional policies and procedures to establish an acceptable standard of practice for the nursing care of patients receiving intraspinal opioids should also be available to the nursing staff.

Pain Cocktails

Pain cocktails are compounded usually liquid doses of narcotics used to decrease opioid doses in an objective fashion. The goals of pain cocktail use are typically two-fold: Evaluate the narcotic analgesic needs of the patient while controlling for subjective bias and decrease the amount of opioid used by the patient. (see *Figure 9-4*, Chapter 9.)

Historically used in conjunction with interdisciplinary pain management programs, the pain cocktail involves the use of an opioid with an adjuvant and/or non-opioid analgesic. Patients who have been on opioid therapy or patients who may be candidates for chronic opioid therapy are placed on scheduled doses of a liquid or powdered opioid (usually methadone), acetaminophen and/or hydroxyzine in a liquid vehicle. The vehicle is usually juice or cherry syrup.

The patient is instructed not to ask about the ingredients or doses thereof while being assured that their pain will be managed. An equi-analgesic conversion of whatever opioid the patient has been taking to methadone is made and the co-analgesic or adjuvant is added. The medication is given every six hours and not on a time-contingent schedule.

Every 48 to 72 hours the opioid dosage is titrated downward while the non-opioids are maximized. The patient's function, pain scores, activity level and therapy performance are monitored. If there is an objective indication of requirements for an upward/downward titration of the opioid, these are made based on the relevant team member's input.

Some of the objective indicators of increased analgesic need are reflected in functional performance in either physical or occupational therapy. For example, the patient may demonstrate significant decreases in the number of repetitions or distance walked following a downward adjustment of the opioid. This is relayed to the physician who then makes the decision regarding the adjustment. It is not uncommon for patients to be off of opioids completely with tremendous increases in their physical and functional capacities. By "blinding" the patient to the nature of the adjustments the bias of fear of pain or the psychological dependence on the agent is controlled for.

Legally, the patient must be told the ingredients of the cocktail but not the dosages. However, at the outset of treatment, an agreement should be made between the patient and the team stating that the patient will not make inquiries of the nature of the cocktail but focus on their program en total.

Patients may not necessarily require inpatient treatment or even an interdisciplinary program. A capsule called "Dolocap" which is compounded by local pharmacies and provided as a prescription medication with instructions for use can be used. The patient may be receiving selected treatments such as physical therapy or biofeedback as an outpatient and taking the "Dolocaps" as prescribed.

It is imperative that the appearance of the capsule or cocktail not vary as adjustments are made. Local pharmacists must have an understanding of the treatment philosophy and rationale as part of the treatment team. The medications in the capsules are typically provided in powder form and not as tablets placed within the capsule as patients may get curious and open the capsule to determine its ingredients.

Nursing Implications

Whether as a nurse on a pain team or as an office nurse in a pain management practice, as narcotic dosages are being adjusted the patient should be monitored for signs and symptoms of abstinence syndrome and increased pain. Encouraging patients to focus on treatment goals and function and not on the pain medications is a very important nursing intervention. Communication with the physician and members of the treatment team regarding the patient's compliance with the regimen and tolerance of the medications is an important nursing function.

Sometimes the nurse may need to do some detective work and telephone area pharmacies to ensure that patients are not having prescriptions from other healthcare providers for controlled-substances filled elsewhere.

When in the hospital setting, standard orders or a pain cocktail form may be used (see *Figure 9-4,* Chapter 9). In the office, or clinic setting the nurse should ensure that photocopies of prescriptions are made and that the patient's record is maintained. It is also good practice for the nurse to establish a rapport with area pharmacists.

Depending on the treatment setting the nurses may be responsible for compounding the cocktail or the pharmacy may assume this responsibility.

Organ System Effects

Central Nervous System

While opioids are found in the intestines and to a lesser extent in the peripheral tissues, they predominate in the central nervous system where they have their principal effects. The most important effects, with respect to nursing management, are analgesia, euphoria, sedation, respiratory depression and constipation.

Analgesia is the primary effect and the others are considered adverse or side effects and are important to consider when administering the opioid and monitoring the patient.

Analgesia—With respect to analgesia, opioids impact both the perception and reaction of the patient in pain. While the perception of pain can be evaluated, the reaction to pain is subject to the singular uniqueness of each patient. It is known that opioids raise the pain threshold and while the pain may not be taken away completely, its severity may be diminished.

Euphoria—Once the medication is administered, the patient experiences a degree of freedom from anxiety and distress along with a pleasant floating sensation. This is the affective response of euphoria.

Sedation—Drowsiness, the impairment of reasoning ability and clouding of mentation, is experienced in varying degrees by the person receiving opioids. This is more common in the elderly than the young and is potentiated by other central nervous system agents, such as the sedative-hypnotics. Usually, the patient is easily aroused when sedated; additionally, it has been noted that normal REM and NREM sleep patterns are disturbed, which is characteristic of all of the opioids.

Respiratory depression—All opioids inhibit the brain stem respiratory mechanisms producing varying degrees of respiratory depression. The respiratory depression is dose-related and can be influenced significantly by sensory input occurring at the same time. A small to moderate decrease in respiratory function may be well tolerated in patients with no prior history of pulmonary impairment or disease.

Nausea/Vomiting—Stimulation of the chemoreceptor trigger zone located in the brain stem may provoke nausea and vomiting. With the advent of PCA, less nausea and/or vomiting occurred in patients receiving opioids. With PCA, as with sustained-release preparations, small amounts of the opioid are delivered over a period of time so that non-opioid receptors in the brain stem are not saturated.

OPIOID ANALGESICS

Legal Requirements

Opioid analgesics are considered scheduled drugs in the United States. Scheduled drugs require the prescriber be assigned a DEA number. The schedule ranges from 1–4. Each state has its own rules and regulations, and it is important for nurses to understand what their state requires with respect to scheduled drugs.

The agents discussed here are either Schedule 2 or 3. Schedule 2 agents must be prescribed in written fashion, and prescriptions may not be pre-printed or refilled. The prescription for a Schedule 2 agent must have the physician's, nurse practitioner's or physician's assistant's name printed, along with their signature, and the assigned DEA number present on the hard copy itself. In some states, the DEA number may not be stamped or pre-printed. The Schedule 3 agents may be telephoned to the pharmacy and may be refilled for a total of a six months supply. Apart from these exceptions, the restrictions noted with the Schedule 2 agents apply to Schedule 3.

Most Commonly Used Opioids

For this course, the opioid agonists will be detailed (see *Tables 7-1* and *7-3*). The most commonly prescribed full agonists, with no ceiling effect and which do not compete with one another for receptor space, are: Morphine, methadone, hydromorphone, and fentanyl. These are also the agents indicated for management of moderate to severe pain.

The following agonists have a ceiling due to their active metabolites or agents with which they are compounded: Hydrocodone, codeine, oxycodone propoxyphene, tramadol, meperidine. They are indicated for the management of mild to moderate pain.

These agents are immediate or sustained-release preparations as detailed below. The U.S.

market for sustained-release opioids has grown by an average of 46% annually since 1996.

When placing patients on chronic opioid therapy, it is important to use the sustained-release agents for the following reasons:

1. Short acting agents have the potential for increased abuse potential due to secondary euphoria.

2. Less sedation and other CNS effects are noted with the sustained-released preparations.

3. Peaks and troughs in analgesic levels do not provide steady-state analgesia.

4. Less analgesic is used overall with the sustained-release preparations.

5. Tolerance does not develop as rapidly.

6. Patients can work while on these agents.

Opioid Data

Morphine (MS Contin®, Oramorph®, Kadian®, MSIR®)

- May be delivered orally, rectally or parenterally.

- Provided in immediate (MSIR) and sustained-release vehicles: MS Contin, Oramorph dosed every 8–12 hours & Kadian dosed every 24 hours.

- A new sustained-release agent by Elan Pharmaceuticals is due to be release soon as Avinza® and will be available in capsule form.

Methadone

- Has a long half life (24 hours) but analgesic efficacy is six hours.

- Has a cumulative effect and should not be used in patients with pulmonary compromise, sleep apnea, poor renal clearance or in the elderly.

- Prescribers do not need a special license if prescribed for pain control.

TABLE 7-3
Opioid Analgesics: Equivalents

Name	Equianalgesic Dose (mg) Oral	Parenteral*	Starting Oral Dose Adult (mg)	Children (mg/kg)	Comments
a. Morphine-like agonists					
Morphine	30	10	15–30	0.30	Standard of comparison for opioid analgesics. Sustained release preparations (MS Contin, OramorphSR) release drug over 6–12 hours. Recent addition of once-a-day sustained release formulation (Kadian).
Hydromorphone (Dilaudid)	7.5	1.5	4–8	0.06	Slightly shorter duration than morphine.
Oxycodone	20	—	15–30	0.30	Available as sustained-release over 12 hr.
Methadone (Dolophine®)	20 acute	10 acute	5–10	0.20	Good oral potency, long plasma half-life (24–36 hours) analgesic half-life is six hours.
Fentanyl		0.1			Transdermal fentanyl (Duragesic) 25 mcg/hour, roughly equivalent to sustained-release morphine, 45 mg/day. Oral transmucosal fentanyl citrate now available for breakthrough pain in chronic cancer pain patients who are opioid tolerant.
Meperidine (Demerol)	300	75	not recommended		Not indicated for use longer than 7 days due to active metabolite.
b. Mixed agonist-antagonists					
Nabuphine (Nubain)	—	10	—	—	Not available orally, not scheduled under Controlled Substances Act.
Butorphanol (Stadol)	—	2	—	—	Also available as nasal spray
c. Partial agonist Buprenorphine	—	0.4	—	—	Sublingual preparation not yet available (Buprenex) in United States; does not produce psychotomimetic effects

*These are standard IM doses for acute pain in adults and also can be used to convert doses for IV infusions and repeated small IV boluses. For single IV boluses, use half the IM dose. IV doses for children >6 months = parental equi-analgesic dose x weight (kg)/100. For infants <6 months see prescribing literature.

Source: American Pain Society. (1999b). *Principles of analgesic use in the treatment of acute pain and cancer pain,* 4th ed. Glenview, IL: Author.

- Edema and urinary retention may occur with chronic therapy.

- Is the least expensive sustained-release preparation.

- Comes in liquid form for each administration/dosage adjustment.

Hydromorphone (Dilaudid, Dilaudid SR)

- Is currently available as short-acting, but studies are in effect for sustained release preparations.

- Has a slightly shorter duration of action than morphine.

Fentanyl (Duragesic, Actiq)

- Has a very short half-life and is not available in enteral form.

- Available as transdermal delivery adhesive patches called Duragesic.

- Transdermal is dosed in 25, 50, 75 or 100 mcg every 72 hours.

- The patches have a 12 hour delay in onset of analgesia; patients will need short acting opioids during this period.

- Do not apply direct heat to patch as it will cause vasodilation and bolus delivery of agent into bloodstream; fever will increase dose rate.

- Available for transmucosal delivery for cancer pain as a lollipop called Actiq.

- Actiq is not to be used in opioid naïve (intolerant) patients.

Hydrocodone (Lortab, Lorcet®, Vicodin, Vicoprofen®)

- Is compounded with aspirin (ASA) or acetaminophen.

- Also available as Vicoprofen (hydrocodone with ibuprofen).

- Not indicated for use in chronic pain.

Codeine (Tylenol #3®, Sulfate 504)

- Ideal as a cough suppressant as codine P04.

- Usually compounded with acetaminophen or ASA.

Propoxyphene (Darvon®, Darvocet-N®)

- Biotransformed to potentially toxic metabolite (norpropoxyphene).

- Overdose complicated by seizures.

- The medication and its metabolite may accumulate with repetitive dosing.

- Medicaid is considering the removal of this from their formulary in the state of Florida.

Oxycodone (Percocet, Percodan, Tylox®, Oxycontin, Oxyir®, Roxicodone®)

- May be compounded with ASA or acetaminophen which limits 24 hour dosing.

- Sustained-release preparation (Oxycontin) has bi-phasic onset of action, which means it has immediate and sustained-release properties and analgesia effects.

- Sustained-release should never be crushed or chewed.

- Non-compounded preparations are now available (Oxyir).

- Available in higher potency immediate-release tablets of 15 and 30 mgm (Roxicodone).

Tramadol (Ultram®, Ultracet®)

- Weak Mu agonist and inhibits the re-uptake of norepinephrine and serotonin.

- Not a scheduled drug.

- Maximum dose is 400 mg/day.

- Lowers seizure threshold.

Meperidine (Demerol, Mepergan®)

- Available compounded with phenergan (promethazine) called Mepergan.

- Has an active, toxic metabolite which can cause seizures when accumulated.

TABLE 7-4
Specific Opioid-Related Side Effects With Nursing Interventions

Facts	Interventions
I. Respiratory Depression	
• Is usually seen in opioid naïve patients and those with a history of pulmonary compromise. • Typically occurs at sleep.	Assess respiratory rate, character and effort. When using opioids for acute pain, have IV access available. Administer naloxone (Narcan) which is an agonist displacing the opioid from the receptor site. Naloxone will reverse the analgesic effects of systemic opioids.
II. Constipation	
• Most common side effect associated with chronic opioid therapy.	Start the patient on a bowel program at the onset of opioid use. Establish the patient's regular bowel habits by history. Start with a senna preparation with a stool softener on a daily to TID basis. Utilize enemas and suppositories as needed to prevent impaction. If feasible, fluids, roughage and fiber should be a part of the daily diet.
III. Nausea/Vomiting	
	May be associated with a particular agent. Sometimes switching to a sustained-release dosing regimen or dosage preparation will help. Changing the opioid or dosage may also help. Administer antiemetics as ordered and re-evaluate.

• Is not indicated for prolonged use.

• Most of the oral preparation is lost in the hepatic first-pass effect and is not recommended.

• Not indicated for patients with renal compromise because of the toxic metabolite.

NURSING INTERVENTIONS FOR PATIENTS RECEIVING OPIOIDS

In addition to the monitoring for and assessing the analgesic, adverse and side effects, nursing interventions will vary depending on the practice setting. In the hospital, nurses are able to perform direct assessments while hospice nurses may need to troubleshoot over the telephone and rely on family members for pertinent clinical information.

In the outpatient cancer setting, daily telephone conferences should be arranged to evaluate the analgesic efficacy of the new agent/dosage when starting patients on new analgesic regimens. In an office practice, the nurse may work with chronic pain patients and therefore have an important role in monitoring and documenting prescriptions, in addition to communicating with pharmacists.

Irregardless of the practice setting, communication and documentation remain the cornerstones of sound nursing practice in the management of the patient receiving opioids. It is important for nurses to understand the pharmacology, adverse effects, side-effects and delivery vehicles of the opioids being administered.

General Nursing Guidelines

- Assess and re-assess analgesic efficacy on a regular basis.

- Communicate the need for increases or decreases in dosing to the person prescribing the agent.

- Know and share facts with the patient, family and persons writing the prescriptions.

- Listen to the patient.

- Recognize, treat and control for side effects whenever possible (see *Table 7-4*).

- Do not fear addiction and/or label patients.

- Be alert for physical dependence and control for withdrawal when feasible.

- Watch for and report development of tolerance.

- Know state laws regarding the use of opioids in managing pain.

- Use the art and the science of nursing.

Remember, when working with patients receiving opioids for pain management, an ounce of prevention is truly worth a pound of cure.

EXAM QUESTIONS

CHAPTER 7
Questions 38–47

38. The prototypical opioid is

    a. methadone.
    b. morphine.
    c. meperidine.
    d. hydromorphone.

39. The route of choice for opioid administration is

    a. parenteral.
    b. oral.
    c. transdermal.
    d. rectal.

40. The metabolism of the opioid resulting in the loss of some of its analgesic properties is referred to as the

    a. hepatotoxic effect.
    b. portal effect.
    c. hepatic process effect.
    d. hepatic first-pass effect.

41. Methadone is different from other sustained-release opioids because methadone

    a. has a 12 hour half-life.
    b is to be used only for heroin addicts.
    c. comes in liquid form.
    d. prescriptions may be telephoned to the pharmacy.

42. A continuous infusion provides

    a. steady-state analgesia.
    b. a vulnerability to abstinence syndrome.
    c. toxic levels of analgesic.
    d. increased nausea/vomiting.

43. Patient controlled analgesia can be beneficial for the patient in pain who

    a. is scheduled for physical therapy.
    b. has chronic non-malignant pain.
    c. is comatose.
    d. is paralyzed.

44. A patient who is receiving intraspinal opioids for post-operative thoractomy pain would realize the best analgesia with the placement of the catheter at the

    a. kappa receptor.
    b. thoracic dermatome.
    c. lumbar dermatome.
    d. cervical dermatome.

45. An indicator of impending respiratory depression with intraspinal opioids is

    a. mitosis.
    b. urinary retention.
    c. spinal headache.
    d. miosis.

46. When you speak with your patient she informs you that the methadone is not holding her. It is dosed every 8 hours. You contact the physician and suggest changing

    a. to percocet and reassess.

    b. to morphine and reassess.

    c. the dose to Q6 hours and reassess.

    d. the dose to Q4 hours and reassess.

47. You are caring for a patient with a history of epilepsy and back pain. You note that the nurse practitioner wrote for Ultram prn for pain. You call and suggest that Ultram may not be the best agent for this patient because

    a. the patient may choke on oral medications during a seizure.

    b. Ultram is contraindicated for back pain.

    c. Ultram lowers the seizure threshold.

    d. Ultram is not a scheduled drug.

CHAPTER 8

NON-PHARMACOLGICAL APPROACHES TO PAIN MANAGEMENT

CHAPTER OBJECTIVE

Upon completion of this chapter, the reader will be able to cite non-pharmacological and psychological interventions for pain management and identify indications that therapeutic exercise is indicated and note the role of biofeedback in pain management.

LEARNING OBJECTIVES

After studying this chapter, the learner will be able to

1. cite three non-pharmacological interventions for pain management.

2. recognize two psychological techniques for chronic pain management.

3. recall the role of the nurse in the use of non-pharmacological interventions.

4. select the theory that led to the use of TENS units.

5. cite the mechanism and duration of action of TENS units.

INTRODUCTION

In many instances, medications alone do not adequately control pain. When developing a comprehensive pain management plan, it is critical to address all of the elements of the pain.

For example, when the question, "what is the pain keeping you from doing that you'd like to do?" is asked, there is little to no point in exploring functional increases if not prepared to assist the patient in the restoration of their physical and psychosocial functioning. In considering non-pharmacological approaches for pain, the impact of pain on a person's functioning is essential if the program is to succeed. Another baseline element is determining treatment goals with the patient. This is generally within the realm of the nursing assessment and data base.

For the purpose of this course, the primary interventions that have been supported in the scientific, nursing and medical literature will be discussed. There are interventions that have anecdotal value and that have been reported but have not been subjected to the rigor of controlled studies. Some of those trends include magnet therapy, copper bracelets and cranio-sacral therapy.

Elements within each of the treating disciplines will be discussed, with applications to diagnostic categories. The primary non-pharmacological interventions to be explored in this chapter are:

• Physical Therapy;

• Biofeedback and Relaxation Therapy;

• Psychological Therapy;

• Occupational Therapy; and

• Acupuncture.

PHYSICAL THERAPY

Physical therapy comprises a variety of interventions and techniques directed at maintaining physical function, integrity and restoration. Some of the interventions have a direct impact on the control of pain, while others manage the pain indirectly. When treating pain, it is important to distinguish between acute, sub-acute and chronic pain. It is important for the prevention of further injury, while attaining and maintaining gains.

Acute care focuses on decreasing symptoms while protecting tissue and muscle from further injury. In the acute phase, activity is limited, modalities are employed and assistive devices may be utilized. These may include a cane, cervical collar or lumbar brace.

Subacute care begins once healing has started and the injured tissues and muscle begin to resort to normal. In subacute care, progressive restoration of function begins.

In chronic care, the therapist rarely works in isolation. Typically, the patient is working with at least one other discipline such as Occupational or Biofeedback Therapy. Restoration of function is usually preceded by selected modalities to decrease spasm and tension in muscles that have been underutilized.

There is also some concurrent, ongoing pharmacological treatment of the pain. This pharmacological management occurs at all phases of the injury, varying in classes of medications used.

TENS Unit

Transcutaneous Electrical Nerve Stimulation (TENS) is indicated for regional and/or musculoskeletal pain. A variety of pain syndromes have been treated with TENS therapy. While it is used primarily for musculoskeletal and chronic pain, TENS units have documented efficacy in neuropathic and postoperative pain.

Mechanism of Action

Based on the famous Gate Control Theory by Melzack and Wall in 1965, electro-stimulation in the treatment of pain is well established and accepted. Larger diameter fibers are stimulated with low level electric current, over-riding the smaller diameter pain conducting fibers. This stimulation shuts the "gate" in the spinal cord, through which the nerve impulse must travel in order to reach the cerebral cortex, where it is perceived as and called "pain." With time, the smaller fibers compensate, override the larger fibers and transmit pain.

Because of this eventual override, the TENS unit should only be used for 30 to 60 minutes at a time and then turned off. Once the electrical stimulus is removed, analgesia has been documented to persist for up to an hour (Johnson, Ashton & Thompson, 1991).

One study looked at the efficacy of TENS therapy in 211 patients with a variety of diagnoses that provoked pain (Meyler, deJongste & Rolf, 1994). In addition to clinical efficacy, the researchers evaluated unwanted side-effects. The researchers found distinct outcomes based on the etiology of the pain. The majority of patients with pain from peripheral nerve damage found the TENS unit to be efficacious (53%), as did patients with anginal pain secondary to ischemic heart disease (75%) and patients with musculoskeletal pain from mechanical degenerative causes (69%).

Patients reporting a lack of efficacy with TENS units were those with prominent psychological and social distress. Of these and patients with pain caused by central and autonomic dysfunction, only 10–25% reported satisfactory pain relief.

Side effects were related to technique in the early phase of treatment in 35% of the patients. This number was reduced once instructions were clarified. The effects were maintained for longer than six months.

Heat/Cold

The application of heat and/or cold is referred to as a modality. Heat may be applied with a heating pad, lamp or hot water bath. Ice, cold compresses or a vapo coolant spray such as fluromethane may be used intermittently either alone or in conjunction with massage. National surveys of patients with chronic pain reveal that 41% use heat or cold at home for comfort (Bostrom, 1996).

Patients may be taught to do "spray and stretch" for spasm and muscle tension. In this technique, the coolant is sprayed onto the affected area and then the area is massaged and the tissues and underlying muscles stretched to decrease spasm.

The use of heat/cold in unresponsive or noncommunicative patients or on insensate areas is contraindicated and not recommended. The inability to discriminate and perceive pain and/or communicate, places the patient at high risk for tissue damage.

Orthoses/Assistive Devices

Splinting a painful limb may decrease pain and preserve function. Such is the case with Carpal Tunnel Syndrome and Reflex Sympathetic Dystrophy (RSD/CRPS). Likewise, the use of soft or semi-rigid collars or braces may be warranted with certain pain problems. For example, in patients with severe degenerative disc or joint disease with and without osteophytes (bone spurs), a soft cervical collar may help pain when engaging in activities with prolonged or sustained use of the upper extremities. Examples of activities are typing, data entry and gardening.

Prolonged use of lumbar braces or supports and abdominal binders used for lumbar support are contraindicated in back pain patients unless there is instability of the spine. Prolonged or consistent use of these aids can cause atrophy of the paravertebral and other muscle groups of the spine with resulting increases in spasm, decreases in function and range of motion.

Case Example

A 78-year-old female patient presented with myofascial neck and cervical pain as a result of a radical neck dissection performed thirty years ago. She has a history of degenerative disc disease of the cervical spine. She works 32 hours a week as a transcriptionist/data entry clerk to supplement her income. She came for an evaluation. Following a course of physical therapy exercises, with a home program and the use of an NSAID and an as needed antispasmodic, she reported continued cervical pain with driving and after approximately three to four hours working at the computer.

She was placed in a soft cervical collar with instructions to use it periodically when driving and doing sustained data entry. She was to remove the collar after two hours and leave it off for two hours. She was to continue her endurance and strengthening exercises. On follow-up visits, an increase in her cervical range of motion and a decrease in the tension over her traps in nuchal musculature was evident. Her pain score while driving and at work had decreased by 60%.

Another example of an orthotic is a heel lift. Of the last 30 patients seen by the author of this course for low back pain, 70% had undiagnosed leg-length discrepancies. Typically, one hip is higher than the other on presentation, and loading on the lumbar musculature is in-equivocal, stressing the joints and muscles.

A leg length discrepancy can cause mechanical back pain which is easily ameliorated. The physical therapist measures the legs and recommends the appropriate size lift to be placed in the shoe.

Diathermy/Cryotherapy

Paraffin baths (diathermy) or ultrasound (cryotherapy) may also be used to patient tolerance

---

TABLE 8-1
Selected Exercises

Flexion Based	Extension Based
Take pressure off of disc and nerves	Allow overstretched muscles to heal; helpful in leg pain

Source: Garfin, J. & Garfin, S. (2002). Low back pain: A quick guide to exercise as acute therapy. *Consultant, 4*(1), 350–353.

---

and satisfaction. These are especially therapeutic for osteo and rheumatoid arthritis.

Exercise

All exercise regimens should be prescribed by the physician, physician's assistant or nurse practitioner and supervised by the physical therapist. Patients should be encouraged to remain independent in self-care and active whenever possible. Exercise enhances these aspects by promoting strength, supporting muscle integrity, range of motion and physical/functional tolerances.

In very ill patients, such as those with cancer, exercises that provoke pain should not be undertaken. When pathological fracture secondary to tumor invasion is likely, all weight bearing activities should be avoided (AHCPR, 1994).

Positioning for comfort can be effective in ameliorating pain. For example, a patient with back pain should not lie prone as it stresses the spine and increases discomfort. Placing a pillow under the knees diminishes the load off the back and promotes comfort. It should be emphasized that this is for bedtime only, as resting, reclining and bed-resting is contraindicated with chronic back pain.

All *therapeutic exercise* should be prescribed by a health professional versed in the treatment of pain syndromes. In patients with chronic back pain for example, the multifidi muscles (the main stabilizers of the back positioned at oblique angles to the spine) become atrophied with disuse. These muscles allow for rotary movements. Rotation exercises and movements, along with flexion and extension exercises help to rebuild these important

muscle groups (see *Table 8-1*) (Garfin & Garfin, 2002).

When prescribing exercise, consideration should be taken of the patient's diagnosis. For example, a patient with back and leg pain from spinal stenosis (a narrowing of the spinal canal) should not have walking or treadmill work as part of their exercise regimen. Prolonged walking and standing will make the pain from spinal stenosis significantly worse. This type of pain is better managed with exercises such as swimming and biking. Likewise, patients with degenerative disc disease with bone spurs should not have flexion activities, as these maneuvers can irritate nerve roots. Too often, prescribers order "exercise" without taking into consideration the patient's diagnosis.

In addition to the strengthening, flexibility and endurance building activities, the physical therapy program should also include cardiovascular elements. The goals of the physical therapy component of pain treatment are to decrease pain, prevent re-injury or pain recurrence and enhance physical and functional tolerances.

When working with patients with neuropathic or dystrophic pain, the therapist works to decrease hypersensitivity and promote function. This is done with sensory stimulation and splinting or combinations of both.

Patients with pain from headache and/or temperomandibular disease (TMD) receive tailored treatment, again directed at the alleviation of symptoms and enhancement of physical/functional tolerances and independence in ADLs. Progressive activities directed at increasing the oral opening and/or ionophoresis to decrease spasm and pain are the interventions for TMD. The trapezii and cervical spine regions are the focal points of headache treatment in physical therapy.

Despite the diagnosis, the main goal of physical therapy is to increase function and decrease pain. While it is difficult to motivate patients who are in pain and suffering, once they begin to exercise, the benefits are well worth the initial discomfort. Patients are provided with individually tailored home exercise programs to maintain gains realized in treatment and to prevent re-injury by staying conditioned.

BIOFEEDBACK AND RELAXATION THERAPY

When considering a typical day, people are barraged with stress from a variety of sources. Some of the stresses are manageable, and others appear insurmountable. Imagine handling the stress that comes with parenting, marriage, bills and then add to that relentless chronic pain, from which there is never a moment's relief. For persons with chronic pain, it takes all the energy they have to handle their pain, so they learn to rely on pharmaceuticals as they do not have the internal resources to handle the stress of life and the stress of pain. There are well documented associations between chronic stress and disease, and pain is no exception.

In pain and headache management, biofeedback and relaxation therapy provides the patient with internal resources from which to draw when the pain levels get too high. It is accepted that muscle tension, stress and pain are very intimately involved, one with the other.

The Procedure

Biofeedback teaches the patient how to manage their stress and subsequent muscle tension through a variety of techniques. The goals of the treatment are an increased sense of control over life

events so as to not let them make the pain worse. Typically, biofeedback is provided in a laboratory environment which is kept quiet and dark (see *Table 8-2*).

A computer is used to measure the amount of muscle tension present in the patient. The patient is attached to the computer via leads and electrodes, which are attached to relevant muscle groups. This is referred to as electromyography. If the patient has shoulder or neck pain, the electrodes may be placed on the trapezii; if there is headache, the electrodes may be placed on the temporalis or frontalis muscles (temples or forehead, respectively).

The degree of muscle tension is then imaged on the computer screen along with therapeutic threshold, which is the goal. The patient is then instructed in techniques to decrease the muscle tension, such as imagery, progressive muscle relaxation, deep breathing and distraction. As muscle tension decreases, the levels on the screen fall to threshold or below, and relaxation is achieved.

Ultimately, the patient is taken off of the computer and taught to spontaneously relax. This of course takes practice, and patients are encouraged to practice at lease once to twice per day. It usually takes 12 visits to accomplish the training.

Techniques

Imagery

Imagery is an ancient technique used for healing. Purposeful mental images are used to accomplish a therapeutic goal. It is considered a cognitive tool. The senses are used to produce mental images, and the energy generated by the images can be directed toward an identified task.

Imagery can be used in a variety of clients to achieve a variety of outcomes.

For example, a patient with burning pain from neuropathy can visualize the pain being consolidated into a ball, which is then lifted and removed from the body. Also, the patient can visualize a

---

TABLE 8-2
Types of Biofeedback Instrumentation

The **Electromyograph (EMG)** is capable of measuring muscle activity. More specifically, the EMG measures the electrical energy emitted by the flow of electrically charged particles in and out of a muscle cell just before contraction. Aside from general relaxation training and anxiety reduction, EMG is therapeutically useful in more specific applications such as neuromuscular reeducation.

Thermal Feedback is used to index peripheral vascular constriction or dilation. During sympathetic activation accompanying a stress response, hands may become cold due to the shunting of blood from peripheral areas.

Electrodermograph (EDR) measures skin conduction levels. Minute changes in the concentration of salt and water in sweat gland ducts produce signals which measure increased skin conductance of electricity. EDR provides an excellent measurement of emotional arousal.

---

band of ice being wrapped around the affected extremity.

Not all patients are cognitively able to perform imagery, so it is important for the person teaching these types of techniques to be qualified. Clients with mental illness, in particular those with psychosis, are not candidates for this type of technique.

Progressive Muscle Relaxation

Progressive muscle relaxation is easily used and has great utility for a variety of pain problems. Patients who carry their tension in their muscles are especially good candidates for this technique. The patient is taught to mentally scan their bodies, sensing areas that might be holding tension. For example, some people clench their jaws or frown subconsciously or reflexively. This is especially important for headache or TMD patients. As part of the exercise, the patient purposefully contracts and relaxes major muscle groups from head to toe.

Deep Breathing

Deep breathing is actually a form of energy release and distraction. The patient takes slow deep breaths and expels the breath through pursed lips, against pressure. While they are concentrating on their breathing, they are not focusing on their pain.

This is usually taught in conjunction with other techniques.

Distraction

Distraction is used as a form of thought stopping, where the patient thinks about pleasant things. The patient can also use other activities as a form of distraction. The patient is encouraged to read, watch television, exercise or engage in a leisure pursuit.

Elements of Biofeedback

There are specific elements of biofeedback relative to the pain problem to be treated. As with physical therapy, biofeedback is usually provided in conjunction with other treatment. Optimum results are realized when more than one pain treatment modality is provided.

Muscle Re-Education

Muscle re-education utilizes surface electromyography (sEMG) to assess, evaluate and treat. Visual feedback and physical therapy techniques are incorporated for overall enhancement of motor control and functional movement. Patients with various diagnoses benefit from this application, those specific to pain management are orthopedic and/or neuropathic conditions.

Headache Program

A headache program is a specific 12 session treatment that focuses on education, posture, nutrition, physiology of stress and pain as well as stress management. Patient education includes written material and audiotapes, sEMG, and temperature training. Patients are encouraged to keep a journal.

Pain Management Muscle Education

Pain management muscle education combines traditional surface electromyograph recording with posture education, pain management education, physiology and muscle relaxation training. Functional outcomes are incorporated with pain management techniques for generalization of behavior into "real life" situations.

PSYCHOLOGICAL THERAPY

Introduction

Wilbur Fordyce was a psychologist who pioneered the use of psychological treatment as an element of pain management. Fordyce was an advocate of the use of operant conditioning for patients with chronic pain. He theorized that if pain behaviors (grimacing, limping, verbalizing discomfort) were ignored and positive health-oriented behaviors (increased activity levels, no use of assistive devices) were emphasized, then the pain behaviors would eventually become extinct.

His work provided a platform, as it were, for further research into chronic pain syndromes and their impact on psychosocial functioning. Working from this type of intervention or theory, behavioral scientists have moved onto cognitive-behavioral assessments/interventions, utilized psychometric instruments to document the effects of the chronic pain on the psyche and used psychotherapeutic and psycho-educational interventions directed at restoring the emotional health of affected individuals.

Psychology and Pain

It has been proposed that psychological variables are both risk factors in and consequences of, pain. For example, chronic pain may raise the risk of suicide, and when pain is coupled with substance abuse, the risk increases. A sample of patients admitted for attempted suicide was analyzed for the presence of somatic disease. Researchers discovered that 52% were shown to have a somatic disease, and 21% were using analgesics for pain on a daily basis (Tearnan, 2001).

Another study looked at the relationship between pain and 20 psychological variables, only two of which were identified as associated with pain: Less emotional repression and greater ergomania (excessive work). Patients with chronic pain also had a relative who had experienced prolonged physical pain (Gamsa & Vikis-Friebergs, 1991).

The majority of patients with chronic pain suffer from reactive depression. This differs from clinical depression in that this depression is situational. Needless to say, psychological and psychosocial treatment and support are essential elements of an effective pain management program or as adjunctive components of a pain management plan. A comparative study analyzed outcomes in patients receiving PT alone with patients receiving PT and cognitive-behavioral group therapy (Nicholas, Wilson & Goyen, 1992). Patients receiving both therapies displayed improvement over the group receiving PT alone in

- measures of functional impairment;
- use of active coping strategies;
- self-efficacy belief; and
- medication use.

Durability of these outcomes was validated at six months post treatment.

Portenoy (1998) divided the psychological dimension of pain management into three types of interventions:

- Cognitive;

- Behavioral; and

- Psycho-educational.

There are elements of the psychological dimension and associated suffering that are unique to the patient with pain. For example, the man with a back injury who cannot provide for his family may have issues related to his identity and self-esteem related to his pain; the person with cancer perceives the increases in pain as a signal that death is imminent.

It takes an experienced professional to assist patients in processing thoughts and perceptions related to their pain and disability. Coping skills must be identified and then enhanced in order for the patient to maximize function.

Cognitive-Behavioral Techniques

Cognitive-behavioral interventions are directive and attempt to change the way patients think about their pain. Feelings of helplessness and hopelessness translate into pessimistic thoughts regarding the futility of their situation. These thoughts along with fears about the meaning of the pain and fears of re-injury are common in patients with chronic pain. Instruction is given to develop awareness of the impact that negative thoughts can have in perpetuating "illness behaviors."

Cognitive-behavioral techniques include thought stopping, problem solving, coping skills enhancement and normalizing emotional distress. Any or all of these interventions can assist the patient with synthesizing and processing thoughts and perceptions related to the pain. This helps self-concept which in turn promotes empowerment to perform in areas that have been previously thought to be impossible. The patient is taught to manage their pain and not let the pain manage them.

Coping skills enhancement is an integral part of the psychological treatment of patients with chronic pain. A study of patients with rheumatoid arthritis found a positive association between coping efficacy and pain. When patients rated their ability to control and reduce pain utilizing spiritual/religious coping methods as high, they were less likely to have joint pain and a negative mood (Keefe et al., 2001).

Literature suggests that the meanings that patients assign to pain may be tied to their behavioral, emotional and cultural responses to pain (Ferrell et al., 1993). Cognitive therapy explores these and other psychological variables of the pain experience.

Psycho-Educational Groups

The group process affords a venue wherein patients are exposed to others with like experiences. Groups may focus on clarification of treatment and problem-solving techniques and they provide members the opportunity to benefit from experiences and strategies of others. Patients with chronic pain report social isolation, so the group experience may help to expand the patient's social network. The group process may also provide an outlet for patients to talk about their experiences.

There are disease-specific support groups available for patients in the community. These may or may not be facilitated by a licensed professional. Some groups are patient-directed. While support groups may have therapeutic benefits, they are not considered therapy.

Selected Psychological and Biofeedback Interventions

- Coping skills enhancement

- Deep breathing

- Progressive muscle relaxation (PMR)

- Distraction

- Guided imagery/hypnosis

Psychometric Instruments

In addition to pain scales, questionnaires are valid psychological instruments that can be utilized in evaluating patients and treatment efficacy. For the purpose of this course, discussion will be limited to the most commonly utilized and tested instruments.

There have been several instruments that have utility in the psychological component of pain treatment. The **Minnesota Multidimensional Personality Inventory (MMPI)** has been validated for use in patients with pain. It comes in a short form, an adolescent form, in Spanish and on tape for patients who cannot read or write. The MMPI can detect depression, hypochondriasis, sociopathic and borderline personality disorders. It also has built-in validity indicators. Criticism of this instrument is its length and cost. Many chronic pain programs use this to test all participants, others use it selectively when there is suspicion of psychopathology.

The **Beck Depression Inventory (BDI)** is a 20 item instrument that rates depression as mild, moderate or severe. The BDI has been used as an instrument to document treatment outcomes.

Quality of Life (QOL) is another measure that may be utilized to evaluate treatment efficacy or outcomes. There are many instruments available. Some are general and others, like the Headache Inventory Test (HIT-6), are disease specific.

Summary

The cognitive-behavioral and psycho-educational interventions are utilized to assist the patient in dealing with fear, depression and anxiety. Family members also benefit from these techniques and can learn some of them for themselves as well as for the patient.

ACUPUNCTURE

In late 1997, the National Institutes of Health issued a statement endorsing the use of acupuncture as an element in a comprehensive treatment plan of certain conditions (Goldstein,

2001). In the United States, physicians are permitted to practice acupuncture in all of the states, but licensure, certification or registration of non-physician acupuncturists are required in 34 states (Goldstein, 2001).

Studies have evaluated the use of acupuncture as a complementary medical technique in the management of cranio-cervical, headache and temporomandibular joint disease (TMD). Acupuncture is intrinsically safe and was initially used for disease management. It has evolved to include pain management.

A placebo-controlled study of 30 patients with tension type headache was conducted with five measures of symptom severity and treatment response. Outcomes indicated that acupuncture was not any more or less effective than placebo (Tavola, Gala, Conte & Invernizzi, 1992).

Acupuncture is contraindicated in patients on anticoagulation therapy and in the first and last trimester of pregnancy. Patients with pacemakers should not undergo electro-acupuncture.

Nursing Interventions

Patients may be hesitant to participate in a physically-oriented approach to their pain and its management. Fear of increased pain and re-injury may make the patient reluctant to undergo an exercise program. The patient may have had physical therapy in the past and found that it made their pain worse.

Likewise, undergoing psychological evaluation or treatment may cause suspicion on the part of the patient. The patient may think that the referral is based in the belief that the pain is psychogenic or "in their head."

The nurse has an important role in the education and implementation of non-pharmacological treatment of the pain patient. It is important that the nurse have an understanding of the different modalities and approaches to the management of pain being prescribed.

The role will vary and the nurse's degree of involvement is dependant on the practice setting. If the nurse is working in a pain management program, reinforcing learned techniques, encouraging patients to utilize proper body mechanics while on the unit, supporting the patient and listening when they become discouraged, are part of the nurse's responsibility.

The nurse must communicate with the therapist, the patient and the person prescribing the program. If the patient appears to have increases in pain levels (which is expected within the first week of physical therapy treatment), an assessment should be made and, if ordered, palliative interventions provided. Patients may be having their narcotics adjusted and may need added coverage during this time.

If the nurse is working in a physician practice, then the nurse will have limited contact with the patient. The nurse should attempt contact with the treating therapist(s) prior to the patient's follow-up medical visit for an update on the patient's progress. It is not uncommon for a patient not to follow through with therapy and fail to disclose this to the prescriber. By establishing communication with the treating professionals, compliance is assessed and re-enforced.

The nurse can also assist the patient in the utilization of some of the psychological and relaxation techniques discussed. It is important that if techniques are going to be taught, then the nurse should be familiar with some of these techniques.

Summary

While pharmacotherapy is important in pain management, it is not necessarily a panacea. Outcomes can be enhanced through the concomitant use of therapies and medications. As with all of the interventions directed at the management of pain, misconceptions, fears and inadequate knowledge must all be addressed if the patient is to be a willing participant in their care and treatment.

EXAM QUESTIONS

CHAPTER 8
Questions 48–53

48. Your peer is caring for a comatose patient and notes an area of lumbar spasm. A suggestion is made to place a heating pad on the area. You respond by informing the nurse that

    a. the use of heat or cold may be harmful in a non-responsive patient.

    b. ice would be better.

    c. a combination of heat followed by ice would be better.

    d. a combination of ice followed by heat would be better.

49. The theory that is the basis for the use of TENS units is the

    a. Acute Pain Theory.

    b. Operant-Behavioral Theory.

    c. Gate Control Theory.

    d. Cognitive-Behavioral Theory.

50. The mechanism of action of the TENS unit is

    a. the larger pain fibers override smaller nerve fibers.

    b. the larger nerve fibers override the smaller pain fibers.

    c. endogenous systems in the spinal cord are depleted.

    d. small frequency electrical stimulation releases GABA.

51. Your patient with back pain tells you he is wearing his TENS unit 24 hours a day, 7 days per week. You inform him that

    a. in order to be effective, it should be used for periods no longer than 30–60 minutes at a time.

    b. he is going to start feeling the full benefits after two to three more days of use.

    c. you are glad he is complying with the instructions.

    d. he should use it 24 hours a day every other day.

52. Your patient has just been referred to a psychologist for pain management. A common treatment goal is

    a. an increased range of motion.

    b. a decrease in psychosis.

    c. a decrease in psychogenic pain.

    d. to enhance coping skills.

53. Your patient has a history of low back pain and schizophrenia. The biofeedback technique that would be contraindicated for her is

    a. deep breathing.

    b. progressive relaxation.

    c. stress management.

    d. imagery.

CHAPTER 9

CHRONIC PAIN AND RELATED SYNDROMES

CHAPTER OBJECTIVE

Upon completion of this chapter, the reader will be able to differentiate between chronic and acute pain and recognize the treatment paradigm and interventions for chronic pain.

LEARNING OBJECTIVES

After studying this chapter, the learner will be able to

1. recognize the difference between chronic and acute pain.

2. recall chronic pain as a disease and not a symptom.

3. list the signs and symptoms of Reflex Sympathetic Dystrophy (RSD) and Complex Regional Pain Syndrome (CRPS).

4. cite a back pain diagnosis that worsens with ambulation/standing.

OVERVIEW

Typically, nurses are trained to approach pain through an acute pain framework. As previous discussions of chronic and acute pain have noted, acute pain is time limited whereas chronic pain is not. In chronic pain, either a definitive etiology is not always present or the pathophysiological process of the pain cannot be ameliorated.

The International Association for the Study of Pain (IASP) definition of pain bears repeating and affords a point of reference for the material to be covered in this chapter. Pain is defined as an unpleasant sensory and emotional experience associated with actual or potential tissue damage or described in terms of such damage (Abram & Haddox, 2000). This definition is less restrictive than others in that it encompasses an important element of the chronic pain experience with the important qualifier: "Or described in terms of such damage" (Mersky & Bogwik, 1994, p. 40–43). Unfortunately, there is not always a clearly defined etiology or cause of the pain. Patients with a chronic pain syndrome often find themselves in an odd quandary; they may actually want an abnormal MRI or CT finding as validation of their pain. They know they are hurting, but no one can find the source of the pain. While acute pain is a symptom of a pathological process or injury, chronic pain becomes the disease or pathological process.

For the purpose of this course, the four most common chronic pain problems will be discussed: Chronic Low Back Pain (CLBP), Reflex Sympathetic Dystrophy (RSD), Neuropathic Pain Syndromes and Neuralgic Pain.

Unlike acute pain, **chronic pain** is not time-limited and may, or may not, be associated with a long-term incurable or intractable medical condition or disease.

Chronic pain:

- May be associated with cancer or a chronic nonmalignant illness (i.e., arthritis, back pain, reflex sympathetic dystrophy, pain from nerve damage).

- May be present in the absence of a definitive etiology.

- Rarely responds to a uni-modal approach.

Philosophy of Chronic Pain Treatment

The patient with chronic pain has real pain irrespective of a negative workup. In chronic pain, a definitive etiology may not be found. Consequently, a cause of the pain is not sought and treatment for the pain is initiated. The course changes from investigational to therapeutic. The goals to improve function and decrease pain are realistic, with complete pain relief never a goal. The outcome focus is on function not on pain with a successful outcome not based on the pain score but instead on function, medication use and quality of life.

Outcomes

When establishing goals for chronic pain treatment, instruments that can quantify identified outcomes are used. Examples of these are tools that measure quality of life; psychological assessment tools such as the Beck Depression Inventory; use of controlled substances which can be evaluated with urine drug screens; and indices of physical functioning, such as exercise tolerance and range of motion measures. An indicator of both psychological and physical functioning may be a return to gainful employment. Pain scores may never change, but function may improve.

Pathogenesis of Chronic Pain

In an acute pain event, the putative element is removed, repaired or restored. The pain was a symptom that an injury has occurred or that there is a pathological process present. Damage causes inflammation and changes within the central nervous system. The pain signals travel to the brain and a set of homeostatic and protective mechanisms are activated. For example, muscle spasms around a break serve to stabilize the area, holding the bones in place, endorphins and adrenalin are released and constrict blood vessels and block pain impulses. As healing ensues, these mechanisms abate.

Not as much is known in the case of chronic pain. The nervous system continues to send pain signals as it reacts to the memory of the initial injury. Less is known about why this occurs. Research has helped identify some of the mechanisms involved in the pathogenesis of RSD and neuropathy.

TREATMENT APPROACHES TO CHRONIC PAIN

The treatment of chronic pain differs from that of acute pain. In chronic pain, the pain is unremitting, so there is no true end point in treatment. Therefore, chronic pain is treated as a disease, whereas acute pain is a symptom. This is the cornerstone of treatment.

If the pain is constant, then an interdisciplinary treatment approach is usually warranted. The patient should be referred to a pain specialist, who can individually tailor and supervise a treatment plan. The goals are twofold: Reduction in pain and restoration of a healthy lifestyle.

The intensity of services depends on the degree of disability. In the chronic pain syndrome, the pain has become the center of the patient's universe. The pain is managing the patient as the patient cannot manage the pain. When the chronic pain becomes a syndrome, every aspect of the patient's life has been impacted by the pain, resulting in physical and emotional disability.

TYPES OF PAIN PROGRAMS

Multidisciplinary Program

A multidisciplinary program includes extensive services with an interdisciplinary focus and the provision of multiple modalities (multi-modal) simultaneously. This type of program is usually reserved for pain that has been refractory to selected modalities and medications. An inpatient setting may be utilized, especially if the patient is on opioids. The nurse's role is one of documentation, facilitation, education and communication. The nurse should re-enforce learned techniques, evaluate the patient's response to treatment and administer medications as ordered. Education classes regarding nutrition and pharmacology are typically in the nursing domain. The nurse is considered an integral part of the team.

Modality Oriented Clinic

These usually afford selected modalities. A "nerve block program" is an example of this type of setting. The focus of the treatment is on the interventions administered with supportive modalities of physical therapy and psychology, sometimes offered in the same setting. Nurses in this setting generally set up for and assist with procedures. Documentation and education are the functions of the nursing role.

Syndrome Oriented Clinic

These treat a particular type of pain problem. Examples are headache clinics or spine programs. The diagnosis drives the modalities offered and the services provided. The nursing role is also contingent on the nature of the population treated.

Typically, the role of the nurse will vary with the practice setting and the nurse's educational preparation. The nurse may function as a Certified Nurse Anesthetist (CRNA) or Nurse Practitioner (ARNP) and be involved in the prescription and/or provision of treatment.

Irrespective of the setting, the **key to positive treatment outcomes** in chronic pain is the early recognition of when the pain is no longer acute. Historically, chronic pain was defined as pain persisting for six months or longer. This type of definition sets everyone up for failure because the longer the patient goes untreated the less likely they are to return to work and the greater the extent of disability. For example, if a person sprains their ankle, healing should take place within days, and the patient should be able to function and be off analgesics in a matter of days to weeks. If in a month the patient cannot bear weight or work and is in need of opioids, the patient has a chronic pain problem.

Treatment Components

Components of chronic pain treatment may be provided through a formal, interdisciplinary program or combinations of selected elements may be warranted. The person prescribing the interventions determines the number of treatment interventions. Ongoing communication with the treatment providers is important. The office/clinic nurse may be responsible for facilitating this. The goal of the treatment components is to restore an optimum level of functioning and to take the patient out of the healthcare system by giving them control over their lives.

Physical Therapy

Physical therapy focuses on enhancing physical tolerances, flexibility, endurance and overall reconditioning. The patient receives an individually tailored exercise program. The patient also has a home exercise program. Modalities are discouraged as they are not effective. A trial of a TENS unit may be warranted.

Psychological Therapy

Chronic pain exerts a tremendous impact on the psychobehavioral and emotional functioning of the patient. Feelings of loss, identity crisis, depression, and self esteem issues are typical in patients with chronic pain. These are compounded by the financial and physical compromises that accompany the pain and disability. Psychological therapy is an important aspect of the treatment plan. A comprehensive psychological evaluation with recommended treatment may be warranted, or a short course of therapy may suffice. See *Figure 9-1* for comprehensive psychological treatment protocols

Family and significant others are included in the treatment plan. Persons in the patient's environment must be educated about chronic pain and the rationale for and goals of treatment. Marital difficulties are not uncommon with chronic pain. Sometimes, unhealthy relationships and patterns of behavior evolve over time with respect to the pain. The spouse or closest person to the patient may be asked their perspective of the pain and its impact on the patient. This can be done through an interview or questionnaire designed for that purpose. A sample is provided in *Figure 9-2* for examples of the type of data that may be used for development of the treatment plan.

When the patient is participating in an interdisciplinary pain treatment program, the entire treatment team participates in the education of the family or significant other. This enhances their understanding of the rationale and goals for treatment. The education is discussed at scheduled weekly team conferences.

Occupational Therapy (OT)

OT provides interventions and education related to functional performance. Patients engage in relevant task simulation with the occupational therapist's supervision. Body mechanics, energy conservation and pacing techniques are taught and employed with OT. A review of *Figure 9-3* provides an overview of some of the evaluation and treatment afforded through OT.

Biofeedback and Relaxation Therapy

Biofeedback is an instrumental conditioning technique used to gain voluntary control over specific physiological responses or combinations of responses of which a person is not normally aware. It is actually a behavioral technique which is based on learning theory, with a process of trial and error learning. Through the use of accurate and immediate feedback of physiological responses, individuals are able to learn voluntary control of specific physiological responses once considered beyond human control.

Feedback from selected body systems is transformed into visual and/or auditory signals. The immediate feedback regarding continued attempts promotes greater frequency of successful outcomes. Examples of these responses include muscle spasm/tension associated with back pain and temperature control associated with sympathetically-maintained pain. The individual is encouraged to modify or change feedback as they maximize skills. *See Appendix A* for a sample format of biofeedback evaluation.

Intensity of Treatment

Selected treatment elements may be offered simultaneously. Chronic pain treatment can be undertaken either inpatient or outpatient in a structured interdisciplinary, multimodal program. If the patient is employed and able to continue to do so, a program may be tailored so that physical therapy, psychological therapy and biofeedback are offered back to back for five mornings a week. The patient may then work in the afternoons. The sessions are then decreased to three and then two and then one day a week with the patient continuing with one or two elements during lunch or at the end of the day. If the patient is dependent on opioids and unable to work and/or function, a multimodal, interdisciplinary program with an inpatient setting is warranted.

Pharmacotherapeutics

Rational poly-pharmacy is typically used in chronic pain. Patients will generally be on at least one agent from three classes. Primary classes of agents used are: AEDs, antidepressants, NSAIDs, antispasmodics and opioids.

When antispasmodics are used, the agents that target neurotransmitters and muscle fibers are preferred for chronic use. Examples of these are baclofen and cyclobenzaprine. Patients who are returning to work and cannot tolerate these agents due to sedation usually can tolerate Skelaxin® 400–800 mg TID or Zanaflex® 2 mg BID to TID.

Opioids may be indicated for patients with chronic pain. Candidates for chronic opioid therapy should meet certain criteria. They should be used in the presence of documented pathology; a myofacial pain problem or back strain does not warrant this aggressive a pharmaceutical approach.

Suggested criteria are:

- Diagnostically verified pathology;

- Pain is refractory to various other pharmacological and non-pharmacological interventions;

- Adheres to narcotic contract;

- Does not escalate dosages; and

- Measurable improvements in function are realized with opioids.

Ideally, the determination of candidacy for chronic opioid therapy should be made by a pain specialist. This is not always possible as there is a need for additional pain management specialists. Regardless of who is overseeing the treatment plan, a contract should be entered into between the patient and prescriber delineating expected behaviors on the part of the patient. Failure to comply with the contract may deem the prescriber-patient relationship to be non-therapeutic, and the patient

is discharged from that prescriber's care. Another consequence may be to taper the patient off of the narcotics and continue managing them within the practice. In any event, the contract controls for lost prescriptions, doctor shopping and other behaviors that compromise the patient and the practice of the person managing the patient. A sample Prescription Controlled Substances Policy is supplied in *Appendix C.*

If the patient is on opioid therapy but cannot stay out of bed or is sedentary, then the medication is not helping and should be discontinued. If the medication can help the patient return to work or a functional lifestyle with quality, then they are considered therapeutic.

A pain cocktail may be utilized if the patient is opioid dependant. Even if the patient is felt to be a candidate for chronic opipoid therapy, the least amount needed should be used. This is best determined objectively. The patient is not told the dosage of the medication, and the opioid is withdrawn incrementally as the patient goes through the program. A standard order form for the pain cocktail should be used as it aids in controlling for consistency in appearance, volumes and scheduling (see *Figure 9-4*).

The patient's tolerance to decreases in the opioid is monitored in all therapies. Signs of abstinence syndrome are monitored as well. If the patient has decreases in function in treatment along with increases in pain, the cocktail may be adjusted. The team will meet on a weekly basis for goal evaluation and revision.

The nurse has the primary responsibility for monitoring the patient's tolerance of the adjustments. The nurse is responsible for administering the medications and may need to administer an extra dose of cocktail if abstinence syndrome is evident. A patient will invariably try to get the nurse to disclose the dosages. The nurse must re-

FIGURE 9-1

Protocols for Psychology Component of Pain Management

Evaluation: Three general types of psychological evaluations are available:

1. Psychological.

2. Neuropsychological/cognitive.

3. Psycho educational.

4. Comprehensive personality evaluation (as indicated).

Reporting: The psychologist will provide a complete review of the psychological evaluation results to the referring physician and interdisciplinary treatment team at the initial staffing. This will include:

1. Review of pertinent psychological evaluation results with a brief psychosocial history relevant to the pain diagnosis.

2. Treatment recommendations.

3. Prognosis for outcome.

4. Recommended psychological and interdisciplinary treatment goals.

Treatment Plan: Upon completion of the initial evaluation, the psychologist establishes an individual treatment plan which should include:

A. Mental status and functioning.

B. Areas of strength/coping.

C. Areas of deficit.

D. Patient goals.

E. Treatment goals.

F. Treatment approaches.

G Proposed length of treatment.

H. Prognosis.

I. Anticipated follow-up/referral needs.

Treatment Implementation: The psychologist initiates treatment based upon the results of the initial evaluation utilizing all or combinations of the following treatment approaches:

A. Individual patient psychotherapy.

B. Family/significant others participation: Family/significant others have the option of being included in the patient's psychological treatment.

C. Psycho-educational group therapy weekly.

D. Re-evaluation and Discharge Summary: The psychologist provides a written progress summary. Patient goals are adjusted in accordance with the patient's progress and re-evaluation. A Discharge Summary is compiled with attained goals, follow-up recommendations and referrals.

direct the patient and reinforce the agreed upon treatment plan.

CHRONIC PAIN SYNDROMES

Chronic Back Pain

The most common pain problem is that involving the back, with up to 80% of Americans suffering from it at some point in time. Back pain is the second most common reason for visits to primary care physicians and the most common cause of disability for people under the age of 45 (Andersson, 1991). While 90% of back pain problems resolve without difficulty, they have a significant impact on the economy. It is estimated that direct and indirect medical costs are in excess of $50 billion annually for chronic, episodic and recurrent back treatment (Green et al., 2000).

Bedrest used to be a commonly prescribed or recommended intervention for the person who sustained a back injury. Patients could be immobilized for up to two weeks. This immobility served to produce muscle atrophy, de-conditioning and back spasms. Typically, the pain would have worsened, making the patient more reluctant to move; thereby perpetuating the immobility, atrophy, spasm, weakness and pain. In time, the pain would go from subacute to chronic.

The best intervention for back pain/injury is exercise. Having said that, an important distinction must be made. In the event of an acute injury, there is a 48 to 72 hour time period where the patient should rest, not necessarily bed rest, but engage in activities with a sedentary level of functioning. The patient should take analgesics and antispasmodics as prescribed. Once the 72 hour period has passed, then gentle progressive stretching and conditioning exercises should be prescribed and provided through physical therapy.

Types of Chronic Low Back Pain

Facet Disease

The facet joints of the spine are primary pain generators. They are subject to degeneration and capsular injury. Facets may be hypertrophied causing a diminishment in the amount of space for nerve fibers as they exit through the neural foraminae. This causes compression of the nerve root(s) provoking radiculopathy or pain that radiates through a nerve pathway. Facet disease is almost always accompanied by degenerative disease and often involves L4–5 and L5–S1 vertebral levels. Patients with facet disease will have difficulty with hyperextension of the spine, which always provokes pain, as does lateral bending.

Degenerative Disc Disease (DDD)

DDD is usually a result of cumulative trauma, age and combinations of factors. The discs lose fluid and do not cushion as they should. This diminishment in size compromises the integrity of the neural foraminae with secondary effects on the nerve root(s). There are indications that the disc itself may be a pain generator in chronic pain of the spine (Anderson, 2001).

Herniated Disc

It is interesting to note that many asymptomatic adults and children have "bulging discs." These are discs in which the interior matter or nucleous pulposus bulges, creating a bubble on the outer annulus fibrosus. When contained by this tissue, the bulge or herniation is termed a "disc protrusion;" when the material breaks through but remains adhered to the nucleus, it is considered "extruded." The degree of herniation or extrusion is not what determines surgery; it is whether or not the disc material compresses a nerve root that drives that aspect of treatment.

If disc material does not compress a nerve root, conservative treatment is indicated. In the non-surgical back, the herniation/protrusion may

FIGURE 9-2
Family Questionnaire

Patient's Name_____

I am *(please circle answer):*   Spouse   Son   Daughter   Significant other

Other_____   My Name:_____

1.   How many hours per day does your family member spend lying down, sitting sleeping or resting (including at night)?
_____ hours per day.

2.   How many hours per day does he/she spend standing, walking, driving, working or doing other active things?
_____ hours per day.

3.   In comparison with the way your family member was prior to having chronic pain, how active is he/she now? *Circle one.*
10%   20%   30%   40%   50%   60%   70%   80%   90%   100%

4.   How much pain has he/she been having lately? *Circle one.*
    0   No pain.
    1   A very low level pain.
    2   A pain level that could be ignored but is noticeable.
    3   Painful, but would allow an individual to continue his job.
    4   A very severe pain which makes concentration difficult.
    5   A very intense, incapacitating pain.

5.   How effective are your efforts to encourage your family member to be as active as possible? #_____
    1. Never   2. Rarely   3. Sometimes   4. Usually   5. Always

6.   If she/he could cope with her/his pain better, what is the maximum level of functioning you think he/she could achieve? *Please explain.*

7.   How well has he/she been coping with his/her pain? #_____
    1. Terribly   2. not very   3. about average   4. very well   5. terrifically

8.   How well have you (family) been coping with his/her pain? #_____
    1. Terribly   2. not very   3. about average   4. very well   5. terrifically

9.   How much time do you and your family member spend talking each day?
_____ hours - telephone
_____ hours - in person

10. What type of activities does the family do together?

11. How satisfied are you with your ability to cope with your family member's pain problem and pain behavior? #_____
    1. Never   2. Rarely   3. Sometimes   4. Usually   5. Always

12. How satisfied are you with your ability to get your family member to understand your need? #_____
    1. Never   2. Rarely   3. Sometimes   4. Usually   5. Always

13. What are the biggest problems you face with your family member? *Please be specific.*

14. Use this space to make any comments you think might help us to understand more about your family as it was before pain and how it is now.

be central wherein the disc contents spare the nerve roots. With multilevel herniations, the discs may contribute to spinal stenosis. If the disc compresses the spine to the degree that bowel and bladder functioning or reflexes are impacted, surgery is warranted.

Spinal Stenosis

This involves a compromise of the nerve root and spinal cord compartments. There is a circumferential compression of the cord and roots which can be mild, moderate or severe. Stenosis is generally secondary to other pathologies of the spine such as facet hypertrophy, herniated discs, DDD and/or bone spurs.

In stenosis, pain is worsened with walking and standing. The Babinski reflex may be positive, and bowel and bladder functioning may be compromised. Neurovascular changes in the lower extremities may occur in severe cases.

Treatment

If treated early enough, the appropriate type of physical therapy may accomplish satisfactory outcomes along with a good pharmacologic regimen. The physical therapy should be appropriate to the diagnosis as certain treatments can worsen pain. For example, physical therapy directed at increasing flexibility may not be appropriate for facet disease, and treadmill work would be contraindicated for spinal stenosis. Exercise to strengthen the back muscles and increase tolerance will help these and most back pain complaints.

Depending on the chronicity of the problem and the degree of patient debilitation, a multimodal approach is the best plan. Combinations of nerve blocks, physical therapy and medications may be indicated. If the patient is in outpatient treatment with one or two interventions has failed, and/or the patient is dependent on opioids, an inpatient pain management program may produce better outcomes.

Case Study

The following is a case study of a patient with a 2 year history of chronic low back and leg pain.

History

A 35-year-old male patient presented with a complaint of low back (lumbar) pain radiating into and down the right leg corresponding with the L5–S1 dermatome. The patient had been employed as a welder on construction sites, favoring work on high structures. He was at work when a board he stepped onto "gave way" causing him to fall approximately 10 feet. He landed in a seated position, immediately felt a "pop" and severe pain across his low back and into his legs, with the left worse than the right.

Treatment Course

He was taken to the E.R, x-rayed and sent home with NSAIDs, antispasmodics and opioids. He had a follow-up with the Workers Compensation physician who sent him to physical therapy for modalities and light exercise. The patient continued to have the pain despite two courses of physical therapy and a variety of medications. An MRI was done six months after the initial injury, and he was diagnosed with a herniated disc lateral to the right, which impinged on the nerve root at L5–S1.

Surgery

He underwent a lumbar laminectomy, and the disc material was removed. The patient's postoperative course was uneventful, and he noticed that while the intensity of the leg pain was lessened, he continued to have low back pain.

Outcome

He was left with chronic low back and leg pain. He was unable to return to work. He had an MRI six months after the surgery which failed to disclose a cause for the pain.

FIGURE 9-3
Sample Occupational Therapy (OT) Pain Management Plan

I. **Evaluation:**

    A. *Patient Interview:* The following information will be obtained from the patient and medical records at the onset of the OT assessment:

        1. Background Information;

        2. Physical Status;

        3. Symptoms Report;

        4. Educational/Vocational History;

        5. Pain Management Knowledge;

        6. A.D.L. Status; and

        7. Patient Goals for Treatment.

    B. *Physical Characteristics of Patient (i.e., posture)*

    C. *Activities of Daily Living*

    D. *Pain Behaviors Observation*

    E. *Endurance*

II. **Treatment Plan:** Upon completion of the initial evaluation, the therapist establishes an individual treatment plan including short and long-term goals.

III. **Treatment Implementation:** Based on the evaluation, the therapist begins occupational therapy treatment.

IV. **Progress Notes:** Weekly progress notes are written on each patient. Any changes in goals are recorded in the progress notes.

V. **Re-evaluation and Discharge Summary:** The therapist re-evaluates the patient at weekly intervals. The data is shared at the interdisciplinary team conferences.

Psychosocial Data

He lost his job. The patient was married and his wife worked full time as an office clerk. His pain and disability caused marital/relationship difficulties. He stated that he was depressed with a low tolerance for frustration. He reported feelings of helplessness and hopelessness. His sleep was poor. He used to enjoy bowling and fishing but had not been able to engage in any leisure activities. He had a sedentary lifestyle with social isolation.

Treatment

He failed three or four courses of physical therapy with modalities of heat, ultrasound and mas-sage. The patient had been on opioids and ibuprofen and was referred to pain management as his physician told him there was nothing more that could be done and that he was not going to continue prescribing opioids.

Pain Management Treatment Plan

An MRI showed scarring which was retracting the right L5 nerve root. Multi-level degenerative disc disease was noted. The patient was referred to a three week inpatient interdisciplinary pain program. A BDI showed depression, which the patient never experienced until the injury. He was diagnosed with a reactive depression. Psychological therapy consisted of individual and group sessions focused on coping skills enhancement, marital therapy and treatment of the depression.

Physical therapy evaluation found diffuse spasm of the paravertebral muscles, several trigger points and decreased flexibility of the trunk with limited range of motion. The patient's walking tolerance was compromised. An individualized exercise program was implemented with a home program for use after discharge. Myofascial release techniques were utilized to decrease the spasm and trigger points.

Occupational Therapy

Occupational therapy focused on postural remediation, leisure exploration, energy conservation and pacing activities. The patient brought in his fishing pole and the occupational therapist took him fishing, demonstrating applications of what he had learned.

The physician did an equi-analgesic conversion of his hydrocodone to methadone, which was administered in juice around the clock. An NSAID and TCA were also prescribed. While engaging in therapies, the dosage of the methadone was decreased to 5 mg every 6 hours. He was discharged on this dose in tablet form. Biofeedback and relaxation therapy assisted in the management of the stress response and helped him learn techniques by which he could better handle frustration.

Outcome

The patient completed his three week inpatient program and was transitioned to a work hardening program where his job tasks were simulated and his functional tolerances developed. After six weeks in this program, he was discharged and returned to work. He was working full-time as a welder. Six months later he came for a clinic visit and presented the Nurse Practitioner (the author of this course) with the hardhat he had gotten on his last job as welder on the new local football stadium. He continued to work full-time in this capacity.

REFLEX SYMPATHETIC DYSTROPHY SYNDROME (RSD/CRPS)

RSD/CRPS is a multi-symptom syndrome typically affecting an extremity. It was documented as far back as the Civil War, referred to as causalgia. Reflex Sympathetic Dystrophy Syndrome (RSD) has been known by a variety of names: Causalgia, sympathetically maintained pain (SMP), sympathetically independent pain (SIP). The terms Complex Regional Pain Syndrome (CRPS) type I and type II have been used since 1995, when the IASP felt that reflex sympathetic dystrophy did not represent the full spectrum of signs and symptoms of the disease. It was felt that the name inferred the mechanism. Since research has identified a variety of pathophysiological events that contribute to the syndrome, RSD was felt to be inaccurate. Many publications, particularly older ones and some new ones, continue to use RSD. This chapter will use RSD/CRPS synonymously.

Pathogenesis

One theory states that injury causes a C-receptor response which is propagated by wide dynamic range (WDR) neurons and central transmission. These WDR neurons remain sensitized and react to large diameter A mechanoreceptors, which are stimulated by light touch. The WDR neurons respond to the A mechanoreceptor activity, now elicited by sympathetic efferent action at the sensory receptor. No cutaneous stimulation is needed for this effect; hence the term sympathetically maintained pain (Hicks, 1999). This model demonstrates two primary features of RDS/CRPS: Pain in the absence of cutaneous stimulation and allodynia or pain in response to light touch. RSD/CRPS may

---

FIGURE 9-4
Pain Cocktail Form

This is the proposed standard order form to be implemented for pain cocktail administration throughout the hospital. It is to be printed on NCR carbon paper with the original in the chart and the copy to pharmacy. The goal for use of this form is to control for error in transcription/administration and to set controls in place for the vehicle of administration. The volume should stay constant with each dosage adjustment.

PAIN COCKTAIL ORDERS

MEDICATIONS	DOSAGE	VEHICLE (30CC)	FREQUENCY	DURATION
METHADONE	_____	RED FRUIT PUNCH	Q6hours or_____	
MORPHINE	_____	RED FRUIT PUNCH	Q6hours or_____	
PHENOBARBITAL	_____	RED FRUIT PUNCH	Q6hours or_____	
OTHER	_____	RED FRUIT PUNCH	Q6hours or_____	
VISTARIL®	_____	RED FRUIT PUNCH	Q6hours or_____	
ACETAMINOPHEN	_____	RED FRUIT PUNCH	Q6hours or_____	
OTHER	_____	RED FRUIT PUNCH	Q6hours or_____	

BEGIN DOSING SCHEDULE @ 12 MIDNIGHT

DO NOT DISCLOSE CONTENTS TO THE PATIENT. IF THE PATIENT INQUIRES DEFER TO THE M.D.

ORDERED BY:_____ DATE/TIME:_____

NOTED BY:_____ DATE/TIME_____

---

manifest following mild trauma. Just twisting an ankle can cause the syndrome. There is evidence of a genetic predisposition to the development of this disorder.

Stages of RSD/CRPS

Stage I

*   Severe pain at the site of injury

*   Allodynia

*   Hyperpathia

*   Localized swelling

*   Muscle cramping

*   Stiffness and limited mobility

*   Hyperhydrosis

*   The skin is usually warm, red and dry and then may change to a mottled bluish appearance and become cold.

In mild cases, this stage responds quickly to treatment. In other cases, progression may be arrested at this state and not progress. Early appropriate treatment is crucial in order to arrest the disease in this stage.

Stage II

*   Pain increases in severity and is more diffuse.

*   Edema spreads and becomes hardened.

*   Hair may become scant and nails become brittle, cracked and ridged.

*   Spotty wasting of bone (osteoporosis) occurs early but may become severe and diffuse with time.

*   Muscle wasting begins.

*   Contractures may occur.

Stage III

*   Marked atrophy

- Severe deformity and contractures

- May spread to other areas

(*Comment:* It was not uncommon 15 to 20 years ago to see patients with Stage III RSD/CRPS. With earlier diagnosis and better treatment efficacy, patients with Stage III RSD are rarely seen in pain practices.)

Aggressive treatment can keep the disease from spreading and progressing. With earlier interventions, pain can be mitigated with function maintained.

Signs and Symptoms

The mildest trauma or injury can cause RSD/CRPS, there are no definitive instruments with which to make the diagnosis of RSD/CRPS; although thermography can discriminate a cooler body surface area from a warmer one and has been used to document the disease. The reliability of thermography as a diagnostic aid remains debatable in the scientific and medical communities. Clinical diagnosis remains the primary means by which the determination is made. As stated, RSD/CRPS can be confused with a variety of other pathologies. It is often confused with neuropathic and neuralgic pain.

Patients will present with pain complaints out of proportion to stimulus that triggers it. The lightest of tactile stimuli can provoke a painful episode (allodynia). Pain is often constant, aching, burning with sharp, shooting spikes. There might be swelling. Pain will be elicited with light tapping of the area, and when the tapping stops, the pain may persist (hyperpathia). There may be temperature changes in the extremity as a result of the vasomotor changes associated with the abnormal sympathetic activity. The area may be cooler and the skin shiny.

The patient will usually guard the affected extremity. There may be secondary myofascial pain and/or atrophy of the muscles as a result of

disuse. Adjacent areas may be painful, and trigger points may be present. Typically, a patient with upper extremity involvement will have marked limitations in range of motion of the entire extremity and the associated shoulder girdle musculature. This is secondary to the patient holding it close to the chest. There may even be neck pain and spasm. Atrophy may be present and discrete in the early stages.

Treatment

RSD/CRPS responds best to combinations of nerve blocks, physical therapy and medications. A nerve block prior to physical therapy can assist in differentiating between functional overlay, (i.e., fear of moving) and pathology. If hand function is compromised, a hand clinic or occupational therapy referral may be warranted. OT can assist with functional ADLs. In addition to maintaining functional range of motion with mobilization and splinting, the physical therapist can provide desensitization procedures to decrease allodynia and hyperpathia. Beta and calcium channel blockers have proven efficacious as is the use of transdermal clonidine. The TCAs and AEDs should also be maximized to mitigate the burning and sharp shooting pain characteristics. TENS units may be therapeutic or the patient may not tolerate the tingling sensation produced by the device.

An important component of the treatment plan is education. Patients will be reluctant to even move the area let alone let someone move it for them or apply splints. RSD in children can pose serous problems with body image and socialization. Referral to psychological therapy may help as can biofeedback and relaxation therapy. Treatment combinations have afforded the best outcomes with this diagnostic group.

Summary

If diagnosed early, aggressive therapy can mitigate the disease. If undiagnosed and untreated, RSD/CRPS can spread to other extremities and can lead to permanent deformity and chronic severe pain.

NEUROPATHIC PAIN

More than two million people in the United States suffer from neuropathic pain (Beydoun, 1999). The IASP defines neuropathic pain as pain that is initiated or caused by a primary lesion or dysfunction in the nervous system (Ong & Keng, 2001). If undiagnosed, it can lead to tremendous pain and functional impairment. Neuropathy can be sensory, motor or both.

Neuropathic pain can also occur in the orofacial region. Not as common as peripheral neuropathy, orofacial neuropathy is difficult to manage and often overlooked (Ong & Keng, 2001). Damage to the peripheral nerves does not always produce pain. Motor neuropathies are not necessarily painful with problems associated with coordination. For example, patients may complain of clumsiness with fine motor tasks and weakness.

Mechanisms

Peripheral neuropathy is a result of damage or an insult to the peripheral nerves. There have been two mechanisms proposed to cause the phenomenon of peripheral neuropathy: Central sensitization in patients with minor sensory impairment and partial nociceptive deafferentation in patients with major sensory deficit. The patients in the first group experience hyperalgesia (pain out of proportion to stimulus) and patients in the second, painful hypoalgesia (Baumgartner, Magere, Klein, Hopf & Treede, 2002). Hypoalgesia is defined as diminished sensitivity to stimuli that would normally be considered noxious. Patients sometimes describe it as a "numb pain."

Etiology

Peripheral neuropathy can result from a variety of causes. The three most common pathologies associated with peripheral neuropathy are diabetes, post-herpetic neuralgia, and low back pain (Perkins, 2002). Alcohol abuse, metabolic disorders, renal disorders, toxins, drugs, peripheral vascular disease, trauma and HIV are some of the other pathologies/events contributing to the disorder.

In basic terms, when the nerves are damaged and inflammation ensues, regenerated nerve sprouts fire haphazardly often with out sufficient stimulus in undamaged fibers, to cause pain. The A-delta and C fibers fire, transmitting pain to light touch, light pressure and sometimes without tactile or mechanical stimulation.

Characteristics of the Pain

The peripheral nerves affected become dysfunctional and produce a variety of bizarre symptoms. Pain is often burning with sharp spikes of shooting pain (neuralgias). Sometimes it feels like "numb pain," or there is decreased sensation for stimuli other than pain. All tactile stimuli become processed as painful and cold or heat becomes painful. Decreased sensitivity to pressure may ensue. Patients will report "pins and needles" (parasthesias) or "painful pins and needles" (dysesthesias). On ambulation, patients will report that the soles of their feet feel as though they are "walking on rocks." Reflexes may or may not be compromised.

TRIGEMINAL AND POST-HERPETIC NEURALGIAS

Trigeminal neuralgia or tic doloreaux is uncommon. It is impressive with respect to the intensity of the pain when present. The tic involves paroxysmal pain in one or more of the branches of the trigeminal nerve. The pain is intermittent and unilateral. The pain can be triggered with the most innocuous of stimuli; a puff of wind or a strand of hair can set off paroxysms of pain. In most patients, the pain is paroxysmal with a sudden shocklike onset; in others, it builds up gradually over several seconds.

80% of patients with trigeminal neuralgia respond to AED therapy, particularly carbamazepine. Other AEDs are not as effective. While thought to be centrally mediated, some studies have suggested a localized, segmental mechanism. If the pain remains refractory to the appropriate medications, surgical decompression of the nerve may be indicated.

Post-herpetic neuralgia is the painful sequelae of reactivation of the varicella zoster virus. After primary infection, the virus remains dormant in the dorsal root ganglion. Emotional or physical stress can re-activate the virus, often after years of dormancy. Shingles occurs in approximately 20% of people. Post-herpetic neuralgia (PHN) will develop in about 10–15% of persons once the rash disappears. The incidence increases to 50% in persons over the age of 60.

Patients complain of burning, aching, shock-like pain. Other sensory symptoms include numbness, and a "crawling" sensation at the site of the rash. Neuropathic itch can occur as sequelae. One case report cited intractable itch as the only postherpetic symptom. In the year following the ophthalmic zoster, a 39-year-old female with desensate skin scratched though her frontal skull into her brain (Oaklander, Cohen & Raju, 2002).

Treatment

Once the diagnosis has been established, the management of pain from peripheral neuropathy and neuralgias is best undertaken with combinations of medications.

Combinations of AEDs and TCAs have produced the best outcomes. Typically, opioids in usual dosages are not efficacious for this type of pain. Agents should be maximized, and if indicated, sustained-release opioids may be also be used.

Physical therapy and the use of orthotic shoes may ameliorate some of the pain. Biofeedback and relaxation therapy may also assist in the management of pain, and any reactive depression can be addressed with psychology individual and group sessions. Support groups may also be an option. If patients do not respond to the appropriate medications and therapies, a chronic pain management program may be considered.

A treatment algorithm, such as the one to follow, is helpful in the development of the treatment plan (see *Figure 9-5*). The AEDs listed are on lable for peripheral neuropathy. Other AEDs and TCAs have been and continue to be used, but they may be an off label indication. Many of the studies of neuropathic pain have used diabetic peripheral neuropathy and trigeminal neuralgia as models.

In the case of neuralgias where the pain follows a nerve pathway, nerve blocks may be used. Sometimes steroids can be utilized in combination with a local anesthetic in a nerve block (see *Figure 9-6).*

Phantom Limb Pain

While not a true or classic neuropathic pain syndrome, phantom limb pain falls into this category as a nerve-related pain state. Patients with amputations will report retaining the sensation of the limb that has been removed. In years past, a solution to severe Stage III RSD was amputation. Tragically, the patients would not only lose the affected limb but retain the memory of the painful limb as though it had never been removed.

The phenomenon of phantom limb pain presumes centralization of the pain. It has also been suggested that patients may be conjuring up memories of the pain apart from any physiological events. Unfortunately, there have not been sufficient, rigorously controlled studies to evaluate pain in this population.

When diagnosing phantom limb pain, it is important to be diligent in evaluating the character-

FIGURE 9-5

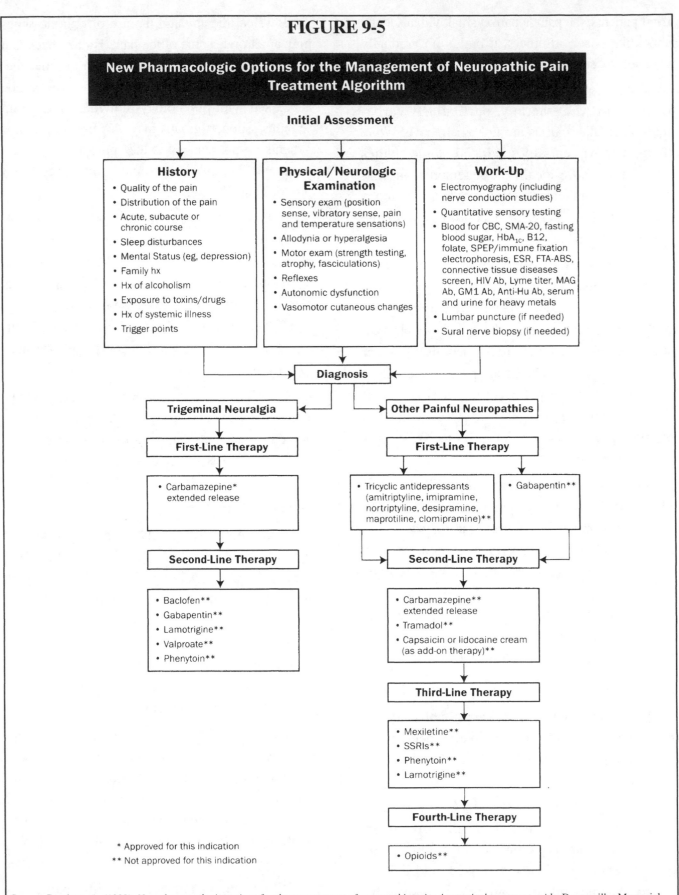

New Pharmacologic Options for the Management of Neuropathic Pain Treatment Algorithm

Initial Assessment

History
- Quality of the pain
- Distribution of the pain
- Acute, subacute or chronic course
- Sleep disturbances
- Mental Status (eg, depression)
- Family hx
- Hx of alcoholism
- Exposure to toxins/drugs
- Hx of systemic illness
- Trigger points

Physical/Neurologic Examination
- Sensory exam (position sense, vibratory sense, pain and temperature sensations)
- Allodynia or hyperalgesia
- Motor exam (strength testing, atrophy, fasciculations)
- Reflexes
- Autonomic dysfunction
- Vasomotor cutaneous changes

Work-Up
- Electromyography (including nerve conduction studies)
- Quantitative sensory testing
- Blood for CBC, SMA-20, fasting blood sugar, HbA$_{1c}$, B12, folate, SPEP/immune fixation electrophoresis, ESR, FTA-ABS, connective tissue diseases screen, HIV Ab, Lyme titer, MAG Ab, GM1 Ab, Anti-Hu Ab, serum and urine for heavy metals
- Lumbar puncture (if needed)
- Sural nerve biopsy (if needed)

Diagnosis

Trigeminal Neuralgia → **Other Painful Neuropathies**

First-Line Therapy (Trigeminal Neuralgia)
- Carbamazepine* extended release

First-Line Therapy (Other Painful Neuropathies)
- Tricyclic antidepressants (amitriptyline, imipramine, nortriptyline, desipramine, maprotiline, clomipramine)**
- Gabapentin**

Second-Line Therapy (Trigeminal Neuralgia)
- Baclofen**
- Gabapentin**
- Lamotrigine**
- Valproate**
- Phenytoin**

Second-Line Therapy (Other Painful Neuropathies)
- Carbamazepine** extended release
- Tramadol**
- Capsaicin or lidocaine cream (as add-on therapy)**

Third-Line Therapy
- Mexiletine**
- SSRIs**
- Phenytoin**
- Lamotrigine**

Fourth-Line Therapy
- Opioids**

* Approved for this indication
** Not approved for this indication

Source: Beydoun, A. (1999). *New pharmacologic options for the management of neuropathic pain: A practical treatment guide.* Dannemiller Memorial Education Foundation. Used with permission of the Dannemiller Foundation.

FIGURE 9-6

**New Pharmacologic Options for the Management of Neuropathic Pain
Dosing of Anticonvulsants**

Trigeminal Neuralgia

First-Line Therapy

Carbamazepine* extended release
• Effective Dose:
  400–1000 mg/day bid

• Administration:
  Start at 200 mg bid and increase by
  100–200 mg every 1–2 days until pain
  relief

Second-Line Therapy

Gabapentin**
• Effective dose:
  900–3600 mg/day tid

Lamotrigine**
• Effective dose:
  200–400 mg/day bid

Valproate**
• Effective dose:
  500–1500 mg/day bid

Phenytoin**
• Effective dose:
  200–350 mg/day qhs

Other Painful Peripheral Neuropathies

First-Line Therapy

Gabapentin**
• Effective dose:
  900–1200 mg/day tid (100–3600 mg/
  day for some patients)

• Administration:
  Start at 300 mg/day qhs (100 mg in
  elderly) and increase by 300 mg every
  3–5 days until pain relief

Second-Line Therapy

Carbamazepine** extended release
• Effective dose:
  400–1000 mg/day bid

Third-Line Therapy

Lamotrigine**
• Effective dose:
  200–400 mg/day bid

Phenytoin**
• Effective dose:
  200–350 mg/day qhs

* Approved for this indication
** Not approved for this indication

©Copyright 1999 Dannemiller Memorial Educational Foundation. All rights reserved. Treatment algorithm and dosing schedule are from a continuing medical education monograph entitled *New Pharmacologic Options for the Management of Neuropathic Pain: A Practical Treatment Guide* by Ahmad Beydoun, MD. Joint sponsorship by the Dannemiller Memorial Educational Foundation and IntraMed Educational Group. Made possible by an unrestricted educational grant from Parke-Davis, a Warner-Lambert Division. The above-mentioned parties cannot be held responsible for errors or for any consequences from the use of information contained in this treatment algorithm/dosing schedule. For additional information, contact Advances in Pain Management, IntraMed Educational Group, 230 Park Avenue South, 10th Floor, New York, NY 10003.

Source: Beydoun, A. (1999). *New pharmacologic options for the management of neuropathic pain: A practical treatment guide.* Dannemiller Memorial Education Foundation. Used with permission of the Dannemiller Foundation.

istics of the pain. Dysethesias may arise from the damaged nerves at the site of the incision. If pain can be evoked with pressure over the incisional line, a neuroma or localized nerve tumor may be present. Differentiation between dysesthesias, neuroma and phantom limb pain is critical to a successful treatment outcome.

Management of phantom limb pain is undertaken through the same paradigm as that of neuropathic and neuralgic pain. If a neuroma is present, injection of a local anesthetic and/or steroid may be utilized.

SUMMARY

Pain is no longer a symptom when it becomes chronic. Chronic pain is a disease with a set of symptoms, and the nurse must be cognizant of this fact. Pain may become chronic as a result of pathological processes that are maintained and do not abate with healing and the passage of time. When this occurs, the nurse must make the cognitive shift from treating the pain as a symptom to treating the pain as a disease.

The role of the nurse in chronic pain management varies with the practice setting. The nurse's role within the treatment context has been addressed within the chapter.

EXAM QUESTIONS

CHAPTER 9
Questions 54–59

54. Chronic pain is

    a. time limited.

    b. always associated with a clear etiology.

    c. a disease.

    d. a symptom.

55. Acute pain differs from chronic pain in that acute pain

    a. is time limited.

    b. never becomes chronic.

    c. is treated with opioids.

    d. has pathological processes.

56. Your patient has chronic back pain. He wants opioids. Based on what you know you inform him that

    a. chronic opioids are only indicated for chronic cancer pain.

    b. chronic opioids are only indicated for acute pain.

    c. he may be a candidate for opioids.

    d. chronic opioids are only indicated for pain with HIV.

Please read the following case presentation and select the best answer to questions 57–58.

Mr. B. has severe back and leg pain from spinal stenosis. He has not been able to work and has seen his physician twice. He is currently receiving physical therapy where he is walking on the treadmill. He is on methadone every eight hours and naproxen twice a day. He comes for his third visit and reports that the physical therapy has made his pain worse. He also says that the methadone does not last.

57. The best explanation for why Mr. B. cannot tolerate physical therapy is that

    a. he is malingering and does not want to work.

    b. he is deconditioned.

    c. walking makes pain from stenosis worse.

    d. pain levels will decrease as his tolerances increase.

58. You inform the physician of Mr. B.'s complaints and he calls Mr. B. What would he tell Mr. B. about his physical therapy?

    a. He is going to discontinue the treadmill and prescribe different exercises.

    b. After this phase, he will not have to exercise again.

    c. He is stopping the physical therapy as he just read that exercise is not indicated for stenosis.

    d. He is going to renew the treadmill prescription.

59. Your patient has twisted her ankle two months ago and is still experiencing excruciating pain. The area is bluish, mottled and so sensitive to light touch that she cannot wear a closed shoe. The source of her pain and symptoms is

    a. phantom limb pain.

    b. post herpetic neuralgia.

    c. peripheral neuropathy.

    d. RSD/CRPS.

CHAPTER 10

NERVE BLOCKS

CHAPTER OBJECTIVE

Upon completion of this chapter, the reader will be able to recall the role of nerve blocks in acute and chronic pain as well as nursing interventions for patients receiving nerve blocks. The reader will also be able to differentiate between sympathetic and non-sympathetic nerve blocks.

LEARNING OBJECTIVES

After studying this chapter, the learner will be able to

1. differentiate between analgesia and anesthesia.

2. cite three potential complications of epidural nerve blocks.

3. recall two nursing interventions for a patient receiving a stellate ganglion nerve block.

4. cite an effect of a stellate ganglion block on the pupil.

5. identify two procedures that may be safely performed in an office setting.

INTRODUCTION

Nerve blocks can be effective diagnostic and therapeutic pain management tools. They can assist in the diagnosis or confirmation of certain pain states and can be utilized in the management of acute and chronic pain. Nerve blocks range in complexity from trigger point injections to continuous infusions of anesthetics or analgesics into the epidural space. It is important to differentiate between anesthesia and analgesia in understanding nerve blocks and their role in pain management. Simply put, the differences are related to the area affected and the agent used. Anesthesia is the use of local anesthetics to decrease nerve impulses. Analgesia involves the placement of opioids in high concentrations at opioid receptors in the spinal cord. Typically, anesthesia and analgesia are referred to as a whole as interventional or segmental procedures.

These procedures are indicated for the management of acute pain, postoperative pain, chronic non-cancer pain and cancer pain. The nurse's role varies with the types of nerve blocks and the practice setting in which the nerve blocks are performed. Typically, the nurse is responsible for pre-procedural preparation, procedural assistance and intra and post-procedural monitoring of patients.

For the purpose of this course, the most commonly performed nerve blocks, spinal cord stimulation and epidural analgesia, will be discussed. Indications and nursing interventions will also be covered.

NON-SYMPATHETIC NERVE BLOCKS

Trigger Point Injections

Trigger point injections are the most commonly performed nerve block. They are typically performed in an office setting. Trigger points are foci of muscle spasm associated with chronic myofascial pain and/or injury. Pain can be provoked with stimulation of the area, which feels rope-like or tense, often crackling with pressure. The palpation gives rise to pain in a referred pattern. Common areas for these trigger points are the trapezius, gluteus, thoracolumbar paravertebrals, gastrocnemius muscles and periscapular soft tissue.

In a trigger point injection, a local anesthetic is injected directly into the foci of the spasm. The anesthetic may or may not be mixed with a steroid. Relief can last for as long as 7–10 days.

Nursing Interventions

An informed consent should be signed. Patients should be educated that the injection may be initially painful and afterward the area may ache. Complications may include:

- Pneumothorax if the injection is too deep. Patients may develop respiratory distress.

- Seizure can result from intravascular injection of the local anesthetic.

In either situation, symptomatic support should be provided. Depending on the practice setting and presence of appropriate support medications and equipment, support services or transfer of the patient to an acute care setting may be warranted.

Greater Occipital Nerve Blocks

Headaches are sometimes the sequelae to blunt trauma to the head or pathology of the cervical spine. The greater occipital nerves (GON) are a pair of nerves which run from the lower posterior aspect of the cranium over the parietal regions to the frontal area. Pain from pathology to the nerves or from spasm at the site of innervation is referred to as Greater Occipital Neuralgia. Patients with cervicogenic pain and/or headaches are candidates for this procedure as well.

Typically, patients complain of sharp shooting pain that travels from the base of the skull forward. The pain is usually paroxysmal, severe and described as "on the head" not "in the head." This is an important differentiation. The pain can be bilateral or unilateral.

GON blocks are usually an office procedure. In the procedure, a local anesthetic is injected 2 cm lateral and 2 cm inferior to the external occipital protuberance. The needle is then forwarded onto the occipital bone and then withdrawn approximately 5 cm before injection. Lidocaine or bupivacaine is injected, and blockade is usually confirmed with pinprick evaluation along the distribution of the nerve(s).

Nursing Interventions

Generally, the nurse performs the pre-procedural teaching and obtains the informed consent. Assisting with the procedure and evaluation of its efficacy can also be elements of the nursing function. If intravascular injection is made, the patient may experience a generalized seizure, which should be treated symptomatically.

Epidural Nerve Blocks/Analgesia

Administration of local anesthetics with and without steroids and/or opioids has proven beneficial for acute and chronic pain. Several studies have documented the use of epidural anesthesia/analgesia for the management of postoperative pain, chronic and cancer pain.

The following was a study of patient satisfaction with postoperative epidural anesthesia/analgesia with a mixture of bupivacaine and hydromorphone. Patients in the study had undergone short segment posterior spinal fusion and instrumentation, a procedure with high risk for severe postoperative pain. All patients (n=7) were either satisfied or very satisfied with their level of pain management on postoperative days 1 3 and at discharge (Lowry, Kittle, Gaines & Tobias, 2001).

A retrospective study was conducted which evaluated records of 313 patients receiving spinal morphine (long-term administration of morphine via implanted epidural ports) (Plummner et al., 1991). Patients were receiving epidural analgesia for both cancer and non-cancer pain. Of the patients studied, only two had their ports removed for inadequate pain relief.

Patient Candidacy

DuPen and Williams (1995) list five areas of importance to explore in the consideration of patients as candidates for spinal analgesia:

1. Presence of "intractable pain."

2. Presence of unmanageable side-effects.

3. Presence of pain syndromes amenable to spinal therapy.

4. Patient/caregiver ability to manage the technology.

5. A successful trial of this type of analgesia.

In this type of procedure, a segmental approach to spine pain is taken with administration of medication at the site of pathology. It has been widely used for the management of discogenic pain.

Environment

These procedures should be performed in an environment that is fully equipped for resuscitation. EKG and pulse oximetry monitoring should be ongoing throughout and following the procedure. Blood pressure is monitored and volume expanding intravenous fluids infused prior to the procedure.

The Procedure

In this procedure, a small catheter is introduced into the epidural space at the appropriate vertebral segment. The epidural space is the com-partment outside of the spinal fluid space. Once the catheter is placed, the guide needle is removed, and the catheter secured. The patient may or may not be mildly sedated. In order to provide feedback as to where the anesthetic is having its effect, the patient must be alert enough to transact with the anesthesiologist.

Agents

A local anesthetic with or without steroid is administered. The most commonly used anesthetic is bupivacacine, as it has an effect that lasts up to 24 hours. The degree of anesthesia is determined by the concentration of the anesthetic. A 15% bupiviacine solution will block sympathetic fibers alone; a 25% solution will block sensory and sympathetic fibers; and a 50% solution will provide a complete motor, sensory and sympathetic blockade.

In a review article, Manchikanti (2000) identified the most commonly used steroids. They are methylprednisolone (Depomedrol®), triamcinolone diacetate (Aristocort®), triamcinolone acetonide (Kenalog®) and betamethasone acetate and phosphate mixture (Clestone®, Slouspan®). It is believed that the steroids exert a nociceptive effect through their anti-inflammatory properties.

Agents introduced into the area of the spinal nerves must be alcohol/preservative free. The only opioid that has been approved for use in spinal analgesia is morphine. The opioid has its effect at the site of the spinal opioid receptors. While the primary effect of the opioid is at the spinal level, there is migration of the opioid into the brain with rostral or cerebral spinal fluid circulation.

Nursing Interventions

It is important that institutional policies and procedures relative to the roles and expectations of nurses caring for the patient receiving epidural/spinal anesthesia and/or analgesia be in place. Nurses caring for patients and infusion systems should be appropriately trained and credentialed, depending on the interventions provided.

Nurses who are managing the infusion systems, changing dressings and adjusting rates of infusions should be credentialed. Nurses should understand the differences in analgesia and anesthesia.

The following is an example of an actual case in which the author of this course was an expert witness. The intials are not those of the actual patient.

Case Study: Mrs. N. was a 78-year-old female with a history of thoracolumbar pain secondary to spinal stenosis and severe degenerative disease. She was admitted with observation status following a high lumbar epidural nerve block, with sensory, motor and sympathetic blockade. She also had a history of cancer and had been on chemotherapy which had impacted her bleeding times. This was noted in her record. Once the procedure was performed, she was transferred from post anesthesia recovery to her bed on an outpatient surgey unit for a 23-hour stay. The nurses on the unit had not been trained in the management of patients receiving this type of procedure. Appropriate orders included neurosensory checks, vital signs and standard orders for catheterization, if needed for urinary retention.

As the night progressed, the nurses noted an *increase* in the patient's paralysis but did not report this to the anesthesiologist who called periodically thoughout the evening to check on her. The patient was also experiencing severe pain at the site of the nerve block and had an episode of urinary incontinence, none of which were reported to the physician. When the physician made rounds early the next morning, he found the patient paralyzed, in severe pain and incontinent of urine. He ordered a stat CT of the spine which showed an epidural bleed and resultant hematoma. The patient was taken to surgery immediately, and the hematoma was evacuated. Unfortunately, she never regained

function and was a high paraplegic. She was subsequently placed in a nursing home.

Outcome: The fundamental issue in this case was that the nurses did not know why they were doing the neurological assessments and how to interpret their findings. The nurses did not know one critical piece of data: With neural blockade, the anesthesia should regress, not progress, with time. There were no policies/procedures or standards of care to assist them and not one educational intervention had been offered by the institution on the care of these patients.

Nursing interventions are contingent on the practice setting. If the procedure is performed in post anesthesia recovery (PAR) and the patient is transferred to the floor, immediate responses to the procedure will be the PAR nurse's area of concern. If the procedure is performed in a pain clinic, the nurse may be responsible for the patient throughout the entire continuum of care from pre-procedural education to community follow-up. Follow-up after discharge with an assessment tool might be conducted to evaluate durability of outcomes.

Infusion Systems

The type of system to be used for the administration of epidural medications is contingent on the duration of therapy. The catheter is always placed as close as possible to the segmental spinal level of involvement. In acute or post operative pain management or for a periodical nerve block, an epidural catheter is used and removed after the procedure. In the case of an evaluation of candidacy for continuous infusion, the catheter is removed after 72 hours. The integrity of the catheter and its connections, along with the occlusive dressing, should be assessed per protocol but no less than once per shift.

For long term analgesic therapy, an internal system reduces the risks of infection, displacement, or dislodgement. Examples of long-term treatment options are:

- **Tunneled epidural catheters:** The catheter is tunneled transcutaneously (under the skin) and attached to either a percutaneous or an implanted epidural port, either of which can be attached to an infusion device for continuous administration with or without PCA. This affords flexibility in permissable volumes and drug combinations (Saberski & Ramiro, 2000).

- **Implanted Pump:** A programmable pump with a limited reservoir is placed in a subcutaneous pocket and is re-filled at regular intervals. The limited reservoir affords limited flexibility in volumes and drug combinations.

Therapeutic Effects

Patients receiving epidural anesthesia/analgesia should have a reduction in their pain and increases in their functional levels. A baseline pain score should be used as a point of reference to evaluate analgesic effectiveness of the procedure. In a structured pain management program, the nurse may also be part of a treating team and may need to have ongoing communication with the physical therapist who is working with an extremity that was blocked for increases in function and range of motion. A functionally focused treatment goal such as, "I'd like to sit long enough to do some fishing," may have been established. This would then become an outcome value to be assessed.

Side Effects

In patients receiving epidural anesthesia with sensory and motor blockade, evaluation of *sensory and motor functions* should be performed using a standardized method. For example, if pinprick sensitivity is the method of neurosensory evaluation, this is what is consistently appraised.

Hypotension may occur. If it does, the lower extremities should be elevated and orders or protocols regarding IV boluses should be followed. Definitive vital sign parameters should be available to the nurse to assist in the determination of the presence of hypotension.

Infection may occur. If the catheter or system is discontinued in the presence of a temperature spike, the catheter tip should be sent for culture and sensitivity. The insertion site of percutaneously placed catheters should be monitored for signs of infection.

In patients receiving epidural opioids for pain management, the primary outcome is analgesia and not anesthesia. The patient should not have persistent numbness or other sensory motor deficits. The primary side effect to monitor is the *respiratory status* of the patient. Some patients will be at higher risk than others for respiratory distress, and the anesthesiologist is well versed in this particular appraisal.

Patients receiving epidural morphine, which is hydrophilic or has an affinity for water and not tissue, may be at higher risk for respiratory depression as the morphine tends to migrate to the cerebrospinal fluid (CSF) and travel to the brain. The circuit of rostral circulation or CSF circulation takes approximately eight hours. This is not the case with fentanyl which is lipophilic or has an affinity to stay bound to tissue. This is an important distinction, as some protocols will call for vital signs to be assessed hourly times four and then go to monitoring every four hours.

The patient receiving morphine will be at risk for respiratory depression at approximately eight hours after the dose is administered. One clue to impending respiratory compromise is the presence of pinpoint pupils, as a sign that the opioid is in the brain and impacting the related cranial nerve. Respiratory depression will be insidious and not sudden, so a decreasing depth rate of and effort at respiration will be important to note and monitor. If this occurs, the infusion should be stopped and orders followed.

Naloxone (Narcan) may be administered, and the patient will need continuous monitoring thereafter, as the naloxone wears off quickly, and the opioid molecules will still be present. With the administration of naloxone, the respiratory depressant effects of epidural analgesia will be reversed but not the analgesic effects, as the analgesia is being affected at the spinal cord and not the brain.

SYMPATHETIC NERVE BLOCKS

It is important to note that all nerve fibers are mixed as sensory, motor and sympathetic and that these nerves run along blood vessels. The sympathetic nervous system controls the involuntary processes of organisms. Some of these functions include vasodilation/constriction, pupillary response and temperature control. These blocks are usually helpful as diagnostic and therapeutic interventions.

Patients who may be candidates for sympathetic blocks include those with neuropathic or sympathetically maintained pain; pancreatic, abdominal or pelvic pain; or phantom limb pain. Patients with a diagnosis of RSD, or as it has been re-named, Chronic Reflexive Pain Syndrome (CRPS), may benefit from epidural nerve blocks. However, nerve blocks that target the sympathetic nervous system are more efficacious.

Patients with CRPS or SMP may have an extremity which is significantly cooler. A successful sympathetic nerve block will dilate the blood vessels, running along the sympathetic fibers, resulting in a consequential increase in the blood flow to the extremity. Some patients may equate the change in temperature sensation with a reduction in the actual pain. Therefore, a good sympathetic nerve block should increase the temperature of the extremity without numbness or weakness, as the sympathetic fiber is selectively blocked, sparing the motor and sensory fibers. If the block causes numbness or weakness, more than just the sympa-

thetic nerves were blocked and the diagnostic and prognostic value of the nerve block would be compromised.

It is always possible for the local anesthetic to be inadvertently injected into a blood vessel or into the spinal fluid. For safety reasons, sympathetic blocks are always performed under conditions where the vital signs (blood pressure and breathing) can be monitored closely. The maximum sustained benefit from a series of sympathetic blocks is usually apparent after a series of three to six blocks. If the patient has not responded at that point, further blocks should be deferred.

Stellate Ganglion Block

A sympathetic block of the upper extremity is called a stellate ganglia block (SGB). The SGB is performed by inserting a small needle alongside the windpipe (trachea). Patients are informed that they may notice a temporary change in the tone of their voice following the block because some of the local anesthetic may partially numb the vocal cords. They are also informed that immediately after the block they should only sip fluids and take small bites of food. The numbness around the vocal cords temporarily places the patient at a slight risk of coughing in response to drinking and eating. The patient may also notice a temporary drooping of their upper eye lid due to the SGB (Horner's Sign).

Lumbar Sympathetic Block

A sympathetic block of the lower extremities is called a lumbar sympathetic block (LSB). For patient comfort and safety, LSBs should be performed with the aid of X-ray imaging of landmarks.

Celiac Plexus Blocks

Celiac plexus blocks are performed for the management of visceral pain, usually pain of the pancreas. This is especially efficacious in the case of pancreatic cancer.

The plexus of center for the innervation of the sympathetic nerves is blocked. This is done under CT imaging. Patients will have a decrease in pain levels. A successful trial with a local anesthetic may be followed by a neurolytic procedure with alcohol or formaldehyde, wherein the nerve plexus is destroyed.

Mercadante (1993) looked at pain scores and opioid consumption in two groups of patients. There were ten patients in each group, and all patients experienced severe pain. The first group of patients received a celiac plexus block while the second group of patients was managed with opioids and adjuvants. The end point of the study was death. Patients in the nerve block group had significantly lower pain scores and less opioid use than patients managed with medications alone. When used in conjunction with opioids, celiac plexus blocks can promote analgesia and enhanced quality of life.

Nursing Interventions

Informed consent is obtained and pre-procedural education provided. Patients should not eat for six hours prior to a sympathetic block. Patients undergoing a stellate ganglion block (SGB) should be monitored for efficacy. One indicator is the presence of Horner's Sign wherein the pupil of the eye is constricted, the eyelid drooping, and the conjunctiva are reddened on the affected side. There may also be nasal stuffiness and/or tearing of the eye on the affected side. The patient will be hoarse and may have difficulty swallowing following the SGB and should be maintained NPO for six hours following the procedure.

A successful block should also enhance the amount of pain relief and improve range of motion and physical/functional tolerances. It is important that the patient is aware that this is the goal of the treatment.

As with the other interventions, it is important to obtain the patient's particular goal(s) in undergoing the procedure. What would the patient like to do that they have not been able to? By placing desired treatment outcomes in realistic, personally relevant terms for the patient, outcomes may be more reliably reported. This also enhances the patient role as a partner in the treatment plan.

The nurse can facilitate this type of transaction between the patient and the physician by utilizing a pain assessment instrument that includes functional and quality of life questions for the patient. This information about the patient's response to sympathetic blockade can serve to indicate the prognosis for rehabilitation following the series of sympathetic blocks.

SPINAL CORD STIMULATION (SCS)

In spinal cord stimulation (SCS), low intensity electrical impulses are used to trigger selected nerve fibers along the dorsal columns of the spinal cord. This neurostimulation has been applied to a wide variety of painful disorders. These include tumors, phantom limb pain, RSD/CRPS, ischemic limb pain, multiple sclerosis, arachnoiditis, peripheral vasular disease and failed back syndrome (Cameron & Elliott, 2002). Historically, Melzack and Wall's Gate Control Theory has provided the paradigm for its use and efficacy. Modulation is the operant function related to neurostimulation. It has been discovered that spinal inhibitory circuits, involving GABA and adenosine transmission are acitivated by SCS. Cerebral blood flow to the periaqueductal gray and other pain-related structures of the brain have also been documented with SCS (Cameron & Elliott, 2002).

SCS replaces the area of intense pain with a non-painful tingling sensation called paresthesia, which remains relatively constant. There is some experimental evidence that SCS may enhance the

TABLE 10-1
Overview of Major Segmental Procedures

PROCEDURE	AREA AFFECTED	PATIENT OUTCOME	NURSING INTERVENTIONS
Epidural Nerve Block: Cervical-Thoracic-Lumbar-Caudal	Segment that is treated and area below.	Depending on concentration of anesthetic, patient may have sensory, sympathetic and/or motor blockade. Pain score should be lowered if effective.	Consent obtained; patient to void before block; IV bolus given and access maintained; vital signs monitored for hypotension; controlled substances used from time of discharge to time of follow-up, with maintenance continued at appropriate intervals.
Epidural Opioids	Generally pain at or below the segment and some systemic effects.	Pain should be managed; if concomitant anesthetic given, sensory/motor function may be impacted.	IV access; vital signs monitored every hour for first 8 hours, if morphine used; less intensive with lipophilic opioids. Monitor for pinpoint pupils and decreasing respiratory rate, volume and excursion as signs of impending respiratory distress. Naloxone should be on hand, Appropriate care of infusion system per standards/protocols.
Stellate Ganglion Nerve Block: Sympathetic Nerve Block	Primarily used for upper extremity pain; injection into anterior neck with needle resting on C6 process; carotid retracted.	Affected upper extremity should be warmer; Horner's Sign should be present; patient may be hoarse and may have difficulty swallowing for 6 to 8 hrs.	Evaluate for efficacy; NPO for first 6–8 hours post procedure, start oral intake with jello to avoid choking. If seizure results from inadvertent intravascular administration of anesthetic, treat symptomatically.
Lumbar Sympathetic Block	Used for lower extremity, sympathetically maintained pain.	Increased temperature of extremities and decreased pain.	Evaluated for efficacy. For safety after procedure, assist with ambulation.

flow of blood to the affected extremity by blocking the sympathetic nervous system.

SCS is a relatively invasive and costly procedure. It is important that patient candidacy be established. The etiology and pathophysiology of the pain should be documented. A temporary trial should be performed prior to the implanting of permanent electrode(s). As part of the baseline evaluation toward that end, a psychosocial evaluation that addresses pain management issues should be conducted, including psychological testing.

A baseline functional evaluation prior to the trial should include a physical therapy assessment. Once the trial stimulator is in place and the surgical area healed, a repeat functional evaluation should be performed to document efficacy. In other words,

patient selection is important and documentation of efficacy should not be limited to a pain score.

Procedure

There are two types of systems that may be used. One procedure involves the percutaneous implantation of electrodes, which are then attached to an external stimulator. The other procedure involves a mini-laminectomy. If the trial is successful, the stimulators and electrodes can be completely implanted with activation and adjustments of settings accomplished with an external battery-controlled transmitter. Either procedure should be performed in the operating room or similarly equipped setting.

Nursing Interventions

Although uncommon, spinal infection and paralysis are potential complications for which the patient should be monitored. Pre-procedural preparation of the patient along with education and informed consent processes are part of the nursing function. Again, depending on the role of the nurse, interventions can range from assistance with insertion of the SCS to in home follow-up on efficacy following discharge. Primary nursing functions are related to evaluation of efficacy and monitoring for complications.

SUMMARY

Nerve blocks can be an invaluable adjunct in the management of pain. Their efficacy is enhanced with concomitant treatment with non-pharmacological interventions such as physical therapy. Patients may be somewhat apprehensive at the prospect of a needle being placed in their spine or neck. Patient education is very important, not only to allay anxiety but for safety reasons as well.

The nurse has a variety of role opportunities when working in a setting where nerve blocks for pain management are employed. These roles may range from assisting with procedures to patient education to research and outcome evaluation. Irrespective of their setting, it is important that policies and procedures for patient protection be in place. The nurse should be adequately prepared to manage systems and care for patients receiving these interventions.

Table 10-1 summarizes the important points and nursing interventions with the main procedures noted in this chapter.

EXAM QUESTIONS

CHAPTER 10
Questions 60–66

60. Differences in anesthesia and analgesia are primarily related to

    a. area affected and agent used.

    b. epidural space utilization.

    c. diagnosis of the patient.

    d. whether an anesthesiologist performs the procedure.

61. The administration of an anesthetic into the epidural space is

    a. within the scope of RN practice.

    b. within the scope of RN practice in a pain clinic.

    c. outside the scope of RN practice.

    d. within the scope of an RN credentialed by the hospital.

62. Two procedures that may be safely performed in an office setting are

    a. epidural block and GON block.

    b. epidural block and trigger point injection.

    c. trigger point injection and GON block.

    d. celiac plexus block and epidural block.

63. Your patient just had a trigger point injection and experienced a seizure. This is most likely the result of

    a. a pneumothorax.

    b. an intravascular injection of the anesthetic.

    c. an allergy to steroids.

    d. an allergy to lidocaine.

64. Your patient has undergone a SGB and has a constricted pupil. This indicates

    a. a successful block.

    b. an inadvertent intravascular injection.

    c. pressure on the cornea.

    d. allergy to lidocaine.

65. Your patient has had an epidural block; you would expect over time a(n)

    a. increase in sensory function and decrease in motor function.

    b. increase in sensory and motor function.

    c. decrease in sensory and motor function.

    d. increase in motor function and a decrease in sensory function.

66. You are caring for a patient receiving epidural morphine. You are observing the patient for respiratory depression. You are monitoring

    a. respiratory rate alone.

    b. respiratory rate and character.

    c. respiratory rate, depth and character.

    d. respiratory rate, depth, character and pupil size.

CHAPTER 11

MANAGEMENT OF PAIN IN SPECIALIZED POPULATIONS

CHAPTER OBJECTIVE

Upon completion of this chapter, the reader will be able to identify populations at high risk for inadequate pain management and/or severe or chronic/re-current pain and recall a treatment approach unique to each population.

LEARNING OBJECTIVES

After studying this chapter, the learner will be able to

1. list four populations at risk for severe or chronic and/or recurrent pain.

2. identify the two types of hyperalgesia present with pain from burns.

3. identify one common pain syndrome in patients with AIDS/HIV.

4. cite a myth regarding pain from burns.

5. recall one nursing intervention that can effect better pain manaement during procedures in children.

6. recognize age as a variable in the assessment of pain in children.

INTRODUCTION

The most common reason for unrelieved pain in U.S. hospitals is the failure of staff to routinely assess pain and pain relief (APS, 1999). Many organizations have developed position papers, standards of care and protocols for the management of pain. The need for healthcare professional education in this area is essential, if practice is to be impacted.

While pain management is a problem across diagnostic groups and demographics, there are populations who are at risk for poorly managed pain and/or severe pain. For the purpose of this course, four groups at risk for severe pain or under-treated pain will be discussed. Two of the groups are at risk because of developmental issues, and two are at risk because of their diagnosis. The four groups to be discussed are:

1. Persons with burn injuries.

2. Elderly patients with pain.

3. Children with pain.

4. Persons with HIV/AIDS.

PAIN FROM BURNS

Patients who have experienced burn injuries are at risk for acute and chronic pain. The extent of the pain involves the body surface area of the burns and the depth of the burns. The type of burn is also a factor. For example, a patient with a severe electrical burn will have pain from the burn and pain from amputations that are sometimes required. Tissue conducts electricity, bone does not. With an electrical injury, there is the entry point and then the exit point for the charge. Typically, a limb is involved at the point of exit and/or entry. Once the initial injury has been treated, the patient may have to return to surgery for progressive amputations. Consequently, subacute pain from the burns as healing progresses is compounded by acute post-operative pain. The patient may suffer from the chronic pain of peripheral neuropathy subsequent to nerve damage.

Pain Mechanisms

The mechanisms of pain from burn injury involve

- a decrease in thresholds for subsequent excitation of spinal neurons.

- greater response to subsequent stimuli.

- expansion of receptor fields.

- recruitment of "silent" nociceptors.

- subsequent primary and secondary hyperalgesia.

    Hyperalgesia is further delineated into:

Primary which is immediate and limited to injury and mediated by peripheral nociceptors and spinal neurons.

Secondary which is immediate and delayed; mediated by spinal neurons and involves the site of injury and adjacent areas.

Combinations of these and other mechanisms make the patient with an injury from burns at high risk for pain and when the pain persists or is not effectively managed, suffering.

Causes of Pain

Burn pain management is similar to cancer pain management in that pain is a consequence of and related to pathophysiological processes *and treatment*. The patient with pain from a burn injury is at risk for pain from the burn, its' treatment and the interventions directed at the preservation and restoration of function.

Burn pain is not different than pain from other causes in that variables and barriers to pain management are present. Fear of addiction and knowledge deficits regarding pain management and pharmacology may impact the care provided. A factor unique to the burn care environment is the professional experience of the nurses. It has been found that the length of time working in the burn setting places nurses at risk for overestimating and underestimating pain.

Factors Impacting Burn Injury Pain

- Initial insult/injury

- Body surface area burned

- Treatment of the initial injury

    — surgery

    — dressing changes

    — expansion devices

    — non-surgical interventions

In a research study, children in a burn unit rated their pain levels before during and after dressing changes. There was a positive correlation between the body surface area (BSA) burned and pain scores. Patients with greater than 70% BSA burned experienced severe pain during dressing changes despite the type, route and dose of opioids. There was also a positive correlation between pain and full-thickness burns (Atchison, Osgood, Carr & Szfelbein, 1991).

When evaluating pain from burns, it is important for the nurse to separate the direct causes of the pain from the elements of treatment that perpetuate pain. For example, poor sleep has been found to have a negative effect on pain in burn patients. Raymond, Neilsen, Lavigne, Manzini and Choiniere (2001) evaluated the impact of sleep on pain in hospitalized adult burn patients. The researchers discovered that not only is the quality of sleep in the presence of acute burn pain poor, but patients with poor sleep experienced higher levels of pain intensity during the day. Nurses should evaluate sleep in their patients and notify the physician of disturbances.

The setting in which the burns are managed is important with respect to pain. One study analyzed the use of analgesics relative to treatment settings (Summer & Puntillo, 2002). Findings of the study that compared the use of analgesics for management of burn pain in outpatient versus inpatient settings was revealing in that

- inpatients received higher doses of analgesics despite no significant difference in pain scores.

- treatment was for procedural and background pain.

- pain intensity was not managed when patients were discharged to outpatient status.

- 50% of the patients in outpatient settings received no analgesics.

Knowing this the nurse should be cognizant of the intensity of pain interventions in the outpatient versus inpatient setting. Cueing the physician of inadequacies in pain management is an intervention the nurse can employ.

Fear of addiction exists in heath professionals and patients alike, despite the nature of the cause of the pain or the setting. Some patients with pain from burns require larger doses of parenteral opioids than the typical post-operative and medical patient. Patients with burns may require analgesics for a longer period of time than patients in other settings. Yet, in patients with burn injuries, addiction is less of a problem than believed.

A survey was conducted in which 181 practitioners treating burn patients were contacted regarding iatrogenic addiction. The practitioners in the survey had an average of over six years on a burn unit and represented the accumulated knowledge of at least 10,000 hospitalized patients. The survey showed that not one case of iatrogenic addiction was found in patients receiving opioids for burn pain when no prior history of substance abuse was reported (Perry & Heidrich, 1982).

It is a given that injuries from burns place the patient at high risk for pain. Burn pain management brings with it challenges peculiar to it, and barriers that can be generalized to other pain problems.

Challenges of Burn Pain Management

- Different pain mechanisms (neuralgic, neuropathic, nociceptive) occur concomitantly.

- Pain can be acute, chronic and recurrent.

- Anxiety plays an intimate role in the pain.

The emotional distress that arises from loss of loved ones, impaired physical functioning, property loss and other financial problems can compound pain. Body image is a psychological variable that may impact the patient's pain. Scarring may be extensive and loss of limb(s) may occur. These and other factors combined make the management of pain related to burns especially challenging. The nurse and physician are not always well equipped to provide for appropriate interventions directed at mitigating issues that perpetuate and enhance pain. An interdisciplinary team should be consulted in the management of the patient, with a pain specialist as a team member.

CASE PRESENTATION

The following is an actual patient who was admitted to a regional burn center and followed by both the burn and the pain management medical team.

V.M. was a 19-year-old male patient who presented to the burn unit with 51% BSA burned with 48% full-thickness injury sustained when his truck hit a tree and exploded. He was thought to be dead by his companions who did not immediately remove him from the truck. He spent four months in the burn unit where he underwent an upper extremity amputation and multiple reparative and restorative surgical/non-surgical procedures.

He was referred to the pain clinic for persistent pain and continued use of opioid analgesics. He had been seen by a different pain management physician while an inpatient and was taking the following medications:

- Amitriptyline 50 mg at HS
- Oramorph SR 30 mg BID
- Celebrex 200 mg BID
- Lorazepam 1 mg BID
- Oxy-IR 5 mg, 1 to 2 before dressing changes
- Ambien 5 mg at HS
- Methadone 5 mg BID

Extent of Injuries

V.M. had burns to his head, neck, face, anterior/posterior trunk, right buttock, left upper arm, left lower arm and hand, right lower arm and left thigh and lower leg.

Treatment

V.M. was status post amputation of his left forearm. He had a dressed open area to his scalp and was status post multiple excision graftings and scar contracture releases. He had undergone extensive physical therapy.

Psychosocial Data

- V.M. was the driver of a truck which exploded on impact.
- His roommate and another friend were in truck at the time of the accident. They sustained minor injuries.
- V.M.'s roommate subsequently moved and sold all of V.M.'s belongings from their apartment.
- After discharge, V.M. moved home with his parents.

- V.M. was previously self-employed as a tree cutter. V.M. had his GED.
- V.M.'s hobbies were hunting, fishing and outdoor activities.

Coping Mechanisms

- Despite a referral to psychiatry, V.M. stated that he was "not letting anybody get inside his head."
- V.M. cried when the pain gets too bad or tried "not to think about it."
- V.M. developed an interest in the Internet and enjoyed bartering on same.

Characteristics/Location of Pain

- V.M. experienced neuralgic pain at site of his left elbow graft. V.M.'s left forearm was amputated below the elbow joint.
- V.M. had hyperalgesia on his antero-lateral trunk and axilla on the left.
- V.M. had constant background pain of a throbbing nature at his scalp which, when exposed to air, was burning in character.

Analysis of Treatment Plan

A stratified approach to this young man's pain had been used with the concurrent use of medications from different classes. Unfortunately, there were no AEDs in the regimen, and the methadone was prescribed at intervals that would not provide steady state analgesia, as the analgesic half-life for methadone is six hours. Although the oramorph was supposed to handle the pain between the methadone doses, it did not.

The OXY-IR (oxycodone without acetaminophen) was not being taken appropriately; he was taking the dose just 10 minutes before starting the procedure. Ten minutes was not enough time for the onset to have taken effect, and he was unable to "catch up" on the pain. The procedure took him close to 45–60 minutes to complete, and the pain lasted at least 90 minutes after the procedure. He had a tremendous amount of anxiety with the dressing changes, so the psychiatrist had prescribed the ambien for this. The patient said this helpcd.

The methadone was changed to an every six hours schedule, and the oromorph was discontinued. The patient was instructed to take one OXY-IR 30 minutes before starting the dressing change and an additional OXY-IR 5 minutes before the procedure, to provide for analgesic coverage after the dressing change. An AED was added to his regimen for the neuralgic pain. Topiramate (Topamax) was chosen, as the patient had gained weight to the point that he was 20 pounds over his ideal, and weight loss is a side effect of this particular AED. The amitriptytline was also contributing to his weight gain, but it was not initially changed.

New Treatment Plan

- Pharmacologic Treatment Plan
    - Discontinue oramorph
    - Begin methadone 5 mg q 6 hours
    - Ambien® with dressing changes
    - Use one Oxy-IR 30 minutes prior and one Oxy-IR 5 minutes prior to dressing changes.
    - Trial of Topamax 15 mg qd for 7 days then BID for 7 days then increase by 15 mg per dose to 30 mg BID and re-assess.
- Non-Pharmacologic Treatment Plan
    - Refer for physical therapy for progressive de-sensitization of left elbow.
    - Refer for biofeedback and relaxation therapy for pain management and sleep hygiene.

Course of Treatment

The patient did quite well on everything but the AED. He could not tolerate either the topiramate or the subsequent gabapentin. He continued to gain weight. A change of the amitriptyline to an SSRI was considered but not done.

As he was undergoing significant reconstructive surgery to replace his ears and reconfigure other features, the methadone was increased to 20 mg every six hours for post-operative pain management. After the acute pain, it was decreased to 10 mg every six hours.

The patient weaned himself with no difficulties from 10 mg of methadone every six hours to 5 mg every six hours and was off all narcotics within six months of the initial pain evaluation. He never overused or abused his medications.

General Treatment Principles

Addiction is not a factor with the use of opioids for burn pain management. Around-the-clock opioids should be used, not PRN or as needed. Scheduled and bolus drugs should be weaned 10–20% as the patient is transitioned to the next stage (Stoddard et al., 2002). Full-thickness burns are painful!

An interdisciplinary approach with the nurse as an active team participant should be used. Non-pharmacologic treatment interventions need to be maximized; biofeedback and relaxation therapy can be used. A stratified approach with appropriate pharmacologic adjuvants should be used. A patient's pain must be managed as aggressively as an outpatient as it was managed as an inpatient.

PAIN IN GERIATRIC PATIENTS

In the elderly, reports of chronic pain vary with estimates at a minimum of 70% (Davis, Hiemenz & White, 2002). Arthritis and neuralgia are the predominant sources of non-cancer-related chronic pain in this population (Davis et al., 2002). Calkins (1991) cited osteoarthritis as the most common condition in persons over the age of 65. Post-herpetic neuralgia is also more common in

Table 11-1

Elderly Patients With Cancer Pain

29.4% of 13,625 patients ≥65 years old reported daily pain. Of these patients, 25.5% received no analgesia.

Source: Bernabei, R., Gambassi, G., Lapane, K., Landi, F., Gatsonsis, C. & Dunlop, R. (1998). Management of pain in elderly patients with cancer. SAGE study group. Systematic assessment of geriatric drug use via epidemiology. *JAMA, 279,* 1877–1882.

Elderly Patients With Nonmalignant Pain

26.3% of 49,971 patients ≥65 years old experienced daily pain. Of these patients, 25.1% received no analgesia.

Source: Won, A., Lapane, K. & Gambassi, G. (1999). Correlates and management of nonmalignant pain in the nursing home. *Journal of American Geriatric Society, 47,* 936–942.

persons with shingles or herpes zoster over the age of 65. In 1996, 383,988 Americans over the age of 65 died of cancer. Many of these patients experienced unrelieved pain (Jost, 2000).

Barriers to Pain Management

There are several specific barriers that have been identified in the under/mismanagement of pain in this group, including:

- Elderly are not inclined to report pain as they believe pain to be an expected consequence of aging.

- Patients with cognitive impairment are at risk for inadequate pain relief.

- Fear of addiction.

- Financial concerns.

By and large no matter what barrier or study, a consistent issue is communication. Pain in the geriatric population is frequently undetected because of patient non-communication and the poor communication and assessment skills of doctors and nurses (Sengstaten & King, 1993). Some patients believe that pain is a natural part of the aging process and should therefore be expected (Pasero & McCaffery, 1996). Elderly patients often underreport pain because of this belief. The elderly are often fearful of addiction, overdose, and side effects, and may refuse medications because they are afraid to use anything unfamiliar or they may have financial concerns or constraints.

Many of the sustained-release, non-opioids and adjuvants used in pain management are expensive. Although Medicare and Medicaid pay for a great deal of pain management, Medicare does not pay for prescriptions. In some cases, both payers discourage the provision of adequate pain management services (Jost, 2000). Even with Medicaid prescription coverage, formularies can be restrictive. Many pharmaceutical companies can provide support either through samples or free medication programs for those who qualify.

Supportive Research

A retrospective, cross-sectional study of 13,625 cancer patients 65 years of age and older, revealed that 4,003 patients reported daily pain. Of the patients aged 85 years and older, 24% had daily pain; of those aged 75 to 84 years, 29% had daily pain; and 38% of those aged 65 to 74 years reported daily pain. Of these patients with daily pain, only 16% received a non-opioid medication, with or without a mild opioid; 32% received a non-opioid medication, with or without a mild opioid; only 26% received a strong opiate; and 25.5% of the patients did not receive any analgesia. The study demonstrated that patients at highest risk for poor pain management included those older than 85 years, minorities, and those with low cognitive performance (see *Table 11-1*) (Bernabei et al., 1998).

In a another cross-sectional study of 49,971 nursing home residents 65 years of age and older with nonmalignant pain, 26.3% experienced daily pain. These individuals were more likely to have impaired function as determined by activities of daily living, exhibited more signs of depression, and participated less frequently in activities. Of the 13,143 residents with pain, 25.1% received no analgesia (see *Table 11 1*) (Won, Lapane & Gambassi, 1999).

Pain Assessment in the Elderly

One study looked at the sensitivity of five pain assessment scales when used by elderly and non-elderly patients at a rheumatology clinic (Purdue Pharma, 2001e). Specifically, researchers examined

- the sensitivity of each scale in detecting change;

- the effect of age on tool sensitivity; and

- the correlation between the subjects' pain intensity ratings on the five tools.

The sample included 61 younger adults and 35 elderly patients receiving cortisone injections. The researches found each of the five scales (Faces Pain Scale for use with older adults, 100 point verbal analogue, verbal 10 point and nonverbal 21 point numeric rating scale and a revised verbal descriptor scale) was sensitive to the differences in the pre and post-pain experience. The Faces Pain Scale correlated less than the others. The verbal numeric scale had the highest failure rate in correct usage in the elderly and non-elderly. Some in the elderly group had mild cognitive impairment, and they found the faces scale and the verbal descriptor scale to be the easiest to use.

Another interesting study compared four scales for use in cognitively impaired older adults. Researchers found that a horizontal, 21 point (0–100) box scale was psychometrically superior to the other three scales evaluated. It was reliable and valid for use by older, mild to moderately cognitively impaired adults (Chibnall & Tait, 2001).

Pharmacological Considerations

Due to age-related changes in renal and hepatic functioning, metabolism and clearance can impact pharmacokinetics. While dated, a study performed over a decade ago clearly illustrates this point. Kaiko (1988) evaluated patient responses to a total of 947 doses of 8 mg or 16 mg of IM morphine. Patients were divided by age into two groups. Four hours after the injection, 71% of the patients 70 to 89 years of age continued to experience pain relief; conversely, only 28% of the patients between 18 to 29 years of age experienced analgesia. Morphine is the only opioid with an active metabolite with analgesic properties: M3G, which may play a role in tolerance, and M6G, which is a potent analgesic (Analgesic tolerance to opioids, 2001). Of note was the finding that total and peak pain relief did not differ in the two groups.

What are some implications for practice? With morphine use in the elderly, more consideration should be given to frequency of the dosages than the amount of medication. These data also translate into practice with other agents. While the analgesia-producing metabolite is peculiar to morphine, other opioids have toxic metabolites and/or effects. For example, propoxyphene (Darvocet) is transformed into norpropoxyphene, a potentially toxic agent. Meperidine (Demerol) has an active metabolite normeperidine which can cause CNS excitability and/or seizures. Consequently, the use of propoxyphene and meperidine should be avoided in treatment of the elderly. If the physician insists on their use, the nurse should carefully monitor for signs of toxicity and provide relevant instructions to the patient and family.

Methadone is another opioid analgesic to be avoided, as it has a 24 hour half-life. This produces an insidious respiratory depressant effect, as the analgesic accumulates in the system. The respiratory depressant effects may not be initially apparent. The patient will appear to be tolerating the agent for the first 24–48 hours and have a respiratory arrest within 72 hours.

When discussing or evaluating the patient's pain management regimen, it is important to query as to the use of over-the-counter agents. Patients do not always equate over-the-counter agents with their prescribed medication regimen and consequently, neglect to mention their use. A commonly used analgesic both over-the-counter and in compounded opioids, is acetaminophen. It is also an ingredient in at least 110 over-the-counter medications.

In daily doses exceeding 4 grams, kidney and liver damage can occur. In the geriatric patient who drinks as little as 2.5 glasses of alcohol per day, this daily dosage is dramatically reduced to no more that 2.5 grams per day (Purdue Pharma, 2001f).

General Nursing Principles

- Communication and assessments must be transactional and appropriate to the cognitive status of the patient being treated.

- In the case of cognitive impairment, scales that are valid and reliable for use in this group should be utilized.

- The factors that place the elderly at risk for poorly managed pain need to be understood.

- The pharmacologic treatment plan should take into consideration the age and mental state of the patient, along with safety considerations.

- Facts related to addiction and pain associated with aging should be known and shared to dispel myths/misconceptions related to pain management.

- The patient's financial status and ability to pay for treatment should be considered.

- Regimens should have a conservative start to control for side effects. For example, an elderly patient should never be started on therapeutic dosages of a tricyclic antidepressant. Low doses should be gradually titrated upward to tolerance.

- The physiology of aging needs to be considered when assessing and treating pain; instruments that are appropriate for age-related visual and auditory hearing deficits should be used.

- Age-related pharmacokinetic and pharmacodynamic changes should be considered.

- Non-pharmacologic treatment interventions such as low impact aquatic therapy should be utilized.

PAIN IN PEDIATRIC PATIENTS

At the opposite end of the age continuum are pediatric patients. Children offer suffer needlessly due to their inability to verbally communicate pain; beliefs that children do not have mature enough nervous systems to transmit and modulate pain; and the failure of healthcare professionals to approach the management of pain in children through developmental paradigms. Children and adolescents experience a variety of pain states including headache, abdominal pain and pain from Sickle Cell Disease. Low back pain has also been documented in children.

While challenging, pediatric pain management can be accomplished. Deering and Jennings-Cody (2002) wrote an excellent article addressing communication with children and adolescents. While not pain specific, they discuss methods and techniques to facilitate the communication process in this age group.

Barriers to Pain Management

- Younger children are unable to conceptualize and quantify pain.

- Older children experience difficulty in describing pain due to lack of experience.

- Pain management in this population is not valued by professionals.

FIGURE 11-1
Wong-Baker FACES Pain Rating Scale

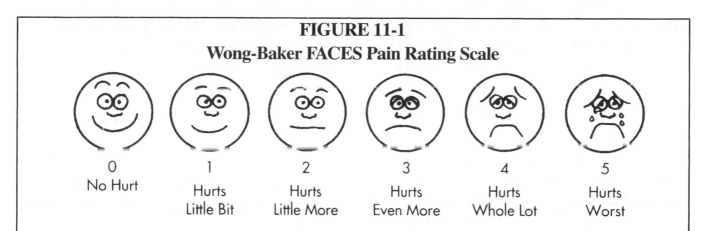

0	1	2	3	4	5
No Hurt	Hurts Little Bit	Hurts Little More	Hurts Even More	Hurts Whole Lot	Hurts Worst

Explain to the person that each face is for a person who feels happy because he has no pain (hurt) or sad because he has some or a lot of pain. Face 0 is very happy because he doesn't hurt at all. Face 1 hurts just a little bit. Face 2 hurts a little more. Face 3 hurts even more. Face 4 hurts a whole lot. Face 5 hurts as much as you can imagine, although you don't have to cry to feel this bad. Ask the person to choose the face that best describes how he is feeling. Rating scale is recommended for persons age 3 years and older.

From Wong, D., Hockenberry-Eaton, M., Wilson, D., Winkelstein, M. & Schwartz, P. *Wong's Essentials of Pediatric Nursing,* 6/e, St. Louis, 2001, P. 1301. Copyrighted by Mosby, Inc. Reprinted with permission.

- Use of opioids is deemed unsafe in infants and children.

- Underutilization of non-pharmacologic techniques occurs.

- Children may not report pain.

Pain Assessment in Children

The Faces Pain Scale is a valid instrument used in children. The scale uses several facial expressions that go from smiling to crying and several in between (see *Figure 11-1*). The child is to choose the face that most closely denotes the level of pain being experienced by the patient. Another instrument is the pain thermometer wherein the child factors pain on a vertical continuum from least to most pain.

Faces Pain Scale

The Faces Pain Scale is the most studied tool and has been found to be valid and reliable. Studies continue in order to perfect assessment techniques. One study evaluated the use of a faces pain scale for children and found that there are currently 20 different faces scales that are being used for children. The researcher postulated that using a happy

face was inappropriate, as hospitalized children are not happy. Therefore, hospitalized children find it difficult to relate to a smiling face when trying to describe what they are feeling. To test her hypothesis, the researcher created two scales for use in a study of 100 healthy children from 5 to 12 years of age. One scale had faces that ranged from a smile to a frown, and the other scale had faces that ranged from a neutral expression to a frown.

Results of the study were compelling in that when the scale with a smiling face was used, the children rated the presence of pain *where there should not have been pain.* Even when using the scale with a neutral face, children had a tendency to rate pain where there should not have been pain. The researcher found that the age of the child was an important variable; the children of 5 and 6 years of age all had fairly high pain rating, regardless of the scale used. However, the 7, 8 and 9 to 12-year-old children rated significantly more pain when using the smiling face scale compared to the scales with neutral faces. The researcher acknowledged some limitations in the study, but the results were very provocative, as the majority of the faces scales do use smiling faces for "No Pain." This study illustrated the need to be sensitive to the developmental levels and differences in children when assessing pain (Purdue Pharma, 2001e).

Babies are at risk for the under-treatment of their pain. This may be due in part to misconceptions regarding their ability to feel pain. They are unable to describe pain, so pain assessment is difficult. As babies develop, their behaviors change dramatically. The changes in the neurological system are toward specificity and organization. Learning begins at birth and is to some degree affected by the environment. Nurses must rely on non-verbal pain indictors and then quantify the indicators to rate the pain, using the rating to evaluate the effectiveness of pain management. Instruments have been developed to evaluate and measure pain in this special population.

The Premature Infant Pain Profile (PIPP) uses specific indices to assess pain. Indices include behavioral state, heart rate, oxygen saturation, brow bulge, eye squeeze, and nasolabial furrow (Stoddard et al., 2002).

Behavioral responses of infants to painful stimuli were evaluated by Johnston, Stevens, Craig and Grunau in 1993. Infants ranged developmentally from premature to full-term to two and four-months-old. The researchers were evaluating developmentally sensitive pain expressions to a variety of procedures.

Study Design

In all, 80 infants were assigned to four groups of 20 infants per group. The sub samples were as follows:

- Premature infants between 32 and 34 weeks gestational age undergoing heel stick procedure;

- Full-term infants receiving vitamin K injections;

- 2-month-old infants receiving DPT subcutaneous injections; and

- 4-month-old receiving DPT subcutaneous injections.

Audio and video recordings were made for 15 seconds from stimulus. Cry analysis was conducted on full expiratory cry with time and frequency measures. Facial action was coded using the **Neonatal Facial Action Coding System (NFACS).**

Study Results

Premature infants were different from the older infants in that they had the ability to communicate through facial actions, but the facial actions were not well developed. The premature infants had higher pitched cries and more horizontal mouth stretch than the older infants. The higher pitched cries were more arousing to the listener, implying distress.

The full-term infants were different from the rest and better equipped to communicate distress to caregivers through facial expression. The full-term infants demonstrated more taut tongue. The two and four-month-old infants were similar to one another with no significant pain-related developmental differences.

When selecting an instrument, it is important to use one that is valid, reliable, developmentally appropriate and practical. The same tool should be used consistently with interpretations standardized.

Procedure-Related Pain

Nothing seems to terrify a child more that the prospect of an injection. Pediatric patients from a local hospital, with ages in the early school-age to adolescent range, were asked to draw their pain. A child life specialist participated in the exercise. Of the 20 pediatric patients that participated in the exercise, all but one included a hypoderrmic needle in the drawing. In many, the needle was not the focal point, but it was present.

Children may endure severe post-operative pain better than undergoing an injection. It has been suggested that procedural pain can have a tremendous and long-lasting impact on children. Research has demonstrated that children who have undergone repeated noxious medical procedures become adults who avoid dental and medical care.

There are several basic nursing interventions that can reduce the amount and degree of emotional and physical distress associated with procedural pain:

- Pre-procedural education of the child and parent.

- Procedural pain can be controlled for by having procedures performed by technicians who are proficient and adept.

- Have procedures performed in a calm environment and not in the child's room.

- Schedule procedures for times when parents can be present.

- Advocate for the effective use of analgesics to ensure compassionate management of pain.

- Use a multimodal approach such as developmentally appropriate cognitive-behavioral techniques (such as distraction), local anesthetics, TENS units or heat.

- Use systemic analgesics/anxiolytics for significantly painful procedures.

Selected Interventions

Pharmacologic and non-pharmacologic interventions are as appropriate for use in children as they are in adults. Novel techniques in the management of pain have been reported in the literature. The use of local and topical anesthetics prior to the performance of painful procedures have been reported in the literature for over a decade; yet they continue to be underutilized, with children being circumcised with restraint and without anesthesia (Ling & Anderson, 2002). Topical anesthetics like EMLA cream can be utilized to diminish needle pain.

TENS Unit

A large placebo-controlled, double blind study was employed to investigate the effect of TENS units in children undergoing venipuncture (Lander & Fowler-Kerry, 1993). Of the 846 children screened for the study, the sample size consisted of 514 children, blocked into six, two year age groups (ages = 5–17 years). Three groups were: TENS, TENS placebo, and control. Baseline values of pain and anxiety were obtained. Following venipuncture, pain intensity was measured with a vertical visual analogue scale, and pain affect was quantified using the Faces Pain Scale. Pain intensity and affect were lowest for the TENS group and highest for the control group. Pain scores were higher in the lower age groups and lowest in the higher age groups. The study demonstrated the utility of TENS units as adjuncts in the management of procedure-related pain in children across developmental levels.

Neonates

A recent study evaluated the use of dextrose solutions with a pacifier in newborns undergoing painful procedures. The researchers found that the use of a 12.5% oral solution of dextrose followed by a pacifier, prior to a heel stick resulted in lower pain scores and shorter crying times in 138 healthy newborn infants (Akman, Ozek, Bilgen, Ozdogan & Cebeci, 2002).

Children and Adolescents

Biofeedback and relaxation therapy has been very effective in pediatric and adolescent patients. There are pediatric and adolescent biofeedback programs available. There are techniques that are specific to certain age groups as younger children cannot factor on a horizontal continuum and may not be mature enough to master certain cognitive techniques. The developmental levels of the child should be taken into consideration when choosing techniques. Developmentally appropriate biofeed-back and psychological interventions are listed in *Table 11-2*.

Pain-Related Research

More than 50% of children with cancer experience cancer-related pain of some type (Leahy & Sigler-Price, 1994). Children are still restrained and not anesthetized prior to circumcision (Ling & Anderson, 2002). Assessments of pain and distress ratings of nurses, parents and children demonstrated that each group rated pain based on their own perspectives: Objective factors did not play a role in the nurses and parents' ratings of distress and pain. The children's ratings were related to their chronological age (Mann, Jacobsen & Redd, 1992).

A population based, cross sectional study was conducted to evaluate the prevalence of low back pain in 1,441 schoolchildren (Watson et al., 2002). The children were 11–14 years of age. The children were surveyed with a questionnaire, and for validation, parents were also surveyed. The researchers found the prevalence of low back pain in one month to be 24%. The incidence was higher in girls and increased with age. Of those with pain, 94% reported disability, with the most common disability related to carrying school bags. Despite this high rate of reported disability, few sought medical attention.

Nursing Guidelines

Developmental Approach

The management of pain in the pediatric population should be approached through a developmental paradigm. Piaget's developmental model is an example of one wherein the developmental levels can be correlated with behavioral indicators of pain and the rational approach by the nurse to ameliorate the pain.

Family Role

The family should be included in the treatment plan. It is important to note, however, that the par-

TABLE 11-2
Developmentally Appropriate Biofeedback and Psychological Interventions

AGE	INTERVENTIONS
0–2	distraction
2–4	deep breathing, distraction
4–6	deep breathing, distraction
6–11	deep breathing, distraction, imagery/hypnosis, PMR
11–adolescence	deep breathing, distraction, imagery/hypnosis, PMR

Source: Stoddard, F., Sheridan, R., Saxe, G., King, B.S., King, B.H., Chedekel, D. et al. (2002). Treatment of pain in acutely burned children. *Journal of Burn Care and Rehabilitation, 23*(2), 135–156.

ents' perception of the pain is not always accurate and can impact that of the child. Parents may also underestimate their children's pain as demonstrated by a study of 110 children aged between 7 and 12 years (Purdue Pharma, 2001e).

In this study, the children and their parents rated the children's postoperative pain. The study was conducted over a period of three days using a seven point faces pain scale. Parents underestimated the pain on a significant level. These findings were not only revealing but should impact the degree of the role a parent should play in their child's pain management.

In a situation where the child has a chronic pain problem, the management of the child's pain should be undertaken using developmental and family systems paradigms. Family education should not be limited to a task-orientation but should include the principles underlying pain management practices.

General Treatment Principles

- Despite the age of the child, pain can be assessed.

FIGURE 11-2
Drawing of Pediatric Pain

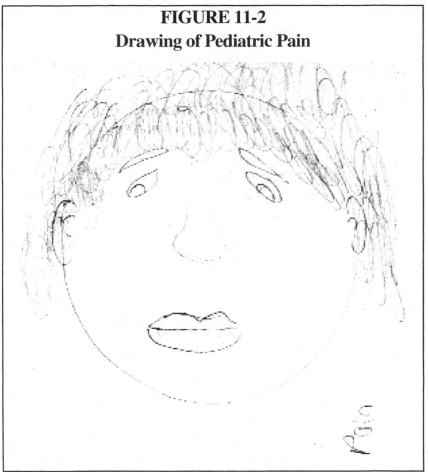

- Children have fully developed nervous systems with respect to pain, its transmission and modulation.

- Developmentally appropriate tools should be used to assess pain and treatment efficacy.

- The majority of analgesics used to manage pain in adults can be used in the pediatric population.

- Use a family systems paradigm to manage chronic pediatric pain.

An adolescent with pain from chronic disease will summarize this section. The patient drew her pain several years ago when involved in a project evaluating how children drew their pain. *Figure 11-2* is her personal pain perspective.

PAIN IN PATIENTS WITH AIDS AND HIV

Patients with Acquired Immune Deficiency Syndrome and Human Immunovirus are at risk for pain from a variety of causes related to their disease. Many types of pain are present, with peripheral neuropathy the most prevalent.

Incidence and Prevalence of Pain

A national sample of 420 patients with AIDS and HIV was surveyed with respect to symptoms experienced with the disease. Within this survey, 11.6% of the patients reported peripheral neuropathy (Holzemer, 2002). It is estimated that 20–30% of patients infected with HIV develop a sensory neuropathy and that the neuropathy is painful in half of these patients (Baumgartner et al., 2002). A study of 95 AIDS patients in Denmark cited an overall incidence of pain at 88%. Constant pain affecting ADLs was described as moderate to severe in 69% of the sample. Patients reported that their physicians did not take their pain seriously (Frich & Borgbjerg, 2000).

Another study that looked at pain in 438 ambulatory AIDS patients found that more than 60% had "frequent or persistent pain" and that those who reported pain had between two to three distinct pains (Brietbart et al., 1996).

As alarming as these data are, further research documented that pain is dramatically undertreated in patients with AIDS, with opioids rarely prescribed.

Researchers from Memorial Sloan Kettering Hospital published a study in which 366 ambulatory patients with AIDS were surveyed. The study disclosed that 226 of those who responded experienced persistent or frequent pain over a two-week period. Inadequate analgesic therapy was documented in 85% of these patients. Of the 110 patients with severe pain, only 8% had been given morphine and only 10% were given an adjuvant analgesic medication.

As noted, pain states associated with AIDS and HIV are not limited to peripheral neuropathy; although it is the most commonly reported chronic painful condition. Of note is the fact that peripheral neuropathy has been documented in the absence of AIDS in persons with HIV. Abdominal pain, headaches, muscle and joint pain, chest pain and other types of pain have been reported by AIDS and HIV patients. Pain is persistent, sometimes severe and universally under-treated.

Barriers to Pain Management

Both patient and clinician-related variables were documented.

Patient related barriers identified in 199 ambulatory AIDS patients were:

- Concern with side effects of medications;
- Fear of addiction; and
- Physical discomfort related to injections.

Clinician-related barriers identified in 492 AIDS care providers include:

- Lack of knowledge about pain management;
- Inadequate access to pain management experts; and
- Concerns about substance abuse and addiction (Ellison, Finley & Paice, 2002).

General Treatment Principles

1. Utilize the WHO analgesic ladder.
2. Use opioids for moderate to severe pain. (Long acting are preferred.)
3. Constipation common to other groups with use of opioids does not commonly affect patients with AIDS (likely due to diarrhea that accompanies disease).

4. Practitioners should be aware that pharmacokinetics of drugs may be altered by malabsorption and other conditions related to AIDS.

5. The use of methadone is contraindicated with certain antiviral protocols.

6. A multidisciplinary approach to the pain is warranted.

7. Health professionals should explore issues such as guilt, depression and fear (Ellison, Finley & Paice, 2002).

SUMMARY

Pain in burn injuries has multiple mechanisms and causes which combine to pose challenges peculiar to this diagnostic group. Pain in the elderly may be under-treated due to misconceptions and poor communication. Pain in children is often ignored. Young children cannot communicate pain due to developmental constraints and a lack of history with pain. Patients with pain from AIDS and HIV are under-treated and at risk for pain from a variety of causes. Nurses can make a difference in all of these groups by knowing and sharing facts, recognizing risk factors for undertreatment and using combinations of opioids, non-opioids, adjuvant agents and non-pharmacologic interventions. Nurses should be cognizant of their own biases and factors that might impact their pain management effectiveness.

EXAM QUESTIONS

CHAPTER 11
Questions 67–72

67. Which of the following statements regarding burn pain is accurate?

    a. Patients may have pain from the injury and treatment.

    b. Pain is limited to treatment as the cause.

    c. Pain is related to the burn injury alone.

    d. Full-thickness burns are not painful.

68. Hyperalgesia

    a. does not contribute to pain from burns.

    b. has three stages in burns.

    c. has four stages in burns.

    d. has two stages in burns.

69. Which statement is true with respect to the use of morphine in the elderly?

    a. it should never be used

    b. more consideration should be given to frequency of doses

    c. more consideration should be given to the amount of doses

    d. doses and frequency are equally important

70. Which statement is true of the cry of premature infants as compared to that of older infants?

    a. Premature infants have a lower pitched cry and less horizontal mouth stretch.

    b. Premature infants have a higher pitched cry and more horizontal mouth stretch.

    c. Premature infants have a higher pitched cry and no difference in horizontal mouth stretch.

    d. Premature infants have a lower pitched cry and more horizontal mouth stretch.

71. When assisting with a painful procedure on a child, the nurse should

    a. advise the parents not to be present.

    b. set up for the procedure in the patient's room.

    c. plan to use distraction techniques.

    d. tell the parents the procedure is brief, so no analgesia is needed.

72. Your patient with HIV tells you that he has been diagnosed with peripheral neuropathy. Based on what you know of this disease with HIV/AIDS, your assessment is that

    a. pain control is indicated.

    b. neuropathy does not manifest until AIDS is present.

    c. the patient is drug seeking.

    d. neuropathy with HIV/AIDS is motor and not sensory.

CHAPTER 12

PATIENTS WITH PAIN FROM CANCER

CHAPTER OBJECTIVE

Upon completion of this chapter, the reader will be able to recall the scope of pain from cancer, pain syndromes resulting from cancer and nursing interventions directed at care of the patient with cancer pain.

LEARNING OBJECTIVES

After studying this chapter, the learner will be able to

1. cite three cancer pain syndromes caused by the cancer itself.

2. list two painful syndromes caused by cancer treatment.

3. indicate a painful sequelae of radiation therapy and a clas of medication used to treat it.

4. cite and intervention for breakthrough pain.

5. recall Foley's classification system for cancer pain.

THE SCOPE OF CANCER PAIN

If a member of the general public was asked which disease is associated with pain, invariably cancer pain would be cited, and they would be correct. In the year 2000 in the United States alone, 1.2 million individuals were diagnosed with cancer and 500,000 people died from cancer (Mantyh, 2002). The most common symptom in cancer is pain, with 30% of cancer patients experiencing pain at the time of diagnosis (Levy, 1996). Chronic pain is prevalent in 30% to 50% of patients undergoing active cancer therapy and in 70% to 90% of patients with advanced disease. (Portenoy & Lesage, 1999). Among cancer patients in pain, 40% to 50% rate their pain as moderate to severe, while 25% to 30% rate their pain as very severe (Bonica, 1990). Approximately 25% of patients in the United States with the diagnosis of cancer die in severe pain (Paice, 1991).

In the mid-1980s, the World Health Organization (WHO) published clinical guidelines for cancer pain relief. Field trials in several different countries documented the efficacy of the WHO guidelines.

Healthcare professionals can provide adequate pain relief in up to 90% of cancer patients using relatively simple drug therapy, yet this goal is far from being achieved. (WHO, 1996). Pain from malignancy remains a widespread problem despite the availability of the WHO guidelines and other high quality clinical guidelines for cancer pain relief, such as those issued by the American Pain Society and the Agency for Health Care Policy and Research, a division of the U.S. Department of Health and Human Services.

BARRIERS TO CANCER PAIN MANAGEMENT

If cancer pain can be managed but remains unmanaged, wherein lies the problem? The problem is inherent in the symptom of pain itself; pain is difficult to quantify. In previous chapters, the subjective nature of pain has been discussed along with the fact that variables exclusive of pain hinder its management. Prior to 1980, less than 15% of the data in textbooks dedicated to oncology covered pain (Paice, 1991). Knowledge is a critical but prevalent healthcare barrier to effective pain management.

Healthcare Barriers

Despite the prevalence of cancer pain, the trend of under-treatment remains pervasive. A recent survey of members of the Eastern Cooperative Oncology Group (ECOG) assessed pain in 1308 outpatients with metastatic cancer. This study documented physician barriers to adequate pain management (Von Roenn et al., 1993).

- Only 51% of the physicians stated that pain control in their own practices was good or very good.

- Approximately 31% of the physicians indicated that they would wait until the patient's estimated survival was six months or less before beginning maximal analgesic treatment.

- 76% of the physicians pointed to inadequate pain assessment as the most important barrier to effective pain management.

- Many physicians also cited concerns about adverse effects of and tolerance to analgesics as limiting factors in providing adequate pain relief.

Unfortunately, additional factors, over which patients have no control, also place them at high risk for inadequate management of their pain. As demonstrated by the following studies, these factors include ethnicity, gender, age and cognitive status.

The ECOG Minority Outpatient Pain Study was a prospective study which was two-fold in its aim: It evaluated the severity of cancer-related pain and the adequacy of prescribed analgesics. The sample consisted of 281 minority outpatients with recurrent or metastatic cancer. Of the first group, there were 168 respondents and of the latter group, there were 180 respondents.

The results of this study were at the very least alarming, demonstrating that patients receiving care at university centers that treat minorities were more likely to receive less than adequate pain relief (77%) than patients treated at non-minority centers (52%). The study also demonstrated a trend toward under-medication in women, with 57% of the men under-treated versus 71% of the women (Cleeland et al., 1997).

Studies have shown that elderly patients are at risk for inadequate pain management. A retrospective, cross-sectional study of 13,625 cancer patients aged 65 years or older, revealed that 4,003 patients reported daily pain. Of the patients aged 85 years or more, 24% had daily pain; of those patients aged 75 to 84 years, 29% had daily pain; and 38% of patients aged 65 to 74 years reported daily pain. Of the patients with daily pain, only 16% received a non-opioid medication, with or without a mild opioid; 32% received a non-opioid medication, with or without a mild opioid; and only 26% received a strong opioid. 25.5% of the patients did not receive any analgesics. The study demonstrated that patients at the highest risk for poor pain management included those over 85 years of age, minorities and those with low cognitive performance (Bernabei et al., 1998).

Patient Barriers to Effective Pain Management

Pain management may be divided into two categories: Reporting pain and taking medications for the pain.

Patients may be reluctant to report cancer pain because

- they are concerned with physicians being distracted from the underlying disease.

- fear that pain means the disease is progressing or worsening.

- concerned with not wanting to be perceived as troublesome; desire to be a "Good Patient."

Patients may worry about taking pain medications because of

- fear of addiction or being perceived as an addict.

- worries about the side effects of the medications.

- concern about becoming tolerant to pain medications (AHCPR, 1994).

Interestingly enough, this data is supported by The Mayday Fund Survey which documented public attitudes about pain and analgesics. Of the 1,000 respondents, 71% reported avoidance in calling the doctor when in pain. With respect to analgesic use, 46% stated that they avoided taking analgesics until the pain "gets bad," and 35% avoided the use of analgesics until the pain became unbearable (Bostrum, 1996).

Mechanisms of Cancer Pain

The pathophysiology of pain from cancer is complex. Animal models have provided valuable data related to the mechanisms that generate and maintain cancer pain. For instance, two years ago a mouse model of bone cancer pain was introduced and mirrored many of the changes noted in patients in pain from bone cancer. Data suggested that different types of cancer pain may be unique, persistent pain states that change with the progression of the disease (Mantyh, 2002). In other words, cancer pain cannot be reduced to a type but is dynamic and should be addressed as such. Basically, there are three classes of cancer pain: Somatic, visceral and deafferentation. Somatic and visceral pain result from tumor infiltration of tissues and the subsequent activation of nociceptors. Secondary inflammation results with the release of pain producing or algogenic chemicals which in turn sensitize the nociceptors. These events may be localized (somatic/visceral) or referred to remote sites (visceral). Injury to the nervous sytsem by tumor infiltration and/or cancer therapy results in deafferentation pain, which may persist even after the cause has been removed. Disruption of the sympathetic nervous system resulting in sympathetically maintained pain may complicate the somatic, visceral and deafferentation pain. Sympathetically-mediated pain presents with hyperpathia, allodynia and vasomotor changes (Payne, 1989).

For the purpose of this course, the complex neurobiology of cancer pain will be addressed by its characteristics, which are important for the nurse to appreciate if cancer pain is to be appropriately assessed and treated.

TYPES/CAUSES OF PAIN WITH CANCER

As noted, the patient with cancer may experience several types of pain at once. Predominantly, pain is caused by the cancer itself (WHO, 1994). Pain can be classified as nociceptive (which encompasses the somatic and visceral components), neuropathic or neuralgic (Portenoy & Lesage, 1999).

- **Nociceptive pain** is caused by noxious stimulation of peripheral sensory nerve fibers. Radiation and chemotherapy can cause somatic pain and chronic visceral pain. Nociceptive pain resulting from cancer are: Neoplastic invasions of bones, joints, muscles, viscera or connective tissue (Portenoy & Lesage, 1999). This type of pain is generally constant and aching. Nociceptive pain may also result from a lack of or decrease in mobility. This type of pain is responsive to opioids and NSAIDs.

- **Neuropathic pain** is caused by abnormal processing of sensory information either in the peripheral or central nervous system (Portenoy, 1998). Examples of neuropathic pain caused directly by cancer include tumor infiltration of nervous tissue, nerve compression, and peripheral nerve damage. (Portenoy & Lesage, 1999). Neuropathic pain may also result from chemotherapy with heavy metal agents. Neuropathic pain is poorly responsive to opioids in "standard dosages." This type of pain is responsive to the AEDs and antidepressants.

- **Neuralgic pain** is caused by damage to specific nerves and follows nerve pathways or dermatomes. It is sharp, lancinating and electric shock-like. Neuralgic pain may be caused by compression of a nerve by a tumor. Chronic neuropathic or neuralgic pain can result from peripheral nerve damage due to radiation-induced fibrosis (Portenoy & Lesage, 1999). As in neuropathic pain, this type of pain is poorly responsive to opioids in "standard dosages." This type of pain is also responsive to the AEDs and antidepressants.

Pain may be related to cancer treatment, such as postoperative pain or neuromas at the site of the surgical scar (WHO, 1994). Finally, pain may be caused by concurrent or pre-existing conditions not related to the cancer, such as arthritis or spondylosis (WHO, 1994) or from decreased mobility, resulting in muscle spasms or decubiti.

ETIOLOGY OF CANCER PAIN

While addressing the types and characteristics of pain is important, it is also imperative to understand the origin of the pain from cancer. As discussed, cancer pain is related to the disease itself and to the treatment of the disease. While there may be other factors that come into play such as the lack of mobility and the problems that result from this, the majority of pain from cancer is related to the disease and its treatment. There are several cancer pain syndromes outlined by Portenoy (1998) that remain relevant to the clinician.

CHARACTERISTICS OF PAIN IN CANCER PAIN SYNDROMES

Pain from cancer may be separated into two basic causative mechanisms: Pain as a result of the cancer itself and pain as a result of the cancer treatment (see *Table 12-1*). The patient in pain from cancer as the primary source of pain may experience additional pain from the treatment of the neoplasm. Pain as a result of treatment may be acute or chronic or both.

Pain Due to Tumor Involvement

Vertebral Body

Neoplastic invasion of the vertebral bodies causes pain that precedes compression of adjacent structures. Therefore, the early recognition of pain from invasion of the vertebrae may prevent the development of serious to catastrophic neurologic deficits.

Severe pain in the occiput and nuchal region is secondary to subluxation of the atlas on the axis with Atlantoaxial Syndrome. This pain worsens with neck movement, particularly flexion. As its name infers, invasion of the C7–T1 vertebrae may

TABLE 12-1
Cancer Pain Syndromes

Pain related to direct tumor involvement:
- Secondary to invasion of bone.
- Base of skull: Usually presents with headache and a variety of neurological findings.
  — Orbital Syndrome
  — Parastellar Syndrome
  — Sphenoid Sinus Syndrome
  — Clivus Syndrome
  — Jugular Foramen Syndrome
  — Occipital Condyle Syndrome
- Vertebral Body: Usually presents with constant, dull aching pain; may be relieved by standing; exacerbated by local pressure, recimbancy.
- Generalized bone pain: Variable presentation; usually worse at night and dull, aching deep intense characteristics; pain can be referred; associated muscle spasm and stabbing pain when there is nerve involvement.
  — Multiple metastases
  — Intramedullary neoplasm
- Due to invasion of nerves: Constant, burning dysesthetic pain; lancinating, shock-like; diffuse hyperesthesia; and localized paresthesia.
  — Peripheral Nerve Syndromes
    Paraspinal mass
    Chest wall mass
    Retroperitoneal mass
- Due to invasion of viscera.
- Due to invasion of blood vessels.
- Due to invasion of mucous membranes.

Pain due to cancer therapy:
- Post-operative Pain Syndromes: Post-incision pain; usually with the following procedures there will be aching, shooting, tingling in the distribution of the perpipheral nerves.
- Post-Chemotherapy Pain Syndromes: Seen most commonly with vincristine, cisplatin, and vinblastine; may have jaw pain, claudication and/or dysesthetic pain in the hands/feet.
  — Painful polyneuropathy
  — Aseptic necrosis of the bone
  — Steroid pseudoheumatism
- Post-radiation Pain Syndromes
  — Radiation fibrosis of relaxed plexi
  — Radiation Myelopathy
  — Mucositis
  — Radiation necrosis of the bone

Adapted from: Portenoy, R. (1989). Epidemology & syndromes of cancer pain. *Cancer, 63*(11), 2298–2307.

result in referred pain to the scapular region, in *C7–T1 Syndrome*. Both the cervical and thoracic regions should be evaluated with radiographs in patients with interscapular pain, as these lesions are missed when one or the other level is evaluated. In *L1 Syndrome*, lesions on the relevant vertebrae may refer pain to the ipsilateral ileac crest or sacroiliac joint. When the areas to which the pain is referred are imaged, the lesion is missed; therefore, the appropriate levels of the spine should be evaluated. Destruction of the sacrum, such as is seen with Sacral Syndrome, may refer severe focal radiating pain to the buttocks, perineum or posterior thighs. Pain is lessened with standing or walking and worsened with sitting or reclining. The earliest associated neurological deficits associated with this syndrome are bowel and bladder dysfunction. Generalized bone pain, which is poorly localized, is caused by multiple bony metastases.

Peripheral Nerve Syndromes

These syndromes are primarily associated with painful mononeruopathies. Painful mononeuropathies are seen with paraspinal masses, with spinal nerve involvement, with chest wall or rib lesions, with intercostal nerve involvement and with retroperitoneal masses. Paraspinal masses mimic radiculopathy. The pain is aching and dysesthetic in quality and focal or referred along the distal route of the nerve location. Chest wall or rib lesions also produce unilateral pains that are dysesthetic and aching, with distribution superficial to the lesion or referred along the distal course of the nerve. Pain from retroperitoneal masses may be localized in the back, abdomen, flank, buttocks or legs, or the pain may be widely distributed (Portenoy, 1998).

Plexopathies

Plexopathies are anatomically delineated as cervical, brachial and lumbar. Cervical plexopathies are typically aching in the distribution of the plexus and are preauricular, postauricular or neck pain. These may result from local invasion of neoplasms in the head or neck or from pressure of enlarged lymph nodes.

Brachial plexopathies, also call Pancoast's or Superior Sulcus Syndrome, are most commonly seen with carcinoma of the lung and breast as well as with lymphoma. Pain is seen in up to 85% of patients with brachial plexus invasion, which precedes other neurological findings (Patt & Burton, 1999).

The most frequently affected area is the lower cord of the plexus at C8–T1. This pain is described as aching and diffuse in the shoulder girdle with radiation to the elbow and medial aspect of the hand. Weakness, numbness, progressive atrophy and dysesthesias are common. Invasion of the upper plexus at C5–C6 is less common and usually presents as pain in the shoulder girdle and upper arm, radiating to the index finger and thumb.

Radiation fibrosis is one of the causes of brachial plexus injury, but the radiation-induced injury typically involves C5–C7, with pain a less prominent finding. There is aching in the shoulder with tightness and heaviness in the upper arm accompanied by lymphadema and absent Horner's Sign (Patt & Burton, 1999).

Tumors of the rectum, cervix, and breast, as well as sarcoma are most commonly associated with consequent lumbosacral plexopathy. This is due to soft-tissue invasion of the tumor, lymphadenopathy or compression from bony tumors. In one study, pain was the presenting symptom in 70% of the patients with lumbosacral plexopathy (Patt & Burton, 1999). The pain may be local, referred or radicular and is aching or pressure-like. Depending on the level, pain may be referred to the abdomen, buttocks, low back or a lower extremity (Patt & Burton, 1999). Dysesthesias may be present (Portenoy, 1998).

TABLE 12-2
Postsurgical Pain Syndromes

Procedure	Nerves Involved	Pain Location
Mastectomy	Intercostobrachial	Posterior part of the arm, anterior chest, axilla; phantom breast
Thoracotomy	Intercostobrachial	Distribution of the nerve
Amputation	Site specific	At incision/area removed (phantom pain)
Radical Neck Dissection	Site specific	Neck, throat

Leptomeningeal Metastases

Pain has been reported in approximately 40% of patients with metastases to the meninges. The most common complaint is unrelenting headache. Other pains have included back pain and segmental pains.

Pancreatic Cancer Pain

This pain is characterized as relentless, boring, midepigastric radiating through and through to the mid-back. Pain is worsened by recumbancy and lessened by the use of the fetal position.

PAIN DUE TO CANCER TREATMENT

Chemotherapy

*O*ral mucositis is most common with the use of methotrexate, doxorubicin, daunorubicin, bleomycin, etoposide, fluorouracil (5F-U) and dactinomycin. It appears approximately 10 days after chemotherapy is initiated. When chemotherapy is used in combination with radiation therapy, the mucocitis can be severe.

Painful polyneuropathy, with sensory and motor involvement, is seen with exposure to vincristine. Cisplatin is more commonly associated with sensory involvement. When dosages are reduced early on, there is a resolution of symptoms. This is why it is important to diagnose polyneuropathy early on in the chemotherapy treatment.

Radiation Therapy

A variety of painful conditions are associated with radiation therapy including the development of new secondary neurogenic tumors. Some painful conditions consequential to radiation therapy include but are not limited to: Mucocitis, myelopathy (less common), plexopathy and soft-tissue fibrosis (Patt & Burton, 1999; Portenoy, 1989).

Postsurgical Pain Syndromes

Several types of surgeries may place the patient at higher risk for sustained pain (see *Table 12-2*). These are mastectomy, thoracotomy, radical neck dissection and amputation (Patt & Burton, 1999). The pain and altered sensation are often due to nerve entrapment, and despite treatment, the pain often is not ameliorated. The characteristics of the pain are burning, sharp and shooting. The onset of the pain is generally 4–6 weeks after the procedure and begins as sharp, shooting pain that dissolves into a burning hyperesthetic/dysesthetic pain. There is an area of sensory loss with associated sensations of tightness.

In a study of postmastectomy patients, the researchers found that postmastectomy pain was higher in patients who had received conservative surgery (33%) as opposed to a modified radical mastectomy (17%) (Tasmuth, vonSmitten & Kalso, 1996). In addition to pain at the surgical site, phantom breast pain was found to be present in 25% of the patients in the same study.

Assessment of Cancer Pain

When assessing pain, it is important for the nurse to remember that there are three dimensions that are to be evaluated: Sensory, evaluative and temporal. The sensory dimension looks at pain intensity. This is where the Pain Score comes into use. While valuable progress is being made in the assessment of pain with the use of the VAS and Faces Pain Scale, this is only one dimension and does give the whole picture.

The evaluative dimension looks at the overall magnitude of the pain: Is it mild, moderate or severe? This also assists in the assessment of the efficacy of interventions.

The temporal dimension addresses elements in terms of fear, suffering and related qualities. This typically involves the use of interview, multidimensional scales and ancillary support.

Pain and Suffering

An important distinction to be made is whether the patient is suffering as opposed to having pain. Pain and suffering may occur simultaneously. It is often difficult for the patient to distinguish between the two. Pain is anatomical, while suffering encompasses not only the physical being but the person as a whole. Suffering is not limited to the physical but encompasses the spiritual, emotional and psychological aspects of the person; the "intactness" of the person is threatened.

The nurse needs to make time for the patient and offer support by listening and assisting them in verbalizing fears and issues that may be affecting their psyche and/or soul.

Psychological State

Stress, anxiety and depression can worsen the intensity and frequency of pain. The nurse needs to evaluate the patient's psychological state by asking some questions in a non-interrogative manner. Is there an increase in anxiety and fear? Is the patient depressed? The patient should be asked what fears they have with respect to the pain and cancer itself.

Depression

The patient may be depressed for a variety of reasons. Reactive depression is usually situational. This type of depression is different from clinical depression, and the differentiation is best made by a qualified individual.

A social service referral or request of a consult with pastoral care does not usually require an order. An LCSW (Licensed Certified Social Worker) is trained to counsel patients and is best qualified to either treat depression or recommend that a psychologist be consulted.

Antidepressants may be used for pain and depression. The determination as whether to use antidepressants for depression is best undertaken by a person trained to make that recommendation.

Anxiety

Anxiety can intensify the perception of pain. Fear of death and the unknown is stressful for anybody but especially so for the person with cancer. The use of anxiolytics may help with the anxiety and stress, but before resorting to more drugs, it is best to attempt a non-pharmacological course of action. In the hospital setting, the nurse may be able to consult a biofeedback technician. Psychologists are trained in consultation, and they can also implement stress management techniques used by biofeedback technicians.

Fatigue and Sleeplessness

These two phenomena are associated with pain. Researchers have noted positive relationships between pain, fatigue and sleeplessness. This may be especially so in the hospitalized patient, where sleep is often disrupted by medical professionals making rounds and medication schedules.

It is important for the nurse to address the psychological state of the patient with respect to pain management. The nurse is in a key position to intercede for the patient in this respect.

Pain

Acute Versus Chronic

When assessing pain from cancer, the clinician must first differentiate between what is chronic and what is acute. Patients often have chronic and acute pain at the same time. When there is a plan in place for the chronic pain, another plan to treat the acute pain, which complements the existing chronic pain plan, must be developed. The patient may have chronic pain from the cancer and acute pain from the treatment. Opioids for the chronic pain will not usually cover the acute pain needs. The nurse must assist the patient in making this differentiation.

Constant or Intermittent

Is the pain continuous or is it intermittent? If the pain has been fairly well controlled and now the patient is experiencing breakthrough pain, the treatment plan must be revised and the source of the breakthrough pain needs to be identified. If the pain is constant, analgesics are to be given around-the-clock.

Location

Where is the pain located? It is important to not only try to pinpoint the location but also any pattern of radiation. For instance, when the patient reports that the pain "starts in the chest and goes to the back," a crucial question is "does the pain go through and through to the back, or does it go around the rib cage or chest to the back." This will aid not only in the differential diagnosis of the source of the pain, but it will also drive the treatment of the pain. With pain going through and through to the back, a visceral origin or adhesions are a consideration; with pain going around the chest, an intercostal nerve entrapment or irritation should be considered.

Intensity

Using a numerical scale such as the Verbal Analogue Scale assists in the determination of the intensity of the pain. It also aids in serving as a point of reference in evaluating the efficacy of a particular treatment intervention.

It must be kept in mind that one patient's "10" might be another patient's "6;" in other words, the pain is subjective, and the value is owned by the patient reporting it.

Characteristics

Characteristics of the pain must be noted; is it sharp, shock-like (neuralgic) or dull, aching (nociceptive) or is their a burning quality to the pain with pins and needles (neuropathic)? Are there pins and needles (parasthesias) present; are they painful (dysesthesias)? Is the pain a result of treatment, or is the pain from the cancer itself? Is this a new pain or a worsening of previous pain?

Once the physician has determined the etiology of the pain, a treatment plan is developed. If the pain is due to new cancer or metasteses of the current neoplasm, the cancer is targeted with chemotherapy, radiation and/or steroids.

Ameliorating/Intensifying Factors

Simple questions such as, "What makes the pain better?" and "What makes the pain worse?" will aid in the management of the pain. If factors like going to radiation therapy or going to physical therapy worsen the pain, analgesics given prior to mobilizing the patient may help alleviate or prevent the worsening of the pain. Sometimes simple interventions such as positioning the patient or massage can help lessen the pain and should be employed and documented whenever feasible.

Establish Goals

The goal of pain management is to make the patient as comfortable and as functional as possible. Managing the pain at the cost of participation in life is not the best treatment option. Quality of life comes from living life and being sedated with opioids does not necessarily translate into quality of life. When the pain is a result of the cancer itself, it is important to attack the cancer (cause of the pain) and treat the pain simultaneously. Family and significant others should be included in the development of the treatment plan. Whenever possible, the patient should be encouraged to relate pain management goals to function.

Goals should be realistic. Complete amelioration of the pain is not usually realistic. Some patients value the pain as it makes them feel as though they are alive (Sweeder, 2002), while others desire a complete alleviation of the pain. Whatever the patient's desire, the nurse should not judge and should work with each patient as a unique entity, not lumping them all in a "cancer pain" class.

TYPES OF PATIENTS WITH PAIN FROM CANCER

As with any other type of pain problem, cancer pain management starts with the development of a treatment plan unique to the particular patient for whom it is being developed. Combinations of pharmacologic agents, the use of nerve blocks and non-pharmacologic interventions are all utilized; they are sometimes used simultaneously to manage the pain of patients with neoplastic disease.

Because pain is a subjective phenomenon unique to the person experiencing it, a pre-morbid history is an essential consideration, if success is to be realized. Not all patients with pain from cancer are managed in an identical way. The person's psychosocial situation, previous pain history along with the type of cancer pain syndrome/problem faced should be considered in the development of the pain management treatment plan.

Foley (1985) described five types of patients with pain from cancer, and each category brings with it the imperative to develop a regimen that is realistic in its goals and interventions. The patient types are listed and then nursing interventions and considerations are discussed. A synopsis of this data is compiled in *Table 12-3*. This can be used for care planning or as a pocket "cheat sheet" in the clinical setting.

The types of patients with pain from cancer are:

- Patients with acute cancer-related pain.
  - Pain is associated with the diagnosis of the disease.
  - Pain is related to the treatment of the disease.
- Patients with chronic cancer-related pain.
  - Pain is associated with progression of the disease.
  - Pain is related to the treatment of the disease.
- Patients with pre-existing chronic pain and cancer-related pain.
- Patients with a history of drug abuse and cancer-related pain.
- Dying patients with cancer-related pain.

NURSING INTERVENTIONS AND TREATMENT CONSIDERATIONS

Patients with Acute Cancer-Related Pain

Pain is associated with the diagnosis of the disease.

Considerations: In this group of patients the pain is the harbinger of the disease. The pain has an intimate relationship to the diagnosis of the disease that has changed the patient's life.

TABLE 12-3
Types of Patients with Pain from Cancer

TYPES OF PATIENTS WITH CANCER PAIN	NURSING INTERVENTIONS	CONSIDERATIONS
Patients with acute cancer-related pain: a. Pain is associated with the diagnosis of the disease. b. Pain is related to the treatment of the disease.	a. Encourage verbalization of feelings related to the pain and the diagnosis; pastoral care consult may be an option. Support the patient's decisions for Rx; help to discriminate between treatment/cancer-related pain.	a. Pain is the harbinger of the disease with an intimate relationship to the diagnosis of the disease that has changed the patients life. b. 20–25% of cancer patient's pain is directly related to chemotherapy, radiation therapy and surgery (Sweeder, 2002).
Patients with chronic cancer-related pain: Pain is associated with progression of the disease. Pain is related to the treatment of the disease.	A Pain Management Team should be consulted. The patient may entertain cessation of the treatment & may require information to aid in this decision. Support the patient's decision.	The patient is likely to need escalations in their narcotics and adjuvant drug therapy should be implemented. The patient may have less hope and may be less tolerant of the additional pain & stress brought on by the pain from the cancer-treatment. The patient may become hopeless.
Patients with pre-existing chronic pain and cancer-related pain.	Obtain additional psychosocial data. Request that a pain specialist be consulted to handle the medication management of the patient's pain. Patient may need higher doses of opioids due to tolerance.	The patient may be opioid tolerant or may have a history of organ problems due to chronic NSAID use. The patient may already have a pain specialist and/or Psychologist with whom they have worked.
Patients with pre-existing history of substance abuse and cancer-related pain.	Urine drug screens should be performed at the outset and throughout treatment, when indicated. Do not discriminate against the patient or withhold medication.	Patient may need higher doses of opioids due to tolerance: Optimize non-opioid treatment. A Pain Specialist should be in charge of the Pain Management treatment plan and a multidisciplinary team approach.
Dying patients with cancer-related pain.	Death with dignity is a right and not a privilege. Facing the dying patient whose analgesic needs may prove lethal is an ethical quandary.	Patients may need large dosages of opioids but may have already lowered pulmonary functions.

Adapted from: Foley, K. (1985). Treatment of cancer pain. *New England Journal of Medicine, 313,* 84–95.

Nursing Interventions: Verbalization of feelings related to the pain and the diagnosis should be encouraged; a pastoral care consult may be an option.

Pain is related to the treatment of the disease.

Considerations: It has been suggested that 20–25% of a cancer patient's pain is directly related to chemotherapy, radiation therapy and surgery (Sweeder, 2002). Despite this, the patient may be willing to endure the pain and discomfort of the treatment as there is hope that the treatment will cure the disease.

Nursing Interventions: The patient should be encouraged and helped to discriminate between treatment-related pain and cancer-related pain. Prophylactic treatment of the pain related to the treatment may be an option; nonetheless, the pain should be treated as ordered.

Patients with Chronic Cancer-Related Pain

Pain is associated with progression of the disease.

Considerations: The patient is likely to need escalations in their narcotics, and adjuvant drug therapy should be implemented.

Nursing Interventions: The nurse needs to assess and re-assess because at this point the treatment plan should be dynamic and changing in order to stay ahead of the pain. Recommendations for adjuvants should be made, and the treatment plan needs to be more stratified as opposed to stepwise in its design.

A pain management team should be in place at this point in the patient's care. If the patient is going to be managed at home, the home care or hospice nurse should be included in team conferences while the patient is still hospitalized whenever appropriate. It is important to include the patient and caregiver/family as part of the team.

Pain is related to the treatment of the disease.

Considerations: The patient may have less hope and may be less tolerant of the additional pain and distress brought on by the pain from the cancer treatment.

Nursing Interventions: The patient may entertain cessation of the treatment and will need information to aid in this decision. The clinical nurse specialist may serve as a resource for additional education/clinical support. The patient should be supported in any decision that is made even if the nurse is philosophically opposed to the patient's decision.

Patients with Pre-Existing Chronic Pain and Cancer-Related Pain

Considerations: The patient may be opioid tolerant or may have a history of organ problems due to chronic NSAID use. The patient may already have a pain specialist and/or psychologist with whom they have worked. The patient may be well-versed in non-pharmacolgic pain management techniques.

Nursing interventions: Additional psychosocial data should be obtained. The nurse should request that a pain specialist be consulted to handle the medication management of the patient's pain. This patient will need a team approach to pain management and may need higher doses of opioids due to tolerance. The family/caregiver should be included on the team.

Patients with a History of Drug Abuse and Cancer-Related Pain

Considerations: Non-opioid treatment should be optimized. Anesthesia should be consulted to evaluate for candidacy for nerve blocks or an intrathecal pump. The nurse needs to realize that the patient may need higher than average opioids for pain management. Urine drug screens should be performed at the outset and throughout treatment. A pain specialist should be in charge of the pain management treatment plan, and a multidisciplinary team approach will required. If the patient has been in Narcotics Anonymous (NA), it is important to note that NA does not endorse opioids for chronic pain. Agents that are not easy to share and ones that have relatively little street value (i.e., fentanyl patch; methadone) should be used.

Nursing Interventions: The patient should be asked to sign a narcotic contract at the outset of treatment. The nurse must know the contract terms and beware of drug-seeking behaviors. Response to pharmacological agents needs to be evaluated. The nurse needs to note and report the results of the urine drug screen. Appropriate consults should be requested. The nurse must realize that this patient may require higher than average dosages of the opioid if they have been actively using. Documentation and communication are the nurse's most important tools.

Dying Patients with Cancer-Related Pain

Considerations: These patients may need large dosages of opioids but may already have lowered respiratory rates and pulmonary function. If the dosage of opioid is increased, respiratory compromise may worsen to the point of death.

Nursing Interventions: Death with dignity is a right and not a privilege. Facing the dying patient whose analgesic needs may cause them to die is an ethical quandary. Optimizing non-opioids and using adjuvant therapy may enhance the opioid treatment plan.

SUMMARY

Patients with pain from cancer may have acute and chronic pain concomitantly and may have several types of pain at once. The etiology of the pain should be determined prior to the development of the treatment plan. Certain cancer treatments place the patient at high risk for secondary pain, and certain cancer syndromes do the same. Patients with pain from cancer may have that pain compounded with additional pain from the cancer treatment.

It is imperative that the assessment of the patient with pain from cancer be comprehensive, and the nurse must consider the entire person in the development of the pain management plan. Patient goals should be assessed and incorporated into the treatment plan.

Ancillary services should be utilized with orders obtained and consults generated based on each patient's needs. Patients with pain from neoplastic disease and/or its treatment should not be simply lumped together as "cancer patients." The variability in the etiologies and types of pain in the presence of cancer has been clearly delineated, as have the types of patients with pain from cancer.

CHAPTER 12

Questions 73–80

73. Mrs. Z. underwent a radical neck dissection and radiation therapy. She has sharp, lancinating and electric shock-like pain. This type of pain is referred to as

    a. neuropathic.
    b. neuralgic.
    c. nociceptive.
    d. visceral.

74. The type of pain described in question #73 responds best to

    a. AEDs.
    b. antihistamines.
    c. NSAIDs.
    d. opioids.

75. Mrs. Z. reports that she also has a constant aching pain. This type of pain is referred to as

    a. nociceptive.
    b. neuralgic.
    c. neuropathic.
    d. visceral.

76. The type of pain described in question #75 responds best to

    a. AEDs.
    b. NSAIDs.
    c. TCAs.
    d. nerve blocks.

77. Mr. W. has a history of chronic pain from RSD and a diagnosis of colon cancer. Based on Foley's classification system, an important consideration in the formulation of Mr. W.'s treatment plan is that he

    a. may be drug seeking.
    b. has terminal disease.
    c. may have a personality disorder.
    d. may be opioid tolerant.

78. Based on Foley's classification, the consult that should be sought for this patient is

    a. pastoral care.
    b. a pain specialist.
    c. a nutritionist.
    d. a pharmacologist.

79. The percentage of patients with cancer who have pain from cancer treatment is

    a. 5–10%.
    b. 15–20%.
    c. 20–25%.
    d. 45–50%.

80. Suffering

    a. is purely physical.
    b. does not threaten the "entactness" of the person.
    c. encompasses the person as a whole.
    d. never occurs simultaneously with pain.

CHAPTER 13

CANCER PAIN MANAGEMENT

CHAPTER OBJECTIVE

Upon completion of this chapter, the reader will be able to recall a paradigm for the treatment of cancer pain as well as recognize pharmacologic and non-pharmacologic interventions for cancer pain management.

LEARNING OBJECTIVES

After studying this chapter, the learner will be able to

1. list three modes of opioid delivery for the treatment of cancer pain.

2. identify the cornerstone in the pharmacologic treatment of cancer pain.

3. identify two classes of adjuvant medications utilized in cancer pain management.

4. recall two basic elements of non-pharmacologic management of cancer-related pain.

5. define steady state analgesia.

6. differentiate between nocieptive and neuralgic pain.

MANAGING CANCER PAIN

The nurse has an important and pivotal role in the management of pain from cancer. Patient encounters may take place in a variety of settings, such as the inpatient room, an out-patient clinic or in the home. The role of the nurse is not limited to administering analgesics but includes the provision of non-pharmacologic intervention(s) as well. Assessment, application of the intervention(s), education and re-assessment are the elements of a dynamic plan of care for the patient in pain. In utilizing the art and science of the nursing profession, the nurse may develop and implement a plan of care that encompasses the entire continuum of the person and their environment. This continuum encompasses the physical, psychological, environmental and spiritual aspects of each individual.

In these applications, communication is an essential and integral key to the success of any treatment plan. The nurse must communicate the elements of the treatment plan and their rationale to the patient and all involved persons and also discuss outcomes or changes with the healthcare team. Additionally, the nurse must help the patient communicate effectively about their pain, including any changes in the characteristics/intensity, as these changes may indicate disease progression. The nurse must also assess the efficacy of various interventions and assist with the establishment of realistic comfort goals and expectations.

The nurse should dispel any related myth and misconceptions. For example, patients may not want to move onto higher potency analgesics such as morphine fearing that the use of the analgesic indicates worsening of the cancer or infers a "ter-

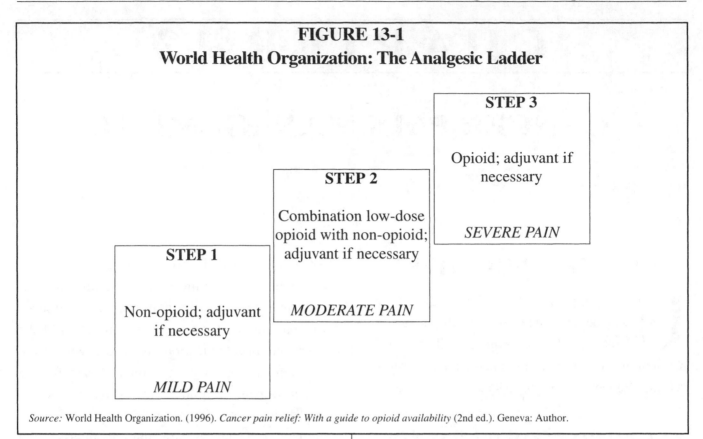

FIGURE 13-1
World Health Organization: The Analgesic Ladder

STEP 3

Opioid; adjuvant if necessary

SEVERE PAIN

STEP 2

Combination low-dose opioid with non-opioid; adjuvant if necessary

MODERATE PAIN

STEP 1

Non-opioid; adjuvant if necessary

MILD PAIN

Source: World Health Organization. (1996). *Cancer pain relief: With a guide to opioid availability* (2nd ed.). Geneva: Author.

minal" status. The patient may also confuse physical dependency or tolerance with addiction or may perceive that the use of adjuvants such as antidepressants means the pain is "in my head" or purely psychological.

An effective approach to managing cancer-related pain includes

- an understanding of the causes and mechanisms of cancer pain.

- a solid foundation in analgesic pharmacology.

- dispelling of myths/misconceptions.

- promotion and maintenance of open lines of communication.

- involvement of the patient and involved other(s) in the development and implementation of the pain management plan.

- a dynamic approach to the assessment and re-assessment of the pain.

- The setting of realistic pain management goals within a functional context.

Pain Management Team

The approach to the management of cancer-related pain should be interdisciplinary and multimodal. This is the same approach to the management of non-cancer-related chronic pain, but elements of the emphasis with the cancer patient will generally be different.

WHO ANALGESIC LADDER

The WHO recommended a "step-wise" approach to cancer pain which basically stated that one class of medication be initiated at the outset of pain treatment then, as the pain progressed or if it did not respond, another class of analgesic or adjuvant could be added (see *Figure 13-1*). This approach is being debated with a more stratified approach to the management of pain from cancer being considered. A stratified approach means that combinations of medications, appropriate to the characteristic/cause of pain, be utilized at the outset of treatment. It helps to understand the mechanisms of the pain so that the appropriate analgesics and adjuvants can be employed in combination with one another.

When developing the treatment plan, causes of the pain must first be established and treated. Studies have suggested that more than two-thirds of pain in cancer patients results from the neoplasm and close to 25% of pain is due to the treatment of the neoplasm (Portenoy & Lesage, 1999; Sweeder, 2002).

PHARMACOLOGICAL THERAPY

(Refer to chapters 5–8 for detailed data related to the medications discussed here.)

Analgesics

Introduction

Opioids will be the cornerstone of the pharmacological treatment plan for moderate to severe cancer pain and when possible, oral dosing should be maximized before going to parenteral routes (see *Table 13-2*). It bears repeating the importance of understanding the distinctions between addiction, dependence and tolerance when working with opioids. This knowledge should be shared with the patient and family, as well as with other members of the healthcare team.

Having said that opioids are the cornerstone, it is important to note that certain types of pain do not respond to opioids. A stratified approach to the management of pain is often most therapeutic. That is, combinations of medications that are selective for the types of pain that the patient experiences and that are administered concomitantly.

The use of adjuvants may also impact the amount of opioids used. Higher, sedating dosages of opioids, which can alter the patient's sensorium, thereby having a negative impact on their overall health status and quality of life, can be avoided.

Lower doses of opioids can be more effective with the concurrent use of adjuvants.

Non-Steroidal Anti-inflammatory Agents

For the management of mild pain the use of NSAIDs alone may be adequate for pain management, but they should be administered around-the-clock and not on a time-contingent (PRN) schedule. Unlike opioids, the NSAIDs have a dosing ceiling, above which toxicity will result without analgesic benefits.

For moderate to severe pain, NSAIDs are valuable adjuncts to opioids. Pain from inflammation and/or metastases respond to this class of medication. Of course it is important to balance analgesia with the potential for toxicity when using NSAIDs. They may not be beneficial in patients who are elderly or debilitated, who have a history of gastropathy or who have recently received anti-tumor therapy (Patt & Burton, 1999).

Ketorolac, comes in an oral and parenteral form (Toradol®). It has significant analgesic benefits, but patients must be selected carefully for the reasons listed above. It may be administered intramuscularly or intravenously and is indicated for short term use only.

Choline magnesium trisalicylate (Trilisate) has a low incidence of GI effects, has less of an impact on platelet aggregation and is better tolerated than most NSAIDs. As such, it may be better suited for patients with cancer pain.

Consideration of the use of agents from the COX-2 class of NSAIDs may be of some benefit as well. Celebrex™, Vioxx and Bextra® are agents in this class.

It bears stating that, despite the fact these agents have essentially the same analgesic effect and mechanism of action, individual responses by cancer patients is not always predicable. Therefore, a lack of response to one agent does not mean the same outcome with another agent. If the patient,

TABLE 13-1
Sustained-Release Opioids

AGENT	DOSAGES	CONSIDERATIONS
Duragesic (fentanyl)	25, 50, 75, 100 mcg patches Q72 hours	Patients should receive short acting opioids at the outset of therapy as analgesic blood levels will not be adequate for first 12–18 hours. Patch should be changed Q72 hours.
Methadone	5, 10 mg tablets; liquid variable Q6 hours	Not for use in elderly or patients with pulmonary compromise. May be crushed or broken. Least expensive of all sustained release agents.
MSContin (morphine)	15, 30, 60, 100 mg tablets Q8–12 hrs	Patients should be told not to break or crush tablets. If pain "breaks through" then short acting dosages should be given between scheduled dosages and all short acting doses converted to sustained-release every 24 hours until consistent analgesia is realized.
Oxycontin (oxycodone)	10, 20, 40, 80 mg	Should not be crushed or broken.

having had an adequate trial, does not respond to one drug another should be tried.

Opioids

Selecting the Agent

In contrast to the NSAIDs, opioids do not have an analgesic ceiling, so the correct dose of opioid is the dose that provides analgesia without serious or poorly tolerated side effects (see *Table 13-2*). When the pain is constant, the dosage should be given around-the-clock, not on a time-contingent schedule (PRN) and sustained-release preparations should be utilized (see *Table 13-1*). For chronic opioid therapy, agents compounded with acetaminophen should be avoided, as chronic acetaminophen use has been associated with increases in liver enzymes.

Around-the-clock dosing not only promotes steady-state analgesia with blood levels of the agent maintained; at least one study has documented a higher rate of patient adherence to the prescribed regimen when this type of dosing is prescribed. An Advanced Practice Extra in the *American Journal of Nursing* cited a study that looked at how well outpatients with cancer-related pain adhered to their prescribed analgesic regimen (Pain treatment in oncology patients is ineffective, 2002). Of the 65 oncology patients who were prescribed either around-the-clock, as needed or a combination of both types of delivery schedules, the highest rate of adherence to the regimen was found in the around-the-clock group (88.9%) versus the "as needed" group (24.7%). This is important, as it has been estimated that an average of one-third of patients fail to adhere to prescribed analgesic regimens (Pain treatment in oncology patients is ineffective, 2002).

Side Effects

Nausea and sedation occur in up to half of the patients early in the course of treatment or with dosage increases (Patt & Burton, 1999). Patients need to be informed that, with continued use, these symptoms should dissipate. The patient should be encouraged to continue use of the medication. Vertiginous nausea (nausea with ambulation) responds well to scopolamine. Anti-emetics may be prescribed in conjunction with the opioid. The use of an antihistamine in conjunction with the antiemetic may also prove useful for controlling the nausea. If the nausea persists, consideration of switching to an equi-analgesic dosage of another opioid should be made, as the patient will not necessarily have the same side effects with another opioid.

The patient should be reassured that as tolerance to the analgesic effects of the opioid develops, a concomitant tolerance to side effects will also be present. The only two effects mediated by opioids that do not disappear with time and dosing are miosis and constipation (Patt & Burton, 1999).

Constipation

"Constipation is the most common adverse effect of long-term opioid therapy" (Plaisance & Ellis, 2002), and the best management strategy for constipation is to control for it at the outset of treatment. Opioids cause constipation through their binding with opioid receptors in the gut, thereby inhibiting peristalsis. When feces' transit time in the gut is slowed, increases in water and sodium absorption in the gut result with the consequence being hard, dry stools. When feasible, patients on chronic opioid therapy should be instructed to increase their intake of fiber and fluid. A daily stool softener should be recommended as well.

Opioids to Avoid

Meperidine is contra-indicated for prolonged use due to the potential for accumulation of the active metabolite (end-product) normeperidine. Normeperidine is an active metabolite that causes CNS excitability and seizures after prolonged use. It also should not be used in patients with poor or compromised renal clearance for the same reason. Oral meperidine is a very weak opioid, with close to 40% of it lost through first-pass metabolism. For example, if a patient were to be converted from 75 mg of IM meperidine, desiring an equivalent oral dosage, 300 mg of the oral dosage would have to be administered for the patient to realize the same analgesic benefits, (APS Guidelines, 1999) and this is a toxic oral dose.

Agonist-antagonist or *partial agonist* agents should also be avoided, primarily because of their ceiling effect (a dosage above which analgesia is not appreciated). With the exception of buprinorphine, they may also precipitate withdrawal from pure agonists, so it is difficult to transition patients from these agents to pure agonists. Naloxone is not as predictably effective in reversing the effects of Buprinorphine.

Delivery Options

Oral

This is the desired route of administration for reasons of mobility, cost and ease of administration/titration. Oral dosages should be maximized before other routes are considered. As noted previously, sustained-release preparations are desirous, and cost should be considered when selecting an agent. While the cost of sustained-release medications is higher than for the immediate-release agents, cost savings may be reflected in decreased labor (Zlotnick, Prince & Frenchman, 1997). Not all sustained-release preparations are covered under Medicaid, and not all patients have prescription benefits.

Zlotnick et al. (1997) analyzed the use of controlled-release versus immediate-release opioids. The study, conducted in a long-term care facility, demonstrated that the use of controlled-release opioids reduced the need for medications and decreased the amount of nursing time spent dispensing medications. This resulted in nurses having more time to meet other patient needs. The researchers also determined that the quality of life of patients receiving sustained-release preparations may have improved.

Conversions

The use of an equianalgesic conversion chart (see *Table 7-3*, Chapter 7) should be utilized when transitioning from one opioid to another and when converting from one route to another. When initiating sustained-release therapy, the total doses of opioids taken in the previous 24 hours should be converted and given in appropriate divided doses of the sustained-release preparation. If breakthrough pain persists, short-acting opioids should be administered between scheduled doses of the sustained-release preparation. The previous 24 hours use of short acting agents should be added into the sustained-release doses until pain is managed with the sustained-release agents as the only opioids. For example, a patient was receiving 60 mg of MS Contin every eight hours but had pain between dosages. The physician ordered 30 mg of immediate-release morphine two to three times per day between the MS Contin dosages. The patient took three doses of the immediate-release agent in a 24 hour period. The physician added 30 mg to each of the MS Contin doses, so that 90 mg's were given every eight hours. The patient continued to have pain in the morning after radiation therapy treatment but had no further breakthrough pain. The physician added one 30 mg dose of the MS Contin to each morning dose. The patient is now on 120 mg of MS Contin in the morning and 90 mg of MS Contin BID.

Oral opioids are primarily available in tablet or liquid form. Fentanyl, which is a potent oipoid, has a short half-life, so it cannot be given in tablet or liquid form. It comes as a lollipop. The fentanyl lollipop is marketed as Actiq, with analgesic effects related to blood level and a 3–5 minute half-life. Actiq comes in six strengths: 200, 400, 600, 800, 1200, and 1600 mcg. Actiq is recommended for breakthrough pain and for cancer pain only. This delivery system is referred to as transmucosal.

Transdermal

There are instances when the patient is unable to take medications by mouth. Fentanyl comes in micrograms in an adhesive patch called Duragesic. The patch is to be changed every 72 hours. At the outset of therapy, short acting analgesics should be used for approximately 12–18 hours, until the

Duragesic is at peak levels. Once the patch is discontinued, analgesia will persist for 12 to 18 hours. The most important factor in the delivery of fetanyl via the patch is temperature. Patients should be warned against the application of heat over the area of the patch.

Rectal

The rectal route of administration is a short term option when the oral route is not an option. The rectal route is contraindicated in the presence of diarrhea, fistula or other rectal abnormality. Morphine and hydromorphone come in suppository form. A pharmacist who is licensed to compound can manufacture methadone suppositories, which have been shown to be efficacious (Patt & Burton, 1999).

Parenteral

Continuous subcutaneous infusions (CSCI):
When pain is poorly controlled despite large doses of oral opioids, CSCI may be used. These may be used in the hospital or at home. There are infusion pumps designed for this purpose which are portable, battery operated and available by lease. They feature alarm systems that make them safe.

When implementing CSCI, the previous 24 hour dose of all opioids are tabulated and divided by 24 for an hourly rate of infusion. When tabulating oral and parenteral dosages, conversion charts should be used. Volumes under 1–2 ml produce less tissue irritation, so appropriate concentrations should be utilized. The anterior chest or supra-clavicular fossa are the injection sites of choice for ambulation. The infusion site should be checked twice daily and changed weekly. Because absorption is rapid, steady-state analgesia levels should be attained within an hour. In addition to the medications previously noted to be avoided, methadone is irritating to tissues and should not be used. Titration should be made based on

TABLE 13-2
Relative Potency of Opioids for Cancer Pain Management

ACTIQ	200MCG	400MCG	600MCG	800MCG	1200MCG	1600MCG
FENTANYL IV	20 MCG	40MCG	60MCG	80MCG	120MCG	160MCG
MORPHINE IV	2MG	4MG	6MG	8MG	12MG	16MG
MORPHINE PO	6MG	12MG	18MG	24MG	36MG	48MG
OXYCODONE PO	6MG					
HYDROMORPHONE PO	1.5MG	3MG	4.5MG	6MG	36MG	12MG

MORPHINE PREPARATIONS

MSIR LIQUID	10MG/5ML
	20MG/5ML
MSIR LIQUID CONCENTRATE	20MG/ML
MSIR TABLET	15MG & 30MG
ROXANOL®	20MG/ML
ROXANOL T	20MG/ML Tinted/Flavored
ROXANOL 100	100MG/5ML

OXYCODONE PREPARATIONS

OXIR CAPSULE	5MG
OXYFAST ORAL SOL.	20MG/ML
*OXYCONTIN	10MG 20MG 40MG 80MG 100MG
PERCOCET	5MG + 10MG W/ACETA MINOPHEN
ROXICODONE	5MG/ML
ROXICODONE INTENSOL	20MG/ML
ROXICODONE TABLETS	5MG &15MG & 30MG
TYLOX	5MG W/ACETAMINOPHEN

*Sustained-release oxycodone

sedation and analgesia per order.

Continuous intravenous infusion: Opioids may also be given intravenously. As with CSCI, dosages should be adjusted based on analgesic needs and side-effects. A continuous infusion with patient controlled analgesia (PCA), when feasible based on function, cognition and age, is desirous.

Bolus dosing produces peaks and troughs in analgesic blood levels, with patients experiencing frequent breakthrough pain. A basal or continuous infusion of the opioid should be programmed into the delivery system, with the capability of a periodic, self-accesssed bolus dose in small amounts programmed as well.

When pain worsens, aggressive upward titration of the opioid is recommended. With morphine as the standard, titration should be performed every 24 hours with a 25–50% dosage increase for moderate unrelieved pain and 50–100% dosage increase for severe unrelieved pain (Levy, 1994; 1996).

With aggressive upward titrations, nursing assessments must be continual. Nursing interventions include monitoring vital signs, respiratory rate and performance, pain relief and side effects.

Spinal Route

While the literature suggests that systemic opioid therapy is effective for most patients with cancer pain, there are patients for whom the systemic approach is inadequate (Portnoy, 1998). It is estimated that 10–30% of patients with cancer pain do not have satisfactory relief from standard management techniques (Young & Ades, 2001). Patients may also experience severe side effects from systemic therapy, despite the use of concurrent antiemetics and/or psychostimulants.

When opioids are administered into the epidural or subarachnoid space, they can provide analgesia without motor, sensory or sympathetic blockade. When the medication is given into the **epidural space,** a small catheter is introduced into the compartment outside of the space containing the spinal cord and cerebrospinal fluid. The medication diffuses through the dura and into the subarachnoid space. When medications are given via the intraspinal route, they are dosed at one-tenth the amount given epidurally and are administered directly into the **subarachnoid space** next to the spinal cord. Whether administered into the epidural space or the subarachnoid space, the medication has a primary effect at the level of the spinal cord and the pain impulses are predominately inhibited before reaching the brain.

There are a variety of delivery systems available for spinally administered opioids. Catheters may be percutaneously inserted or tunneled so that the proximal end is brought percutaneously or connected to an implanted port. A programmable pump, which is periodically filled with an opioid, may also be used. In selecting a delivery device, the anticipated duration of treatment is an important consideration. Generally speaking, the implanted pump is indicated for longer term spinal therapy, as it is more cost effective in the long run with less of an infection risk.

Naloxone should be on hand in the presence of compromise of respiratory rate and/or function and/or a decreased level of consciousness/responsiveness. It must be kept in mind that naloxone will reverse the analgesic effects of the systemically administered opioid, thereby precipitating withdrawals and the onset of pain.

ADJUVANTS

(Applications for use in cancer pain will be discussed; please refer to Chapter 5 for details of agents.)

While opioids are the cornerstone of therapy, not all types of pain respond to opioids. Therefore, adjuvants, (helper drugs) should be utilized. This is especially true of patients with neuralgic and/or neuropathic features to their pain. A sometimes overlooked complaint in patients with cancer is muscle pain/spasm which responds to antispasmodics and NSAIDs. Anxiolytics are believed to have synergistic effects when used in conjunction with opioids.

Adjuvants, unlike opioids, are not indicated for all types of pain. For example, if an opioid is given for pain relief, no matter what the pain, relief will generally be realized, maybe not completely, but some degree of relief will be experienced. The adjuvants are more specific for certain types of pain, so they do not have the broad utility of the opioids. Adjuvants do not have a dose-response mechanism; meaning when a dose of neurontin is given, relief does not appear within an hour of the dose.

Antidepressants

Antidepressants come in two primary classes, tricyclics (TCAs) and selective serotonin reuptake inhibitors (SSRIs). Most of the research has been focused on amitriptyline and imipramine (TCAs) and their use in chronic non-cancer pain has been studied (Patt & Burton, 1999).

Antidepressants are particularly beneficial in the presence of neuropathic pain and for neuralgic pain when combined with an anti-epileptic drug (AED). Patients with neuropathic pain from cancer treatment may benefit from management with this class of medications.

Patients will report a decrease in the "burning" characteristics of the pain. The added benefits of the antidepressants are improved sleep, enhanced mood and analgesia. The analgesic effects are usually seen within 3–7 days (Patt & Burton, 1999). Side effects that are most commonly associated with this class of medication are dry mouth, sedation and weight gain.

Anti-Epileptic Drugs

This class (AEDs) has been utilized as first-line agents for neuralgic and neuropathic pain, when used in conjunction with antidepressants. Pain involving nerve entrapment, radiation fibrosis and other nerve damage, such as that from certain chemotherapeutic agents, responds to this class of medications.

One of the newer agents, gabapentin, has a low side effect profile and does not warrant regular laboratory studies. The most prevalent side effects with this agent are weight gain and dizziness. Topamax, or topiramate, and Zonegram have weight loss as a side effect and may not be appropriate for patients with pain from malignancy.

Benzodiazepines

Clonazepam, a benzodiazepine with anticonvulsant action, is thought to decrease neuronal firing. It is well absorbed, has a low potential for toxicity and no blood level requirements. These factors have made it extensively utilized for patients cared for at home with hospice (Cole, 2002).

The AHCPR (1992) recommends benzodiazepine use for procedures only because their analgesic efficacy has not been documented. The American Pain Society (APS, 1999) lists them as adjuvants but recommends their use in cancer pain in the presence of "recurrent anxiety" and pain related to muscle spasm. The APS recommends that if benzodiazepines are to be used with opioids, there should be a downward titration of the opioids.

Psychostimulants

This class of medication is useful in offsetting the sedating side effects of opioids. Dextroamphetamine and methylphrenidate have been found to enhance the analgesic effects of opioids in patients with cancer pain, as well as improving their appetite, decreasing fatigue and relieving depression (Cole, 2002). Pemoline, another agent, comes in chewable form which can be absorbed through the buccal mucosa (Cole, 2002). The APS (1999) recommends the use of psychostimulants to combat sedation from opioids.

Lidocaine

Lidocaine may be administered via the parenteral, transdermal or transmucousal routes. Neuralgic pain is responsive to this local anesthetic. The patient receiving parenteral lidocaine should be on telemetry. The transdermal formula comes in a patch called "Lidoderm®," as an ointment, and the viscous transmucosal vehicle.

Steroids

Steroids have specific indications for chronic cancer pain. They are indicated for suspected malignant cord compression and for shrinkage of tumors, especially those associated with lymphoma (APS, 1999).

INVASIVE TECHNIQUES

In addition to the spinal administration of opioids, there are other techniques which may be employed in the management of cancer-related pain. It is important to consider anticipated survival time when considering candidacy for these types of invasive procedures. Other considerations include the duration of pain relief required, the immediate and long-term risks of the procedure, likely survival time and availability of the required expertise to perform the technique.

Some of the techniques include **nerve blocks,** where a nerve is isolated and anesthetized. The sensory, motor or sympathetic fibers may be selectively blocked, or they may all be anesthetized.

With visceral pain, a nerve plexus innervating the organ may be blocked. This is the case with the **Celiac Plexus Block,** which is used for pain from pancreatic cancer. Once a trial with a local anesthetic has been considered successful, the nerve plexus may be destroyed using alcohol or formaldehyde. Destruction of a nerve is referred to as a **neuroablative** procedure.

NON-PHARMACOLOGICAL APPROACHES TO CANCER PAIN

For the purpose of this course, non-pharmacologic techniques for cancer pain management will be divided into two categories: Physiatric and psychologic (Portenoy, 1998). This division clearly delineates the physical from the psychological as the non-pharmacological pain management approaches are discussed. Of course, the distinction is not so clear cut when managing the patient with pain from cancer. The psychologic interventions may be further subdivided into cognitive, behavioral and psycho-educational (Portenoy, 1998).

Physiatric

These therapies comprise a variety of interventions and techniques directed at maintaining physical function, integrity and restoration. Some of the interventions have a direct impact on the control of pain, while others manage the pain indirectly. While there is not a lot of scientific documentation of their use, these interventions are commonly used as they have minimal risks (Portenoy, 1998).

Some of the interventions include:

- **TENS Unit (Transcutaneous Electrical Stimulation):** Indicated for regional and/or musculoskeletal pain. Studies have shown that TENS for cancer pain produces short-term relief in 70–80% and long-term relief in 15–20% of patients (Bonica, 1990).

- **Heat/Cold:** Heat may be applied with a heating pad, lamp or hot water bath. Ice, cold compresses or a vapocoolant spray, such as fluromethane, may be used intermittently. Use in unresponsive or non-communicative patients or on insensate areas is contraindicated and not recommended.

- **Diathermy/Cryotherapy:** Paraffin baths or ultrasound may also be used to patient tolerance and satisfaction.

- **Exercise:** Patients should be encouraged to remain independent in self-care and active whenever possible. All exercise regimens should be prescribed and supervised by a physical therapist. Exercise enhances self-care ability by promoting strength, supporting muscle integrity, range of motion and physical tolerances. When not feasible, family members should be instructed in passive range of motion and positioning techniques. Positioning for comfort is also very effective in ameliorating pain. Passive exercises that provoke pain should not be undertaken. When pathological fracture secondary to tumor invasion is likely, all weight bearing activities should be avoided (AHCPR, 1992).

- **Orthoses/assistive devices:** Splinting a painful limb may decrease pain. Likewise, the use of soft or semi-rigid collars or braces may be helpful. In addition to decreasing pain by providing support, these can also decrease pain by limiting sudden pain-provoking movements (Portenoy, 1998).

Psychologic

Psychosocial support is an essential element of an effective pain management program. Portenoy (1998) delineates the psychological dimension of pain management into three types of intervention:

- Cognitive
- Behavioral
- Psycho-educational

There are elements of the psychological dimension and associated suffering that are unique to the patient with cancer-related pain. For example, the patient with cancer may view the pain as the harbinger of the disease; pain started and a diagnosis of cancer ensued. Cognitive interventions include relaxation and distraction techniques, systematic desensitization, hypnosis, cognitive restructuring and thought stopping, any and all of which can assist the patient with synthesizing and processing their perceptions of the pain related to cancer.

Meaning of the Pain

It has been noted that pain to the patient with cancer means challenge, punishment or is perceived as the enemy (Ferrell, Taylor, Sattler, Fowler & Cheyney, 1993). Related literature suggests that the meanings that patients assign to pain may be tied to their behavioral, emotional and cultural response to pain (Ferrell et al., 1993). Cognitive therapy explores these and other psychological variables of the pain experience.

Cognitive therapy is also important to the development of coping skills enhancement. Coping skills provide for pain management and for management of fears and anxiety associated with cancer treatment and disease progression.

The behavioral and psycho-educational interventions are utilized to assist the patient in dealing with fear, depression and anxiety. Family members also benefit from these techniques and can learn some of them for themselves as well as for the patient.

Behavioral strategies are directed at the reinforcement of non-pain behaviors on the part of the patient while ignoring pain behaviors. Pain behaviors can include complaining, grimacing, guarding or limping and draw attention to the pain that the person is experiencing. The pain, as opposed to the person, becomes the focal point of attention and interactions. Friends and families are taught to ignore these unhealthy behaviors and focus on healthy appropriate behaviors.

Some of the psycho-educational techniques include related education and constructive problem solving with the goal to empower the patient in pain. Feelings of helplessness and hopelessness can paralyze the patient in pain. These techniques equip the patient to overcome these feelings.

SUMMARY

The nurse plays an important role in the management of pain related to cancer. In the assessment of the patient and their pain, the nurse should have a solid base of knowledge in the cancer syndromes that place the patient at risk for pain. The nurse should also have an understanding of the cancer treatments that precipitate pain.

The nurse engages in social interactions within a variety of settings when caring for the patient with pain from cancer. These interactions may take place in a hospital unit, an outpatient treatment center or clinic or in the patient's home.

Knowing when to treat, what to treat and why to treat cancer pain and cancer pain syndromes lies within the parameters of nursing care. Patient education can be undertaken only by an educated nurse. If the nurse has inadequate knowledge of or entertains myths and misconceptions related to pain management, the therapeutic potential of that nurse and any meaningful difference to be made in the pain of the patient may never be actualized.

With respect to pain and its management, the nurse should master the fundamentals of pain and related pharmacology and understand the range of non-pharmacolgic options for the patient with pain from cancer.

The nurse must be sensitive to the patient's privacy and maintain respect for the patient with pain from cancer. All patients have the right to maintain their dignity. Just because a patient is dying, they should not have to relinquish control over their lives to another person simply because that person has the power to control their pain and suffering.

EXAM QUESTIONS

CHAPTER 13
Questions 81–87

Please read the following case presentation and select the best answer to qestions 81–87.

History

Mrs. B. is a 59-year-old female with pelvic pain secondary to cervical cancer. She has had a complete hysterectomy and is not a candidate for further surgical procedures. Her pain is primarily in her low back and pelvis. She has been on meperidine injections 50 mg per dose every four hours with percocet two tablets every four hours as needed for breakthrough pain. You note that she is reluctant to take her medication for pain and on questioning she tells you of two concerns. Her first concern is that she is afraid if she uses the medication as prescribed now when she "really needs it, at the end, nothing will work," and she is "afraid of becoming an addict." Her concerns are compounded by the fact that the meperidine wears off in about an hour after administration, and she used to be able to use only one percocet.

Psychosocial Data

Mrs. B. lost her husband to metastatic disease as a result of lung cancer four years ago. She has two grown children, neither of whom lives nearby. She lives alone but is very close to her sister who plans to move in and take care of her "when the time comes" that she needs around-the-clock care. She has a good social support network with her bridge club and Sunday school class at the church she has attended for the past thirty years.

Description of the Pain

She has an unremitting aching pain across her entire lumbo-sacral region that is worsened with sitting. She has peaks in intensity with movement, and prolonged standing, but the worst pain is realized with sitting. On a scale of 0 to 10, her pain score when resting/reclining is a 7; within 20 minutes of her injection a 4; and within 45 minutes of her pills a 5. When she sits, her pain score is a 9 to 10.

Impact of the Pain

The pain is keeping her from her favorite pastimes, bridge and church attendance, neither of which she has been able to do for the past four weeks because of her inability to sit for longer than 5–10 minutes at a time. She reports feeling "depressed and hopeless" that she will ever play bridge again or attend her Sunday school class. Her sleep is poor, as the pain wakes her up every two to three hours.

Chart Review

Mrs. B. has bony metastasis to the lumbar spine and most of the pelvic region. She is at risk for, but has not yet sustained, pathological fractures. In the past 24 hours, she has taken six percocet (30 mg oxycodone) and three injections of the meperidine (150 mg). Her pain score for the past 24 hours has not been below a 7/10.

81. The inherent problem with this regimen is

    a. a lack of steady state analgesia.

    b. the inability of patient to use medications as ordered.

    c. too much acetaminophen usage in a 24 hour period.

    d. that parenteral analgesics are not indicated until death is imminent.

82. An adjustment to the regimen that is most appropriate with Mrs. B.'s pelvic and lumbosacral pain is

    a. oral demerol.

    b. increase the percocet to 4 tablets.

    c. sustained-release opioid around-the-clock.

    d. wean narcotics due to the risk of addiction.

83. The adjuvant that might help Mrs. B.'s pain and her sleep is

    a. a tricyclic antidepressant.

    b. a non-steroidal anti-inflammatory drug.

    c. an antiepileptic drug.

    d. lidocaine.

84. What would you tell her regarding her fear of addiction?

    a. Addiction is common with chronic use of opioids.

    b. Addiction rarely occurs from using opioids for pain.

    c. Addiction results from using injectable opioids.

    d. Addiction indicates a need to increase opioids for analgesic effects.

85. When assisting Mrs. B. in establishing her pain management goals, which is the most realistic?

    a. a pain score of zero on a scale of 0 to 10

    b. comfort level that would allow her to play some bridge and periodic church attendance

    c. an optimum treatment plan with no room for improvement

    d. increased sitting tolerance for a sustained eight hour day

86. What non-pharmacolgic treatment modality might benefit Mrs. B.?

    a. deep massage to bony prominences

    b. TENS Unit

    c. cervical collar

    d. aggressive exercises to increase strength and walking tolerances

87. You want to assist Mrs. B. in some relaxation and thought-stopping techniques. With her permission, what other participants might you realistically want to include to reinforce and assist with the interventions?

    a. her physician

    b. her children

    c. her sister and her pastor

    d. her neighbor

CHAPTER 14

ACUTE AND RECURRENT PAIN

CHAPTER OBJECTIVE

Upon completion of this chapter, the reader will be able to recall acute and recurrent pain states, with related nursing interventions.

LEARNING OBJECTIVES

After studying this chapter, the learner will be able to

1. identify the incisions that place the patient at high risk for pain.

2. cite a factor that impacts post-operative pain.

3. recognize the mechanism of pain in sickle cell crisis.

4. identify a primary non-pharmacologic treatment for migraine.

5. recall the mechanism of action of triptans.

INTRODUCTION

Acute pain is something everyone has experienced. The differences between acute and chronic pain are important in that the differences drive treatment. Patients with chronic pain have to adapt their lifestyles in order to function despite the pain; whereas patients with acute pain arrive at a point of relief when the pain ceases. Acute and recurrent pain are different than chronic pain in that acute pain is time limited; once healing occurs, the pain resolves. Acute and recurrent pain are different than episodic pain in that certain physiological processes are triggered, and pain results. There may or may not be a pattern to the episodes and nurses assist patients in identifying patterns. This is important so that the episodes may be prevented and/or the intensity of the pain decreased. While the extent of disability that accompanies recurrent pain is not as encompassing as that with chronic pain, there are periods when the person with recurrent pain cannot participate in activities of daily living. Poorly managed acute and/or recurrent pain can set a person up for chronic pain.

The nurse can assist in the management and prevention of acute and recurrent pain so that function is maintained and disability and abnormal behavioral patterns do not manifest. Pain from surgery, pain associated with sickle cell crisis and headaches are the types of acute/recurrent pain addressed in this chapter.

POST-OPERATIVE PAIN

Post-operative pain has always been perceived as inevitable, and some degree of pain and discomfort is a realistic expectation. Unfortunately, post-operative pain has been given low priority by surgeons. Recent surveys support this statement by documenting that a large proportion of surgical patients still receive inadequate post-surgical analgesia. This is true on a national and international scope (Rawal, 2001). Post-operative pain management continues to be inadequate despite the publication of national guidelines and standards of care for pain management.

Factors Influencing Post-Operative Pain

Patients experiencing pain following surgery generally experience higher pain levels than anticipated. Certain procedures place the patient at higher risk for post-operative pain than others. For example, procedures that place the patient at risk for muscle spasm will produce more discomfort. Procedures involving facet or spine joints, which are primary pain generators will produce moderate to severe pain. While dated, *Table 14-1* is still relevant.

Additional factors that impact postoperative pain include

*   site, nature and duration of procedure.

*   type of incision, amount and degree of intra-operative trauma.

*   physiologic make-up of the patient.

*   presence of serious surgical complications.

*   anesthetic management of the patient pre-intra-and post-operatively.

*   quality of post-operative care.

*   pre-operative cognitive preparation of the patient.

*   psychologic make-up of the patient.

The location of the incision will also impact the intensity of the pain post-operatively. Incisions in the thoracic, upper abdominal and abdominal region tend to cause more localized and/or incisional pain. Coughing, deep breathing and arising to an upright position place unique pressures and tension on incisions in these regions. Transverse abdominal incisions tend to hurt less than those which are diagonal or vertical.

Patient variables may have a role in the perception and expression of pain related to surgery. The emotional make-up of the patient will affect the degree of anxiety and fear experienced. Patients with more "hospital stress" have been shown to have more pain and less improvement after discharge (Bonica, 1990).

Physiology and Pathophysiology of Post-Operative Pain

As with any injury, local tissue damage from surgery releases algogenic or pain producing substances that stimulate and sensitize nociceptors. These in turn produce nociceptive impulses transmitting pain to the neuraxis via A-delta and C fibers. Upon reaching the neuraxis, these impulses produce segmental reflex responses. These include a marked increase in skeletal muscle tension with a concomitant decrease in chest wall compliance. Consequently, positive feedback loops are initiated and additional nociceptive impulses are generated from muscles.

Moreover, these impulses trigger sympathetic neurons. This in turn increases cardiac work and myocardial oxygen consumption along with deceasing tone of the GI and urinary tracts. Related endocrine changes manifest when the impulses reach the hypothalamus and limbic system, causing a number of metabolic effects that result in a catabolic state. These effects occur less so with regional anesthesia than with general anesthesia. These processes are represented in *Figure 14-1*.

Ambulatory Surgery

It bears mentioning that many patients undergoing surgical procedures do not stay in the hospital setting post-operatively but are discharged to home. Post-operative pain is the most common symptom following ambulatory surgery. The incidence and degree of post-operative pain in this population has not been adequately studied. Because the incision and degree of localized trauma is reduced through laproscopic procedures and the patient is discharged early, the myth persists that related pain is mild in severity. Contrary

TABLE 14-1
Intensity and Duration of Postoperative Pain After Various Operations

STEADY WOUND PAIN (%)

Site or Type of Operation	Minimal	Moderate	Severe	Mean Duration of Moderate to Severe Pain in Days (Range)
Thoracotomy	5–15	25–35	60–70	4 (2–7)
Gastrectomy	5–20	20–30	50–75	3 (2–6)
Cholecystectomy	10–20	25–35	45–65	2 (1–5)
Hysterectomy	15–25	30–40	35–55	2 (1–4)
Colectomy, appendectomy	15–25	30–40	20–30	1 (0.5–3)
Nephrectomy, pyelolithotomy	5–15	10–15	70–85	5 (3–7)
Laminectomy	5–10	15–20	70–80	4 (2–7)
Hip (replacement)	5–10	20–30	60–70	3 (2–6)
Shoulder/elbow reconstruction	15–20	25–35	45–60	3 (2–6)
Major hand or foot	10–15	15–20	65–70	3 (2–6)
Open reduction, graft/amputation	10–15	20–30	55–70	2 (1–4)
Closed reduction	30–35	40–50	15–30	1 (0.5–3)
Vascular	30–40	35–40	20–35	1.5 (1–3)
Bladder and prostate	10–15	15–20	65–75	1 (0.5–4)
Anorectal	15–20	25–30	50–60	2 (1–5)
Vaginal	15–55	35–40	15–20	1 (0.5–3)
Scrotal	30–40	35–45	15–35	1 (0.5–3)
Maxillofacial	20–30	25–35	35–55	2 (1–6)
Ventral hernia	30–40	35–45	15–25	1.5 (1–3)
Minor mastectomy	45–50	40–45	5–15	0.5 (0–1)

Source: Bonica, J. (1982). Postoperative pain: Parts 1 and 2. *Contemporary Surgery, 20,* Jan. and Feb.

to this belief, recent studies have demonstrated that 30–40% of discharged outpatients may experience moderate to severe post-operative pain during the first 24–48 hours (Warfield & Kahn, 1995). Although the pain decreases with time, it is still severe enough to interfere with sleep and activities of daily living.

Preemptive Analgesia

In preemptive analgesia, patients receive pre- and intra-operative regional anesthesia, which is continued for a period of time following the surgical procedure. Preemptive analgesia was developed on the premise that peripheral injury is followed by changes in neural plasticity, which can lead to a decrease in pain threshold and increased pain to stimuli. By anticipating and controlling for the pain before it occurs, it is believed that patients will have a shorter duration of post-operative pain.

Data suggests that while effective, outcomes could be enhanced with prolonged administration of the anesthetics in the post-operative period (Purdue Pharma, 2002c).

Effective Management of Post-Operative Pain

Pharmacological Agents

Opioids are the mainstay of post-operative pain management. While effective in the proper dosages for mild to severe pain, when given with an adjuvant, pain relief can be optimized with opioid use.

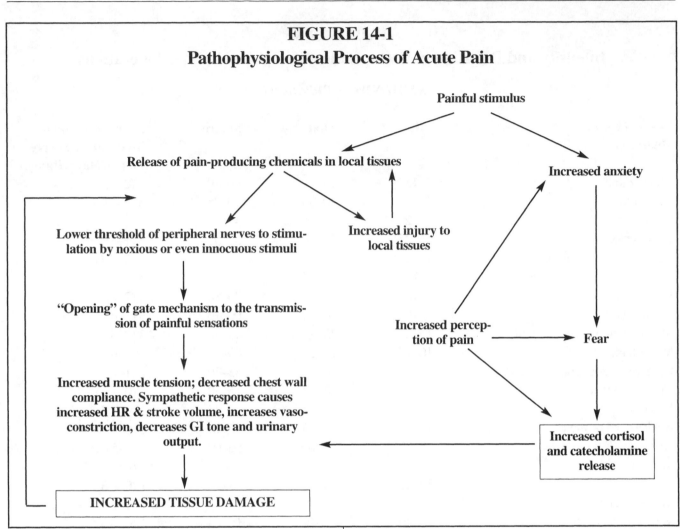

FIGURE 14-1
Pathophysiological Process of Acute Pain

Concomitant use of an NSAID will produce more efficacious outcomes. Rawal (2000) has adapted the WHO analgesic ladder for the management of acute pain. The ladder designates agents utilized to mitigate mild, moderate and severe post-operative pain (see *Figure 14-2*).

Opioid analgesics may be administered with PCA, with or without basal infusions. The use of a basal infusion controls for steady-state analgesia. With patients discharged within 24 to 48 hours of surgery, PCA may not be initiated. Despite the availability of IV access, IM injections are still used over IV. This is especially significant in children where there is an inordinate fear of needles.

Intermittent administration of opioids continues to be ordered, despite the fact that moderate to severe pain is a given, following certain surgical procedures. The efficacy of intermittent versus con-

tinuous morphine administration was studied in 181 pediatric patients aged 0–3 years following abdominal and thoracic surgery. The study design utilized a double-blind approach and demonstrated no difference in the pain levels between the intermittent and continuous administration in the infant to one year of age groups. Continuous administration was favorable in the 1–3-year-old age group, due to fear of injection and needles (van Dijk et al., 2002).

Non-Pharmacologic Interventions

Splinting to control incisional tension and pain is easily accomplished. The nurse instructs the patient in the use of a small pillow or folded blanket to apply pressure against the site of the incision. This reduces the amount of pain experienced with coughing, deep breathing and mobilization.

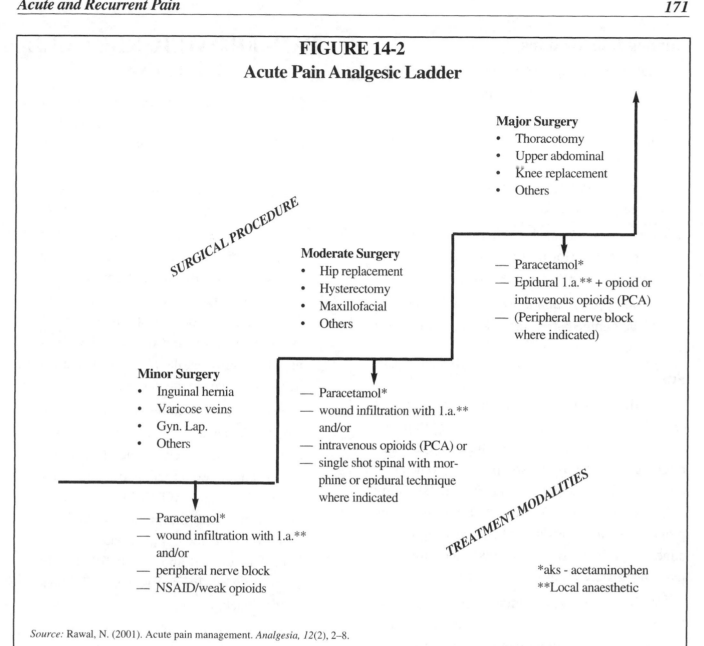

FIGURE 14-2
Acute Pain Analgesic Ladder

SURGICAL PROCEDURE

Major Surgery
- Thoracotomy
- Upper abdominal
- Knee replacement
- Others

— Paracetamol*
— Epidural 1.a.** + opioid or
  intravenous opioids (PCA)
— (Peripheral nerve block
  where indicated)

Moderate Surgery
- Hip replacement
- Hysterectomy
- Maxillofacial
- Others

— Paracetamol*
— wound infiltration with 1.a.**
  and/or
— intravenous opioids (PCA) or
— single shot spinal with morphine or epidural technique
  where indicated

Minor Surgery
- Inguinal hernia
- Varicose veins
- Gyn. Lap.
- Others

— Paracetamol*
— wound infiltration with 1.a.**
  and/or
— peripheral nerve block
— NSAID/weak opioids

TREATMENT MODALITIES

*aks - acetaminophen
**Local anaesthetic

Source: Rawal, N. (2001). Acute pain management. *Analgesia, 12*(2), 2–8.

The nurse can use cognitive and behaviorally based interventions to decrease anxiety and fear. Pre-operative patient education related to the procedure and pain management techniques and interventions can equip the patient in anticipating the discomfort and maximizing the pharmacological interventions ordered for post-operative pain management. For example, patients may not realize that they have to request pain medication, assuming that whatever is ordered will be automatically given. Fears of addiction can be addressed with facts presented.

The nurse can instruct the patient in techniques such as distraction and deep breathing. The nurse can assist the patient in assuming a position of comfort or provide related instructions. More complex cognitive-behavioral techniques warrant a consult with a psychologist or biofeedback technician. The nurse can request an order for such services and place the consult.

A TENS unit may be employed as an adjunct. This would require a physical therapy consult.

Nursing Interventions

Walker and Wong (1991) outlined steps nurses can take to help their patients in pain:

Work with the existing analgesic prescription: Titrate the analgesic to the appropriate range and give as ordered.

Consider alternative prescriptions: Research other analgesics and/or dosages.

Talk with the physician: Provide relevant data: Can the patient perform prescribed activities? Be assertive and make suggestions.

Put the new prescription to work: Begin evaluating efficacy immediately; consider future analgesic needs.

Summary

As the first line responder to the surgical patient in pain, the nurse with knowledge of the mechanisms of post-operative pain, analgesic pharmacology and the use of non-pharmacologic alternatives can effect pain management. By being assertive, proactive and informed, the nurse can provide interventions directed at increasing knowledge, dispelling myths and misconceptions and reducing anxiety.

With a sound knowledge base in cognitive-behavioral pain management techniques, the nurse can utilize these techniques to mitigate pain or request consults for more advance techniques. In understanding pain management pharmacology, the nurse can better evaluate the efficacy of the agents and determine the need for changes in the treatment plan. All of these interventions can maximize relief and promote post-operative recovery.

PAIN FROM SICKLE CELL DISEASE

The following is a story that ran in the *New York Daily News* and was reprinted in the *Partners Against Pain* (Sickle cell-pains and gains, 2002) newsletter:

Ivor Pannell came home from the hospital ... with a prescription for an opioid medication ... to relieve ... pain caused by his sickle cell anemia. He called the pharmacy closest to his apartment in Queens to ask if it had the drug, and accepted Medicaid. The answer to both questions was 'yes.' When he went to the drugstore a few minutes later, however, the pharmacist claimed he did not have the medicine...

Pannell went to 11 different pharmacies in a half-mile square of Astoria that morning and was refused at every one of them. He returned home exhausted, in pain and without medication... When his wife came home from work that night, she took the prescription to the 1st pharmacy her husband had visited and had it filled right away. Deborah Pannell is white. Her husband is black.

Sickle cell anemia affects 72,000 Americans, many of whom are black and Hispanic. A cardinal feature of the disease is episodic pain caused when the sickle-shaped cells occlude blood vessels and cut off blood flow to an area of the body. This is called a vaso-occlusive crisis (VOC) and can lead to infections, stroke or end-organ damage. A crisis can be as brief as an evening or last as long as two to three weeks. Typically, a mild crisis can be managed with a weak opioid and an adjuvant. A severe crisis can warrant treatment with morphine-equivalent opioids. Pain from the disease can be an antecedent to crisis and an effect of crisis. When pain is not managed it can lead to many of the conditions that trigger a crisis in the first place.

Incidence and Characteristics of Pain

Although pain characterizes the disease, there is significant variability in the timing, frequency and severity of a painful crisis. In general, 20% of patients have pain rarely; 60% have one or two episodes per year; and 20% have two or more episodes per month (Payne, 1999).

Pain associated with VOC is usually severe with the back, legs, knees, arms, chest and abdomen the frequent sites of pain. The quality of the pain has been related to bone and abdominal pain in other studies. The average length of crisis has been estimated to be 7.9 days.

Treatment

Pain can be managed at home in the early stage of the crisis with protocols incorporating analgesics and cognitive-behavioral techniques. If ineffective, the patient may need to go to the physician's office where parenteral analgesics, IV fluids and oxygen can be administered. It is felt that if dosed appropriately, oral analgesics can be as efficacious as parenteral. Additional studies to address this are indicated.

If the pain cannot be managed in the office setting, the patient may need to go to the ER. Most crises can be managed in the ER setting with the patient discharged home. If patients need to be hospitalized, then PCA is indicated for the management of the pain. The model for the management of pain from VOC is the same as that of cancer pain. The WHO stepwise approach should be utilized maximizing opioids, non-opioids and adjuvants. Patients with concomitant chronic pain and acute pain from VOC can be treated in comprehensive pain management programs, using the model for chronic non-malignant pain management.

Nursing Interventions

Once again, misconceptions regarding addiction prevail in this population. The need for chronic opioid therapy is compounded by the fact that the majority of sufferers from pain with VOC are black. As previously noted, ethnicity is a variable contributing to the inadequate management of pain. Studies have demonstrated that substance abuse is not a factor in patients with VOC. Three studies evaluated the presence of addiction in a total of 814 patients; of these, addiction was confirmed in eight patients (Payne, 1999). This correlates with the less than 1% of patients found to be addicted in the Porter and Jick (1980) study of addiction in hospitalized patients.

Depending on the practice setting the role of the nurse will vary. The primary nursing role is that of assessing pain, implementing treatment and reassessing pain. The nurse should communicate efficacy to the person managing the patient. If the nurse works in a physician's practice, then contact should be made with the patient's pharmacist to discuss the treatment plan. If the pharmacist is assured that the prescriptions are legitimate, cases like the one described with Mr. Pannell may not occur.

Education regarding the timing of pain treatment is important as is provision of written protocols for use at home. If home care is used, the nurse caring for the patient in the primary care setting should communicate the plan with the home care coordinator, allaying concerns with the use of opioids, if warranted.

The ER nurse is in the position to evaluate what has been done at home and in the office, documenting analgesics already given and the efficacy of same. The ER nurse should have written protocols on hand for management of pain from VOC.

HEADACHES

In 1988, a committee of international experts appointed by the board of the International Headache Society (IHS) published a classification of headaches, creating a standardized system for the diagnosis of headache disorders. There are four primary headache classifications: Migraine, with and without aura; tension-type headache; cluster headache and miscellaneous headache disorders (see *Table 14-2*). For the purpose of this course, migraine and rebound headaches will be discussed, as these types are either a new classification (rebound) or warrant use of a new class of agents (migraine). Not all headaches are the same. Patients may call a headache a "migraine" but when formulating a treatment plan for headaches the proper diagnosis is critical to its success.

International Headache Society (IHS) Criteria

In order for a headache to be considered a migraine certain criteria must be met. The IHS have delineated the following as criteria for migraine without aura:

Migraine Without Aura

A. Migraines lasting 4 to 72 hours (untreated or unsuccessfully treated).

B. Headache pain has at least two of the following:

- Unilateral location

- Pulsating quality

- Moderate or severe intensity

- Aggravation by routine activity

C. During migraine at least one of the following occurs:

- Nausea and/or vomiting

- Photophobia and phonophobia

D. At least five attacks fulfilling criteria A, B and C.

E. No evidence of underlying disease.

Incidence and Prevalence

Studies have shown that incidence differs by age and gender. In males, migraine with aura peaked at the age of 5, and migraine without aura peaked in boys between the ages of 10 and 12. In young girls, the incidence of migraine with aura peaked between the ages of 12 and 13, and migraine without aura peaked between the ages of 14 and 17 (Kaniecki, 2000).

A landmark study using a mailing of a 20 item questionnaire had 20,468 respondents. Of the 12 to 80-year-old population that responded, 12% suffered with migraine. Overall, 18% of females and 6% of males had one or more migraines per year. Migraines peaked at age 40 in both men and women. Prevalence was lower in blacks than in whites and highest in the lowest-income groups (Kaneicki, 2000).

Pathogenesis

The traditional model for the pathogenesis of migraine has been the "vascular hypothesis." According to this hypothesis, the head pain phase of migraine was due to extracranial vasodilation, and neurological symptoms were due to intracranial vasoconstriction. The current hypothesis involves activation of 5-HT-containing and norepinephrine-containing neurons (A and B respectively), which can induce complex blood flow changes in the intra and extracranial vasculature. In addition, the physiologic effect of 5-HT (serotonin) within the vessel wall may initiate the inflammatory response of migraine. Activation of nociceptors of the trigeminal system by pro-inflammatory mediators generate pain, which is then processed and perceived by neurons in the thalamus, brain stem and cerebral cortex. This nerve sensitization may contribute to facial pain and some of the associated symptoms of mirgraine such as photophobia (sensitivity to light) and phonophobia (sensitivity to sound).

It is believed that individuals may have a lowered threshold for migraine in response to predisposing factors such as physiologic or genetic configuration, gender, age, stress and hormonal changes.

TABLE 14-2
IHS Criteria for Headaches

Migraine Without Aura

A. Migraines lasting 4 to 72 hours (untreated or unsuccessfully treated)

B. Headache pain has at least two of the following:
- Unilateral location
- Pulsating quality
- Moderate or severe intensity
- Aggravation by routine activity

C. During migraine at least one of the following occurs:
- Nausea and/or vomiting
- Photophobia and phonophobia

D. At least five attacks fulfilling criteria A, B and C.

E. No evidence of underlying disease.

Episodic Tension-Type Headache

A. Headache pain accompanied by two of the following symptoms:
- Pressing/tightening (nonpulsating) quality
- Bilateral location
- Not aggravated by routine physical activity

B. Headache pain accompanied by both of the following symptoms:
- No nausea or vomiting
- Photophobia and phonophobia absent or only one present

C. Fewer than 15 days per month with headache

D. No evidence of organic disease.

Rebound Headache

A. Diffuse, bilateral headache every day or nearly every day, aggravated by mild physical or mental exertion.

B. Waking with early morning headache

C. Restlessness, nausea, forgetfulness, asthenia, depression

D. Medication withdrawal symptoms when ergotamine, a barbiturate, or codeine is involved

Source: Silberstein, S., Lipton, R. & Goadsby, P. (2002). Epidemiology and impact of headache disorders. In *Headache in clinical practice* (2nd ed., pp. 28–29). London: Martin Dunitz.

The role of 5-HT, a neurotransmitter, has been recognized in the pathogenesis of an attack, and 5-HT receptors are divided into seven subtypes. This is important because Triptans, the newer agents for migraines, target the subtypes within the 5-HT system. With the use of triptans, the entire migraine is treated, not just the pain.

There are triggers for headaches that have been identified, and patients should be educated as to what they constitute. (See Appendix D, Headache Triggers, for a reproducible list.) Patients may be asked to keep a headache diary. Many pharmaceutical companies provide forms for diaries, and the ACHE web site has documents that can be downloaded and used for practice settings.

Menstrual Migraine

Hormones may trigger migraines. Researchers have identified a link between estrogen and progesterone and migraine. Migraine occurs more frequently in women (18%) than men (6%) and develops more frequently in the second decade.

Interestingly, migraine is more common in males during childhood.

Menstrually-related migraine begins at menarche in 33% of women, occurring *mainly* at the time of menses. True menstrual migraine occurs *exclusively* at the time of menses and appears to be related to falling sex hormones. It occurs at the time of the greatest fluctuations in estrogen. Prevalence of menstrual migraine ranges between 26% to 60% in headache clinic patients; with a lower incidence in non-headache clinic patients (Silberstein, 2002).

Treating Menstrual Migraine

It is important to note that, if the cycle is predictable, menstrual migraine can be prevented. Patients are instructed to self-medicate 72 hours prior to the onset of their pain, regardless of whether the pain starts with menses. Medications should continue to be used 48 hours after menses begins. Usually, combinations of NSAIDs, triptans and/or diamox (CNS diuretic) or compazine, with

FIGURE 14-3 *1 of 2*

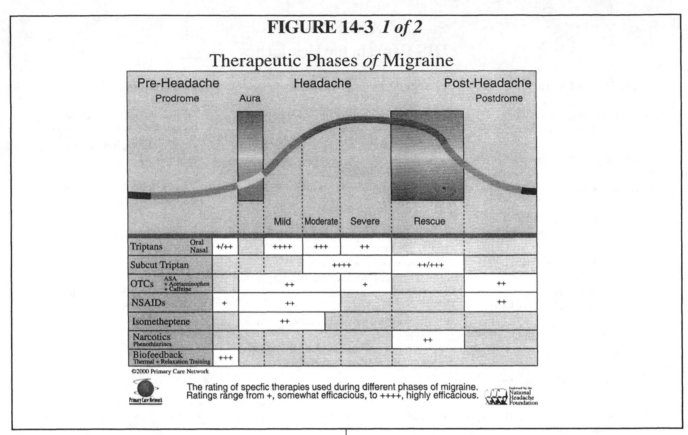

Therapeutic Phases *of* Migraine

		Pre-Headache (Prodrome / Aura)	Headache (Mild / Moderate / Severe)			Post-Headache (Rescue / Postdrome)	
			Mild	Moderate	Severe	Rescue	
Triptans	Oral Nasal	+/++	++++	+++	++		
Subcut Triptan				++++		++/+++	
OTCs	ASA +Acetaminophen +Caffeine		++	+			++
NSAIDs		+	++				++
Isometheptene			++				
Narcotics Phenothiazines						++	
Biofeedback Thermal + Relaxation Training		+++					

©2000 Primary Care Network

The rating of specfic therapies used during different phases of migraine. Ratings range from +, somewhat efficacious, to ++++, highly efficacious.

Primary Care Network   Endorsed by the National Headache Foundation

magnesium are ordered. Early studies showed magnesium deficiencies in women with menstrual migraines.

Patients are asked to keep a diary of attacks and menses. The diary is reviewed by the nurse, who documents patterns.

Phases of Migraine

A migraine attack generally occurs in three phases and treatment can be initiated in each phase (Cady & Farmer-Cady, 2000) (see *Figure 14-3*). The first is the **premonitory phase** which occurs prior to the onset of the headache. Symptoms in this premonitory phase are either prodrome or aura; prodrome is more common and involves changes in mood or energy level, alterations in sensory processing, food cravings, fluid retention and muscle pain in the head and neck, among other symptoms. It is important to help patients identify prodromal activity as a therapeutic opportunity. Treatment of the migraine can be initiated during this phase.

Auras, occurring in 15% of migraines, are generally visual consisting of flashes of light, geometric patterns or loss of a visual field. Some auras are somatosensory with paresthesias in the lips and fingers or in other areas.

The **headache phase** begins with a mild headache that progresses in severity over 30 minutes to several hours. The headache is typically unilateral but may be bilateral and has throbbing, pulsating, pounding and/or stabbing characteristics and is aggravated with routine physical activity. Other symptoms as outlined in the HIS criteria for migraine may be present. This phase may last from 4 to 72 hours. Sleep tends to ameliorate the pain.

The post-headache or **postdrome phase** may last for one to two days. Typical symptoms include irritability, fatigue, inability to concentrate and muscle pain. These may produce disability in some migraineurs who may require therapeutic intervention.

FIGURE 14-3 *2 of 2*

Impact Based Recognition *of* Migraine

Historically, the diagnosis of migraine is based on a pattern of symptoms. However, this approach ignores the most obvious feature of migraine, which is the disability it produces. Given the time constraints of clinical practice, the consensus of the advisory committee is that migraine and its variants can be recognized by exploring the following four questions:

1. How do headaches interfere with your life?	2. How frequently do you experience headaches of any type?	3. Has there been any change in your headache pattern over the last six months?	4. How often and how effectively do you use medication to treat headaches?
Recurrent headaches that produce significant disability should be considered migraine until proven otherwise. Headaches that restrict important activities such as work or home responsibilities suggest a need for aggressive therapy.	The frequency of headaches alerts the provider to chronic headache disorders and the possibility of analgesic overuse. This will also help to differentiate migraine from cluster headache. Frequent headaches raise the issue of adding a preventive medication.	An affirmative answer indicates the need for a more in-depth evaluation whereas a negative response reassures the physician and patient that serious underlying disease is unlikely. **Comfort Signs:** • Onset under age 40 • Family history • Menstrual association • Variable HA location • Meet IHS criteria	Generally patients should not use acute treatment medications more than two days a week. Being pain free *and* fully functional within 2 to 4 hours are the goals of acute therapy. Inability to achieve these goals suggests the need to change medication.

Evaluating Migraine Headaches

The evaluation of migraines and other headaches is best undertaken with a dualistic approach: Symptom evaluation and functional impact. In the former, information relative to the headache and associated symptoms is evaluated; with the latter, the focus is on the impact the headache has had on functioning. When arriving at a differential diagnosis, both are important, as criteria must be to met for migraine to be diagnosed.

It is important to assess the impact of the headache on function because a true migraine will impact functioning, and the impact on functioning aids in the determination of candidacy for prophylactic treatment. So, in assessing the patient with migraine use of an "Impact Based" approach may prove beneficial. Data is sought based on the disability of the migraine, not just the symptoms it produces.

Treating Migraine Headaches

Effective migraine management depends on several factors. The nurse has an important role in facilitating successful implementation of the treatment plan, which involves patient education, delineation of expected patient behaviors and appropriate use of prescribed pharmacologic and non-pharmacologic interventions.

The International Headache Consortium cites goals of migraine therapy (Tepper, 2002) as follows:

- Treat attacks rapidly and consistently.

- Restore the patient's ability to function.

- Minimize the use of back-up and rescue medications.

- Optimize self-care and reduce use of headache resources.

- Be cost-effective.

- Have minimal or no adverse effects.

TABLE 14-3
Prophylactic Treatment for Migraines

Beta Blockers	TCAs	AEDs	NSAIDs	Calcium Channel Blockers
propanolol	nortriptyline	divalproex sodium	indomethacin	verapramil
naldolol	amitriptyline	topiramate	naproxen	nifedipine
atenolol	imipramine	gabapentin		
	desipramine			

Candidacy for prophylactic and abortive treatment must be determined. There are certain criteria to warrant migraine prophylaxis.

In determining a patient's need for prophylactic therapy, function is a critical determinant. Patients warranting preventative treatment are those with disabling primary headaches, who usually meet one of the following criteria:

- Frequent migraine (6 or more per month).

- Chronic migraine (15 or more headache days per month).

- Chronic tension-type headache (15 or more headache days per month).

- "Analgesic rebound headache" (a daily headache with the use of analgesics more than three days per week).

- Headache refractory to routine treatment.

- Contraindication to acute therapy (Silberstein, Lipton & Goadsby, 1998).

Stratified Approach

Studies have demonstrated that treatment of acute migraine with a stratified approach is more effective than using a step-wise approach. In stratified treatment, the patient takes more that one agent simultaneously instead of taking one medication waiting for an effect and then taking another. The choice of agent should depend on the severity of the symptoms and associated disability. Disability can be determined using a disease specific quality of life instrument such as the HIT-6 or MIDAS. In the stratified approach for a patient with less impact, an NSAID and adjuvant may be used. For patients with higher disability a triptan with an adjuvant might be used.

Treatment Options

Prophylactic Treatment

Patients with three or more disabling migraines per month are considered candidates for prophylactic treatment. The goal is to prevent the onset of headaches through the use of a variety of agents (see *Table 14-3*). Efficacy of the prophylactic agents is assessed with follow-up visits. If the patient is not tolerating side effects or if the prophylactic plan is not preventing migraines, other agents may be initiated.

Abortive Treatment

Agents directed at aborting the migraine may be used with the prophylactic program. Some agents are migraine-specific such as triptans and dihydroergotamine. The ergotamines, an older class, and the triptans, a new class of medications selective for 5-HT subtypes, afford relief for all of the symptoms of migraine. These are contraindicated inpatients with ischemic heart disease, peripheral vascular disease and uncontrolled hypertension.

The most common and earliest triptan was sumatriptan or Imitrex, which is available for subcutaneous, intranasal and oral administration. Other triptans have varying onsets and durations of action (Aurora, 2000).

Greatest Effect	Fastest Effect	Least Reccurence
sumatriptan	sumatriptan	naratriptan
rizatriptan	rizatriptan	frovatriptan
zolmitriptan	zolmitriptan	almotriptan

The use of the triptans usually follows attempts at management of the headache with an NSAID, magnesium or butalbital, acetaminophen and caffeine tablets. They are most effective when taken early in the course of the migraine.

Rebound Headache

Rebound headache is a headache that is persistent, waxing and waning in severity but never going away. Characteristics of "Rebound Headache" or "Analgesic Overuse Headache" are as follows:

- Diffuse, bilateral headache every day or nearly every day, aggravated by mild physical or mental exertion.

- Waking with early morning headache.

- Restlessness, nausea, forgetfulness, depression.

- Medication withdrawal symptoms when ergotamine, a barbiturate, or codeine is involved.

Treatment of Rebound Headache

Treatment of rebound headache consists of many of the agents discussed thus far in this chapter. Patients who experience frequent headaches are at increased risk of overusing acute headache medications. Prior to the implementation of a prophylactic program, analgesics must be discontinued. A period of "analgesic washout" is afforded the central nervous system, and headache symptoms are managed with IV protocols. In addition to the IV treatment, non-pharmacological treatment is provided with biofeedback/relaxation therapy, physical therapy for interventions directed at decreasing cervicogenic tension/spasm, with effects on headache and psychological therapy. Active exercise is promoted with a home program implemented. Patients are educated with respect to triggers and taught to identify potential triggers impacting their headaches. (See Appendix D for a listing of Headache Triggers.) Patients may also be instructed to maintain a headache journal to aid in the development of insight, so as to maximize use of non-pharmacological techniques (see *Figure 14-4*).

Nursing Role

The nurse plays an important role in education of the patient with respect to treatment principles, food triggers, use of diaries and medications. The nurse may coordinate home administration of the IV protocols or may administer the protocols in the hospital or physician's practice setting.

IV Protocols

IV protocols that have been successfully used to abort migraines and treat rebound headaches are

- hydrocortisone;

- depacon;

- mangesium;

- DHE; and

- throrazine.

Outcomes in Headache Management

Enhanced quality of life is an important indicator of success in headache management. This outcome is relevant for any type of headache, whether migrainous or rebound in nature.

Criteria for determining outcomes with respect to success of a prophylactic program have been proposed by Lipton and Silberstein (2001), as follows:

- Decreased frequency and intensity of headache.

- Enhanced functioning with decreased disability.

- Reduced use of abortive headache medications.

- Increased efficacy of acute headache medications.

SUMMARY

Acute pain is time-limited, but episodic pain can be debilitating. The reduction in painful events is an indicator that a pro-

FIGURE 14-4
Headache Journal

Date:
Bedtime previous PM:
Awaken time:

HA: STRESS:
Breakfast Time:
Foods: _____
_____

HA: STRESS:
Lunch Time:
Foods: _____
_____

HA: STRESS:
Dinner Time:
Foods: _____
_____

Drinks for day:
Caffeinated beverages: 1 2 3 4 5 6 7 8 9
Water: 1 2 3 4 5 6 7 8

Relaxation Tapes:
Time:
Name of Tape: _____
Tension Before: Tension After:
Comments:_____
_____

Relaxation Tapes:
Time:
Name of Tape: _____
Tension Before: Tension After:
Comments:_____
_____

Physical Therapy Exercises:
Stretches:
Cardiovascular: Type: _____
Amount of Time: _____

Medication: Type and Time taken
Daily Medication: _____
_____

Rescue Medication: _____
_____

Other:_____
_____

Comments:_____
_____
_____

HA = Headache, Measure HA, and Stress 0 (none)–10 (max)

phylactic program is effective. Migraines can be debilitating, as can rebound headaches when they begin to control the person, instead of the person controlling the pain.

EXAM QUESTIONS

CHAPTER 14
Questions 88–93

88. The incisions that place the patient at high risk for pain are

    a. thoracic, horizontal and transverse.

    b. diagonal, thoracic and transverse.

    c. transverse, vertical and diagonal.

    d. upper abdominal, diagonal and vertical.

89. One factor that impacts post-operative pain is the

    a. culture of the surgeon.

    b. gender of the surgeon.

    c. quality of the postoperative care.

    d. time of day of surgery.

90. The mechanism of the pain from VOC is

    a. psychogenic.

    b. due to a decrease in magnesium.

    c. due to occlusion by round blood cells.

    d. due to occlusion by sickle shaped cells.

91. Ideally pain from VOC could be managed

    a. in emergency rooms.

    b. in ICUs.

    c. in the home with protocols.

    d. on medical/surgical units.

92. The percentage of persons who have migraine is estimated at

    a. 10%.

    b. 12%.

    c. 17%.

    d. 20%.

93. Frequent migraine is defined as

    a. 3 per month.

    b. 4 per month.

    c. 5 per month.

    d. 6 or more per month.

CHAPTER 15

ORGANIZATIONAL AND PROFESSIONAL ISSUES

CHAPTER OBJECTIVE

Upon completion of this chapter, the reader will be able to recall the origin of the JCAHO Pain Management Standards, the focus of each of the six pain management chapters and analyze applications of the standards to clinical practice situations with delineation of various nursing roles within practice settings.

LEARNING OBJECTIVES

After studying this chapter, the learner will be able to

1. identify one agency that collaborated with the JCAHO in the development of the standards for pain management.

2. cite two interventions directed at the management of pain in the hospital setting.

3. identify the focus of each of the six chapters of the pain management standards.

4. recall one institutional and one patient expectation for pain management.

INTRODUCTION

Many organizations have been decidedly pro-active in their stance to the problem of inadequate pain management and related professional issues. Some organizational activities have included development of relevant curricula; publication of standards of expected behaviors in healthcare organizations and for healthcare professionals; and development of guidelines and criteria for the assessment and treatment of pain in all forms and types.

ORGANIZATIONS RESPOND TO THE PROBLEM OF UNDER-TREATED PAIN

A congressional mandate designated January 1, 2001 through December 31, 2010 as the "Decade of Pain Control and Research" (Kondamuri, 2001). This mandate, along with the new JCAHO Pain Control Standards and position papers, and consensus statements of other organizations have thrust the problem of pain and challenges in its management into the limelight.

At their 2001 meeting, the **American Medical Association House of Delegates** approved a resolution calling for the AMA to collect and disseminate data about pain management education for medical schools and residency programs. A similar resolution was passed at the meeting of a multidisciplinary group of pain experts at the **University of Kentucky College of Medicine** and the **Hospice of Bluegrass in Lexington.** The participants developed an Objective Structured Clinical Examination (OSCE) to evaluate cancer pain management skills among medical students (Purdue Pharma, 2002a).

The **Agency for Health Care Policy and Research (AHCPR)** has developed standards for the management of pain in cancer, surgery and trauma. In addition to these clinical standards and guidelines, the AHCPR has also developed patient-oriented materials for educational purposes.

The **American Academy of Pain Management (AAPM)** and the **American Pain Society (APS)** have developed guidelines, principles and standards of care related to the management of pain. Both agencies have stressed the need for the education of healthcare professionals in pain management. The APS and the AAPM joined with the **American Academy of Addiction Medicine (AAAM)** in developing a consensus statement regarding the use of opioids for pain management (AAPM, AAAM & APS, 1997). In fact, the APS created the phrase, *"pain: the 5th vital sign,"* stressing the role of early and ongoing assessment of pain (APS, 1999).

The **National Cancer Policy Board** just released its official "Recommendations on Symptom Control and Palliative Care." The recommendations emphasize training, education and increased federal support to overcome barriers to adequate symptom control and palliative care in cancer patients (Purdue Pharma, 2002a).

Joint Commission of the Accreditation of Health Organizations (JCAHO) Responds

In March of 1999, the outcome of a two-year collaboration between the **University of Wisconsin-Madison Medical School** and the **JCAHO**, was a set of Pain Standards to be implemented nationwide. The collaborative effort was funded by the Robert Wood Johnson Foundation; the management of pain became a priority for the first time in the history of healthcare (JCAHO,

1999). A panel of experts assisted JCAHO in the endeavor.

National organizations including the APS and AAPM, along with patient advocate groups, also assisted in the development of the Standards of Care which were implemented in the year 2000. In addition to the University of Wisconsin and JCAHO with their panel of experts, several organizations developed other guidelines on analgesic treatment, pain assessment, methods for pain relief along with position papers and consensus documents relative to the issue at hand.

The development and implementation of explicit standards, a landmark endeavor, is certain to impact the knowledge and practice of healthcare providers and administrators by making the management of pain a priority in U.S. hospitals and outpatient surgery facilities. Hopefully, changes in attitudes regarding patients in pain, as well as the use of controlled substances for pain management, will follow.

JCAHO STANDARDS

Settings

JCAHO's revised standards for pain management cover the following healthcare settings:

- Ambulatory care
- Behavioral healthcare
- Home care
- Healthcare network
- Hospitals
- Long-term care
- Long-term care pharmacies (JCAHO, 1999)

Documents

Anyone who has undergone a survey by a reputable credentialing organization knows that simply having policies and procedures in place does not translate into implementation. Evidence that written policies have been enacted will be required for review. Documentation of compliance with the JCAHO standards should be present for review. Records to be reviewed will include but not be limited to:

- Patient records
- Staff bylaws
- Staff credentialing
- Policy and procedure manuals
- Outcome documents
- Organizational standards (Weiner, 2002)

Implementation

In early 1999, JCAHO sent the proposed Pain Control Standards to accredited healthcare organizations, professional groups and associations, consumer groups, and purchasers. The JCAHO Pain Control Standards were included in the 2000–2001 *JCAHO Standards Manual.* In 2001, JCAHO surveyors assessed compliance with the standards through reviews of policies, procedures, documentation and interviews with patients, families and facility staff.

Overview

Focus of the chapters:

- Rights and Ethics
- Assessment of Persons with Pain
- Care of Persons with Pain
- Education of Persons with Pain
- Continuum of Care (Revised)
- Improvement of Organization Performance (Revised)

Expectations

JCAHO delineated expected behaviors both from within a variety of settings within healthcare organizations and the healthcare providers. As pain involves a social transaction with patients consid-

ered active participants in the transaction, JCAHO specified expected patient behaviors as well.

Providers

The expected behaviors of the providers are noted below:

- Develop and implement policies and procedures supporting safe medication prescription or ordering.
- Monitoring of patient is conducted during the post-procedure period.
- Patients are taught that pain management is an expectation.
- Relevant continuum of care is included in the discharge process based on the patient's assessed needs at the time of discharge.
- The organization provides mechanisms to collect data to monitor performance.

Patients

The expected behaviors of the patient include:

- Clarifying expectations regarding pain and pain management.
- Discussing pain relief options/alternatives.
- Working with healthcare professionals to develop a pain management plan.
- Asking for pain relief at the onset of the pain.
- Participating in the assessment of the pain.
- Reporting unrelieved pain.
- Knowing their medications and asking questions about addiction and dependence.

In order for patients to enact these behaviors, they must be apprised of their rights and responsibilities relevant to their pain and its management. The organization, toward that end, should post patients rights and responsibilities in all patient care areas. Furthermore, standardized pain assessment scales and instruments should be utilized and consistent throughout the organization. These should be posted in all patient care areas and patient rooms with instructions for their use.

Organizations

The organization may create a pain management committee to oversee and regulate the development and implementation of pain management interventions, standards and procedures. The organization should collaborate with the clinical staff in

- the establishment of policies and procedures and practice standards.

- the selection, development and distribution of relevant educational materials for patients, and when appropriate,

  — establish procedures to assess pain status in non-inpatient settings, such as short stay, outpatient surgery and procedure settings.

  — develop educational programs for relevant providers in pain assessment and management.

  — determine competency in pain assessment and treatment during orientation of all new clinical staff.

- holding periodic staff awareness events regarding pain assessment and management.

- including a commitment to pain management in the mission statement of the facility.

- developing a patient and family bill of rights.

EXAMPLES OF IMPLEMENTATION

Rights and Ethics

Patients have the right to the appropriate assessment and management of their pain:

1. Assessment:

   a. On presentation, the patient's pain is assessed utilizing the appropriate pain assessment tool/scale.

   b. The vital signs flow sheet has an area for a pain score, re-enforcing that pain is considered a fifth vital sign.

   c. A poster is present in every patient care area stating the right of pain management along with a copy of the standardized developmentally appropriate pain assessment tool which is used consistently throughout the institution.

2. Management:

   a. The institution has in place formal procedures to support the involvement of the patient, family or surrogate in making decisions regarding the management of pain. This also applies to the terminally ill and dying.

   b. Supplemental resources such as the APS Principles for Analgesic Use or the AHCPR Guidelines for Cancer, Acute or Procedural Pain Management may be utilized. Resources available need to be specific to unit specialties.

3. Maintenance:

   a. Pain assessment/management are considered a dynamic process with standards of care explicit as to the re-assessment of pain and interventions directed at its management.

   b. Personnel performing the interventions have been documented as clinically competent in pain assessment and management.

   c. An element of staff updates include at least one course in pain management.

   d. Pain management is included in outcome measurement/satisfaction data collections (i.e., patient satisfaction surveys include pain management).

Assessment of Persons With Pain

Pain is assessed in all patients upon presentation to the institution.

JCAHO refers to the Whole Patient Assessment relative to pain. Inclusive in this concept is consideration of personal, cultural, spiritual and ethnic beliefs (Weiner, 2002).

a. If the patient has pain, then further inquiries regarding the pain including: The character, quality, onset, location, duration, radiation and intensity are determined.

b. The patient's input is also solicited with respect to aggravating and ameliorating factors and the perceived impact that the pain is having on their life.

c. Objective indicators of the pain are documented by the intake person.

d. Assessment tools should differentiate between acute and chronic pain. (See sample tools from Chapter 3). For example, a patient may be presenting with pain from an inflamed appendix and may also have a history of chronic back pain. While one does not directly impact the other, there may be variables such as analgesic tolerance that may impact the acute pain event.

e. The assessment tool is disease and developmentally appropriate.

Care of Persons With Pain

The institution establishes policies and procedures in support of appropriate prescribing and ordering of pain management interventions.

a. Interventions directed at the management of pain are appropriate with respect to the type of pain being managed.

b. Nurses are competent in handling delivery systems for opioids, such as PCA and Epidural Systems.

Education of Persons With Pain

Patients, residents and families are educated about effective pain management.

a. Education is documented in progress notes.

b. Interdisciplinary teaching or education forms may be used if relevant to the treatment setting. For example, a patient in a rehabilitation center may be educated in pain management by a variety of disciplines.

c. Roles are defined for patients and families.

d. Patient education materials are available and prominent.

Continuum of Care

The discharge plan takes into consideration the patient's continuing pain management needs.

a. The discharge instruction sheet outlines pain management interventions.

b. The patient is referred to a pain management specialist upon discharge.

Improving Organizational Performance

The organization collects data to monitor its pain management performance.

a. This can be part of the institution's information outcomes system or quality improvement activities.

b. Patient satisfaction can be assessed in the area of pain management in addition to the other traditional indicators.

c. Telephone surveys can be conducted once the patient has been discharged.

d. The institution should aggregate, analyze and disseminate data via committee or quarterly reports.

e. Relevant action plans should be developed to address deficiencies: For example, if assessment is the problem, staff education might be warranted.

f. When appropriate, performance should be benchmarked.

Historically, the provision of pain management has been implicit. With standards of care, such as those implemented by JCAHO, there is finally an explicit set of expected behaviors identified for all parties involved in the assessment and management of pain. The examples of implementation of the JCAHO standards are just that, examples. Each institution and set of professionals must make their own interpretation and determine what works for their particular circumstances and setting.

ORGANIZATIONAL GUIDELINES

The organizations listed in Appendix B have developed and disseminated guidelines for pain management. Some are disease-specific and others have a demographic approach. Irregardless, they have taken a proactive stance providing the information needed to positively affect pain management interventions and outcomes. They are listed so as to be a resource and can be contacted for copies of their respective guidelines.

Nursing Practice in Pain Management

The nurse is uniquely equipped to assist in the development, provision and evaluation of pain management interventions and treatment plans. The nurse is trained to approach patients holistically; if there ever was a disease or symptom warranting such an approach, pain management is it.

The nurse has access to the patient and to the person directing the treatment. This gives the nurse a unique perspective that can be used to maximize outcomes. The nurse is the communication conduit between the physician, nurse practitioner and physician's assistant, the patient and ancillary staff. The nurse can apply the art and science of nursing to positively impact the care of the patient.

PROFESSIONAL ROLES IN PAIN MANAGEMENT

Primary Care Setting

Primary Nurse/Team Leader is a role that is typically found in the primary care setting. The scope of the role is contingent on the practice level of the nurse caring for the patient. The LPN and/or RN share responsibilities. Both can play a role in the development of practice guidelines or participating in committee work toward that end. Nurses can also make a difference by imaging sound, scientific pain management principles for peers. Discussions with the person writing the orders can also effect change.

The RN, if educationally qualified, can create a position as a pain management clinician or clinical specialist. If the institution has a Clinical Ladder Program, a Pain Resource Nurse level can be introduced, wherein a trained RN serves as a resource to a designated group of nurses, for a designated shift and/or a designated practice area.

Nurses in critical care settings come in contact with pain all the time. ER nurses have patients that come time and again for pain relief or for controlled substances. The ER nurse can create a Pain Management Data Base or tracking system for delineating referrals made, medications given and the status of each patient visit. This can be used to hold the patient accountable for their follow-through care and to alert those not familiar with the patient that they are a repeater.

The nurse may be part of a pain team for the hospital, wherein consults are seen and standards of care, and policies and procedures developed. Education of the nursing staff is generally a function of this role.

Secondary Care Setting

Nurses may be employed in skilled care units or intermediate units caring for patients awaiting transfer into rehab beds. The nurse may deal with sub-acute or chronic pain issues in this setting. Knowledge of pain management principles is important to optimize functional outcomes in these patients.

The nurse may work in a pain clinic or pain management program. The role of the nurse in this setting is primarily involved with education, re-enforcement of techniques learned in therapies and medication administration and monitoring.

If the nurse works for an anesthesia-based pain practice, there is a heavy procedural orientation, and the nurse may function within a broad continuum from setting up for and assisting with procedures, to community follow-up. The nurse may function as case manager for the patient's program.

A nurse practitioner may see patients in a pain practice. In this respect, the nurse practitioner functions much like a pain physician. If the nurse practitioner has a DEA number, an understanding of diversion, abuse and addiction are crucial to that nurse practitioner's practice.

Tertiary Care Settings

Case Managers

The nurse may work as a case manager for an insurance company dealing with injured workers. Decisions at this level involve finding the appropriate treatment setting for patients. Choices in the type of pain management intervention(s) are a function of this type of role. The nurse's client is not only the patient but the third party payer as well. It is often up to the case manager to return the patient to gainful employment. Understanding the scope of and indications for certain treatment interventions is important.

Hospice/Home Care Nurse

The nurse in this role manages patients across the life-span and deals with a variety of diagnostic categories and pain types. The hospice nurse does not care only for patients with cancer; patients with pain from AIDS are also receiving hospice care.

In addition to the administration of parenteral opioids, the hospice/home care nurse may be asked to administer IV headache protocols or handle epidural infusion systems. In this role, the nurse can share pain management knowledge with patients, families and peers.

EXAM QUESTIONS

CHAPTER 15
Questions 94–100

94. The APS stands for

    a. American Pain Society.

    b. Analgesic Pain Society.

    c. American Pharmacology Society.

    d. Analgesic Principle.

95. The fifth vital sign is

    a. blood pressure.

    b. pain score.

    c. pulse.

    d. temperature.

96. The JCAHO Pain Standards state expectations for healthcare

    a. institutions only.

    b. institutions and nurses.

    c. institutions, staff and patients.

    d. staff only.

97. Taking a patient's pain score on admission comes under which chapter of the JCAHO standards?

    a. Care of Person's with Pain

    b. Improving Organizational Performance

    c. Assessment of Person's with Pain

    d. Continuum of Care

98. Upon discharge, you note that the patient is referred to an RSD specialist. This is in compliance with which chapter of the JCAHO standards?

    a. Care of Patients

    b. Assessment of Patients

    c. Rights and Ethics

    d. Continuum of Care

99. You note that the new Patient Satisfaction Questionnaire now has a question about pain management. This is in compliance with a standard in which chapter of the JCAHO standards?

    a. Continuum of Care

    b. Care of Patients

    c. Improving Organizational Performance

    d. Assessment of Patients

100. Upon orientation to your hospital, you note that it has policies and procedures for both parenteral and epidural patient controlled analgesia. Your hospital is demonstrating compliance with standards within which chapter of the JCAHO standards?

    a. Care of Person's with Pain

    b. Organizational Performance

    c. Assessment of Patients

    d. Continuum of Care

This concludes the final examination. An answer key will be sent with your certificate so that you can determine which of your answers were correct and incorrect.

APPENDIX A

Biofeedback Psychophysiological Evaluation

CHIEF COMPLAINT/ONSET:

GOAL:

SLEEP HISTORY:

PAST HEALTH HISTORY: **ETOH/TOBACCO/HERBS/MEDS:**
Medical

ER Visits Average past 3–6 Months:
Psychiatric: Yes____ No_____   **NUTRITIONAL:**
PATIENT PROFILE: 1.   Caffeine intake_____
                                                            2.   Appetite_____

                                                            Weight_____

                                                            EXERCISE:

                                                            SOCIALIZATION:

STRESSORS: **LITIGATION ___YES ___NO ___NA**
                                                            CURRENT PAIN MANAGEMENT TECHNIQUES:

SURFACE ELETROMYOGRAPHY

Surface EMG recording was used to evaluate muscle function in areas of pain before, during and following active test movements as follows (uv = microvolts):

MUSCLE ACTIVITY: **SYMMETRY:**

0 = No hyperactivity, normal (EMG <4uv)   0 = Normal = Symmetrical (0–19%)

+ = Mild hyperactivity (5–9uv)   + = Mild Asymmetry (20–34%)

++ = Moderate hyperactivity (10–14uv)   ++ = Moderate asymmetry (35–49%)

+++ = Marked hyperactivity (15uv plus)   +++ = Marked asymmetry (50% or greater)

Biofeedback/Pain Management Initial Evaluation *page 1 of 2*

Therapist: _____ Date: _____

Signature: _____

TREATMENT PLAN:

A. Education to include visual and/or auditory feedback, handouts and audiotapes as noted:

B. Surface EMG per diagnostic guidelines

SUMMARY:

RECOMMENDATIONS:

EVALUATION OF DURABILITY OF OUTCOMES IN 6 MONTHS:

Biofeedback/Pain Management Initial Evaluation *page 2 of 2*

Therapist: _____ Date: _____

Signature: _____

APPENDIX B

RESOURCES AND WEB SITES FOR HEADACHES AND PAIN

There are a plethora of pain management/headache resources available to the patient and the healthcare practitioner. In addition to disease-specific resources, there is a listing of resources dealing with Complimentary and Alternative Medicine as well. It is a good idea to familiarize yourself with the site/publication before offering it to your patient.

Most of us are familiar with the idiom "knowledge is power." Well, this is especially true when dealing with patients who are in pain. It has been documented that when patients perceive loss of control, it has a deleterious effect on their pain.

Keep in mind that "over-the-counter" is not synonymous with "benign" and when dealing with AEDs, SSRIs and other neurological agents, drug interactions should be taken very seriously.

RESOURCES AND WEB SITES FOR HEADACHES

Academy for Guided Imagery
PO Box 2070
Mill Valley CA 94942
(800) 726-2070

American Academy of Neurology
1080 Montreal Ave
St Paul, MN 55116-2325
(651) 695-1940

American Council for Headache Education (ACHE)
875 Kings Hwy, Suite 200
Woodbury, NJ 08096
(800) 255-ACHE (800-255-2243)
www.achenet.org

ACHE Support Group
875 Kings Hwy, Suite 200
Woodbury, NJ 08096
(800) 423-0043

Glaxo Wellcome Migraine Resource Center
www.migrainehelp.com

Healthfinder
www.healthfinder.gov

National Headache Foundation
888-NHF-5552 (888-643-5552)
www.headaches.org

National Institutes of Health
(301) 496-4000
National Institute of Neurological Disorders and
    Stroke
www.ninds.nih.gov

TMJ Association, Ltd.
5418 W Washington Blvd
Milwaukee, WI 53213
(414) 259-3223

Trigeminal Neuralgia Association
PO Box 340
Barnegat Light, NJ 08006
(609) 361-1014

RESOURCES AND WEB SITES FOR PAIN

Agency for Health Care Policy and Research
US Department of Health and Human Services
Rockville, MD

American Chronic Pain Association (ACPA)
Self-help organization for chronic pain patients and
    families
916-632-0922

Academy for Guided Imagery
PO Box 2070
Mill Valley CA 94942
(800) 726-2070

American Pain Foundation
111 South Calvert Street, Suite 2700
Baltimore, MD 21202
www.painfoundation.org

Ankylosing Spondylitis Association
511 N LaCienegra Blvd. #216
Los Angeles, CA 90048
(800) 777-8189

Arthritis Foundation
PO Box 19000
Atlanta, GA 30326
(800) 283-7800

ARMS—Carpal Tunnel Information
PO Box 471973
Aurora, CO 80047-1973
(303) 369-0803
www.certifiedpst.com/arm

Chronic Fatigue Syndrome (CFIDS)
PO Box 220396
Charlotte, NC 28222-0398
(800) 442-3437

Crohn's and Colitis Foundation
444 Park Avenue South
New York, NY 10018
(800) 932-2423

Fibromyalgia Network
PO Box 31750
Tucson, AZ 85751-1750
(800) 853-2929

International Endometriosis Assoc.
8585 North 76th Place
Milwaukee, WI 53223
(800) 992-3636
(414) 355-2200

Interstitial Cystitis Association
PO Box 1553
Madison Square Garden, NY 10159
(800) 453-7422

Lupus Foundation of America, Inc.
4 Research Place, #180
Rockville, MD 20805- 3226
(800) 558-0121

National Chronic Pain Outreach
PO Box 274
Millboro, VA 24460
(540) 862-9437

National Foundation for Depressive Illness, Inc
PO Box 2257
New York, NY 10116
(800) 248-4344

National Multiple Sclerosis Society
733 3rd Avenue
New York, NY 10017-3288

National Osteoporosis Foundation
150 17th Street NW, #500
Washington, DC 20036-4603
(202) 223-2226

Overactive Bladder Hotline
300 West Pratt Street, Suite 40
Baltimore MD, 21201
(800) 828-7866

Peripheral Neuropathy
PO Box 2055
Lennox Hill Station
New York, NY 10021
(800) 247-6968

Phantom Pain Information
(410) 614-2010

Reflex Sympathetic Dystrophy
116 Haddon Avenue #D
Haddonfield, NJ 08033
(609) 795-8845

Sickle Cell Disease Association of America, Inc.
200 Corporate Pointe, Suite 495
Culver City, CA 90230-7633
(800) 421-8453

TMJ Association, Ltd.
5418 W Washington Blvd
Milwaukee, WI 53213
(414) 259-3223

Trigeminal Neuralgia Association
PO Box 340
Barnegat Light, NJ 08006
(609) 361-1014

Vulvar Pain Foundation
PO Drawer 177
Graham, NC 27253
(336) 226-0704

VZV Information Line
Shingles and PHN
40 East 72nd Street
New York, NY 10021
(800) 472-8478

COMPLEMENTARY AND ALTERNATIVE MEDICINE RESOURCES (CAM)

The mind-body connection takes on special relevance with pain, which is a sensory-reactive phenomena impacting the entire individual. Certain interventions which have been somewhat esoteric historically are quite mainstream. These include acupuncture, biofeedback and self-hypnosis.

Many patients in pain have been told they have "to learn to live with the pain." Unfortunately, no one equips them to live with the pain, so they look for alternatives to the traditional medical system that has offered no respite.

Shark cartilage, magnet therapy, blue-green alga and megavitamin therapy are some of the alternatives that I have seen used by patients by the time they see me in my practice.

While there are some alternatives that have been proven effective, (acupuncture, chrondroitin, and biofeedback) others are less so. It is important to know what patients are accessing, using and why.

This is not meant to be an exhaustive offering of the alternatives, but it can certainly serve as a start.

CAM Journals

- Alternative Therapies in Health and Medicine

- Integrative Medicine

- Journal of Alternative and Complementary Medicine

- Scientific Review of Alternative Medicine

- Complementary Therapies in Medicine

- Focus on Alternative and Complementary Therapies

Herbal Medicine

- NIH Office of Dietary Supplements
  http://odp.od.nih.gov/ods/databases/ibids.html

- American Botanical Council, Austin, TX
  www.herbalgram.org

- Dukes Phytochemical & Ethnobotanical Databases www.ars-grin.gov/duke/index/html

- USDA Nutrient Laboratory
  www.nal.usda.gov/fnic/foodcomp/

Websites

(http :....)

- Medline

- Yahoo

- cpmcnet.columbia.edu/dept/Rosenthal

- healthy.net

- dietary-supplements.info.nih.gov

- altmed.od.nih.gov

Stay Informed

- MEDICAL QUACKERY

  — QuackWatch - www.quackwatch.com

  — National Council Against Health Fraud - www.ncahf.org

  — Museum of Questionable Medical Devices - www.mtn.org/quack

APPENDIX C

PRESCRIPTION CONTROLLED SUBSTANCES POLICY

In order to provide better care for our patients, we utilize the following policy for prescription medications. Please read the policy and sign the original, which will then be placed in our files.

Non-Clinic Prescriptions:

Patients who come for pain management frequently must take medicines for a variety of ailments, such as high blood pressure, diabetes, heart disease, etc. You will need to fill these prescriptions through your primary care physician. If you do not have a primary care physician, we will be happy to give you the names of at least three primary care physicians or you can refer to your provider directory.

Prescriptions from Our Clinic:

Non-narcotics such as non-steroidal anti-inflammatory agents (Motrin), neuropathic pain medicine (Neurontin) etc., are normally written by your primary care physician. If your doctor prescribes such medication from the clinic, the prescriptions are normally written with enough refills to cover you until your next scheduled visit. If you are unable to attend your appointment, we can authorize enough medicine to last until the next visit. We can only do this one time. Refills will only be provided from ___ AM to ____ PM, Monday through Thursday by calling _____, extension ___.

Narcotics such as Percocet, Lortab and Vicodin are federally controlled substances. You may be given prescriptions for such medications, or your pain doctor may not choose them for you. No refills will be given without a patient being seen in clinic. Lost, misplaced prescriptions or not-due prescriptions will not be refilled prior to the regularly scheduled visit under any circumstances. We will not issue prescriptions for controlled substances if you receive them from any other physician. Your signature below denotes your understanding and agreement to these stipulations

_____   _____
Patient's Name   Signature

_____   _____
Physician   Date

_____
Nurse

APPENDIX D

COMMON HEADACHE TRIGGER FOODS

Suspected headache triggers that may be found in food or beverages include: Tenderizers such as MSG (mono-sodium glutamate), hydrolyzed fat (or hydrolyzed protein), Tyramine, Nitrate and Nitrite compounds. Nutrasweet and Equal contain aspartame, and both have been associated with headache in susceptible individuals.

Alcohol, red wine and beer are drinks most commonly mentioned by patients to be headache triggers. Caffeine may help constrict blood vessels during a migraine attack; it is used in combination products to increase pain relief (e.g., Excedrin Migraine is a combination of aspirin, acetaminophen, and caffeine); habitual consumption of too much caffeine, however, can make headaches worse.

It is important to read labels carefully and ask questions. Content may vary among brand names available in the market because of preparation, processing or storage. It is best to eat freshly prepared foods to avoid the risk of eating foods that may have been aged, fermented, pickled or marinated.

It is best not to exclude all foods from your diet, but be aware of/or journal what you have eaten. Note when you have an increase in headache pain, or have onset of headache following any ingestion of foods that may be suspected triggers. Note if a pattern occurs.

Dietary Triggers	Foods Substitutes
Chocolate	Decaffeinated chocolate
Nuts	
Peanuts, peanut butter, sunflower seeds	
Sesame seeds, pumpkin seeds	
Raisins	
Sauerkraut	
Yeast products	
Sourdough bread	
Homemade bread	Commercial breads
Bananas, citrus fruit	Reduce to 1/2 serving or None
Alcoholic beverages	None or clear liquors
Red wine, beer, ale	Such as Vodka, Gin
Dark liquors	Chardonnay, White Zinfandels
Onion	
Beans, pinto, lima, navy, garbanzo	
Pizza	
Avocado	
Processed Meats	Fresh Meats
Hotdogs, pepperoni,	
Sausages, bacon, ham	
Bologna, salami, pickled meats, dried herring, chicken livers	
Picked/Fermented food	

Yogurt, buttermilk   Yogurt in 1/2 cup portions
Sour cream, soy sauces
Nutrasweet, Equal (aspartame)
Canned figs
Aged Cheese   Cottage cheese, cream
   Cheddar, Gruyere, ripened cheese   cheese, American cheese
   Stilton, Blue, Roquefort, Romano,   Velveeta, or synthetic cheese
   Provolone,

Caffeine

How much caffeine is too much?

Some patients are sensitive to the small amount of caffeine in one small 5 oz cup of brewed coffee (110 mg). Many who complain of headaches on weekends, take less caffeine on weekends than during the week or they get up later, thus drinking their coffee later in the morning. Headaches that occur under this circumstance could be due to caffeine withdrawal and are more likely to occur in people who are accustomed to drinking more than 300 mg of caffeine per day.

PRODUCT	CAFFEINE CONTENT
Cocoa and chocolate	
Chocolate candy bar	25 mg
Cocoa beverage (6 oz)	10
Coffee	
Decaffeinated (5 oz)	2
Drop (5 oz)	146
Instant, regular (5 oz)	53
Percolated (5 oz)	110
Over-the-Counter Medication	
Anacin®	32
Extra-Strength Excedrin®	65
Excedrin Migraine®	65
No-Doz®	100–200
Vanquish®	33
Vivarin®	200
Soft Drinks (12oz)	
7-Up®	0
Coke®	34
Pepsi®	34
Dr. Pepper®	38
Tea (5oz)	22–46

GLOSSARY

Acute Pain - Normal predicted physiological response to adverse chemical, thermal, mechanical stimulus and is associated with trauma, surgery and acute illness. It is generally time limited and serves to protect the organism from harm.

Addiction - A neurobehavioral syndrome with genetic and environmental influences that results in psychological dependence on the use of substances for their psychic effects and is characterized by compulsive use despite harm. Addiction may also be referred to by terms such as "drug dependence" and "psychological dependence." Physical dependence and tolerance are normal physiological consequences of extended opioid therapy for pain and should not be considered addictions.

AEDs - Anti-epileptic drugs; used as adjuvants in neuralgic and/or neuropathic pain.

Agonist - Agent, such as an opioid, that binds with a corresponding receptor in a stereo-specific fashion.

Allodynia - Pain triggered by non-painful tactile stimulation of the skin.

Analgesic Overuse - Regular intake of barbiturates or sedatives (more than four times a week); narcotics or ergotamine tartrate (more than twice a week); over-the-counter analgesics, resulting in rebound headache.

Analgesic Tolerance - The need to increase the dose of an opioid to achieve the same analgesic level. Analgesic tolerance may or may not be evident during opioid treatment and does not equate with addiction.

Antagonist - Competes with agent, such as an opioid, for the receptor site.

C.A.R.F. - Commission for the Accreditation of Rehab Facilities. A not-for-profit organization which promotes accreditation programs in the medical-vocational rehabilitation fields.

Chronic Pain - Pain state that persists beyond time of normal tissue healing. It may be associated with a long-term incurable or intractable medical condition or disease. Frequently there may not be a clearly identifiable cause.

Epidural Space - The space outside the dura mater (outer membrane around the spinal cord).

Equianalgesic - The dose of a replacement drug affording the same analgesic efficacy as an initial and/or substitute drug.

First Order Pain - Pain that lasts as long as the original painful stimulus persists.

Histamine - A biologically active substance produced in many cells of the body; histamine causes vasodilation, increased permeability of blood vessels and bronchial constriction.

Hyperalgesia - The maintenance of pain signal/impulse once the stimuli has been terminated.

Hyperesthesia - Increased sensitivity of skin to touch and light pressure.

Hyperhidrosis - Sweating.

Hyperpathia - A painful syndrome with increased reaction to painful stimulus, especially repetitive; concomitant with increased threshold.

Incidence - The rate of onset of new cases of a disease in a defined population over a given period of time, is usually expressed as the number of new cases per 1000 person-years of follow-up.

Intractable Pain - Pain of moderate to severe intensity that persists despite aggressive use of conventional systemic opioids and adjuvant drugs.

J.C.A.H.O. - Joint Commission for the Accreditation of Health Organizations.

Migraine - Headache with duration of 4 to 72 hours accompanied without aura by:
2 of the following
- unilateral
- throbbing
- moderate to severe pain
- exacerbated by movement
1 of the following
- nausea and vomiting
- photophobia and sonophobia

Modulation - Amplification or suppression of the nociceptive signal.

Nociception - The process of detection and signaling the presence of a noxious stimulus.

Nociceptors - Nerve endings of small thinly myelinated or unmyelinated sensory fibers which transmit painful stimuli.

Neuropathic Pain - Pain that is initiated or caused by a primary lesion or dysfunction in the nervous system.

Opioid - Any of a group of synthetic drugs with a chemical structure similar to opium which is the natural agent; neurochemical agent which binds to receptors to produce analgesia.

Pain - An unpleasant sensory and emotional experience associated with actual or potential tissue damage or described in terms of such damage.

Pain Threshold - The point at which a nociception is recognized or perceived as pain.

Pain Tolerance - The period of pain endurance before initiating a response; varies between individuals.

Paroxysmal Hemicrania - Severe, unilateral headache that is responsive to indomethacin; stabbing pain with autonomic features.

Patient Controlled Analgesia (PCA) - A method for administration of an analgesic affording the patient the ability to self-administer pre-programmed doses of analgesics; placement is usually parenteral but may also be epidural; doses may be administered over a basal or continuous infusion.

Peripheral Neuropathy - Pain resulting from an insult to the peripheral nerves and can be secondary to a variety of etiologies, including metabolic disorders, infections or post-infectious and disorders that are toxin or drug induced, immune mediated, hereditary, paraneoplastic or cryptogenic.

Physical Dependence - A physiologic state of neuro-adaptation which is characterized by the emergence of a withdrawal syndrome if drug use is stopped or decreased abruptly, or if an antagonist is administered. Physical dependence is an expected result of opioid use. Physical dependence, by itself, does not equate with addiction.

Post-Herpetic Neuralgia - A chronic painful condition that sometimes results following a herpes zoster infection. Pain is described as severe, lancinating, stabbing, shooting or steady and burning.

Prostaglandins - Pain producing biological substances in the peripheral tissues which sensitize nociceptors; end products of the arachodonic acid cascade.

Pseudoaddiction - Pattern of drug-seeking behavior of pain patients who are receiving inadequate pain management that can be mistaken for addiction.

Pseudotolerance - The need to increase dosage that is not due to true physiologic tolerance but is due to factors other than tolerance. This phenomenon may occur as a result of either physiological or behavioral factors.

Rebound Headache - Diffuse, bilateral headache every day or nearly every day, aggravated by mild physical or mental exertion. Waking with early morning headache; restlessness, nausea, forgetfulness, asthenia, and depression. Medication withdrawal symptoms when ergotamine, a barbiturate or codeine is involved. Tolerance to acute/abortive migraine medication. No response to preventive migraine medication.

Rostral Circulation - Circulation of CSF through the brain and spinal cord. Typically takes 8 hours for a full circuit.

RSDS - (Reflex Sympathetic Dystrophy Syndrome) CRPS (Complex Regional Pain Syndrome) - Prototype for a variety of sympathetically maintained pain conditions. Continuous pain, usually of a limb; burning in character and disuse consequent to an injury or noxious stimulus. This syndrome presents with variable sensory, motor, autonomic and trophic changes.

Subarachnoid Space - The space between the arachnoid (middle layer surrounding the spinal cord) and the pia mater (inner layer).

Substance Abuse - The use of any substance(s) for non-therapeutic purposes or use of medication for purposes other than those for which it is prescribed.

Subterfuge - Obtaining controlled substances through deception, also called "doctor shopping."

Suffering - The reaction of the organism to the experience of pain.

Sympathetically Maintained Pain - Pain maintained by sympathetic efferent innervation or by circulating catecholamines.

Thermogram - Diagnostic test which measures heat emission from the body surface using a special infrared video camera.

Tolerance - A physiologic state resulting from regular use of a drug in which an increased dosage is needed to produce the same effect, or a reduced effect is observed with a constant dose.

Visceral Pain - Pain from organs or smooth muscles.

BIBLIOGRAPHY

Abbott, P., Short, E., Dodson, S., Garcia, C., Perkins, J. & Wyant, S. (2002). Improving your cultural awareness with cultural cues. *The Nurse Practitioner, 27*(2), 44–51.

Abram, S. (2000). Systemic opioid therapy for non-cancer pain. In S. Abram & J. Haddox, *The pain clinic manual* (2nd ed., pp. 135–138). Philadelphia: Lippincott, Williams, & Wilkins.

Abram, S. & Haddox, J. (2000). Pain glossary. In S. Abram & J. Haddox, *The pain clinic manual* (2nd ed., p. 467). Philadelphia: Lippincott, Williams, & Wilkins.

Agency for Health Care Policy and Research. (1994). Clinical practice guideline no. 9: Management of cancer pain. (AHCPR Publication No. 94-0592). Rockville, MD: U.S. Department of Health and Human Services.

Agency for Health Care Policy and Research. (1992). Clinical practice guideline: Acute pain management: Operative or medical procedures and trauma. (AHCPR Publication No. 92-0032). Rockville, MD: U.S. Department of Health and Human Services.

Agency for Health Care Policy and Research. (1992). Quick reference guide for clinicians number 1. Acute pain management in adults: Operative procedures. (AHCPR Publication No. 92-0019). Rockville, MD: U.S. Department of Health and Human Services.

Ahmad, M., Ackerman, W., Munir, M. & Saleem, M. (2001). NMDA receptor antagonists recent advances in chronic pain. *The Pain Clinic, 3*(2), 25–31.

Ahmedzai, S. (1997). New approaches to pain control in patients with cancer. *European Journal of Cancer, 33*(suppl 6), S8–S14.

Akman, I., Ozek, E., Bilgen, H., Ozdogan, T. & Cebeci, D. (2002). Sweet solutions and pacifiers for pain relief in newborns. *The Journal of Pain, 3*(3), 199–202.

Ali, Z., Meyer, R. & Belzberg, A. (2002). Neuropathic pain after C-7 spinal nerve transection in man. *Pain, 96,* 41–47.

American Academy of Pain Management. (2002). What is pain management? [Available online: http://www.aapainmanage.org.aapm/whatis.html]. Accessed September 2002.

American Academy of Pain Medicine, American Pain Society & American Society of Addiction Medicine. (2001). Definitions related to the use of opioids for the treatment of pain. Consensus Document: Author.

American Academy of Pain Medicine, The American Academy of Addiction Medicine and the American Pain Society. (1997). The use of opioids for the treatment of chronic pain: A consensus statement from the American Academy of Pain Medicine and the American Pain Society. *Clinical Journal of Pain, 13,* 6–8.

American Pain Foundation. (1999). *Fact sheet on pain.* [Available online: http://www.painfoundation.org/fact.htm]. Accessed November 2002.

American Pain Society. (1999). *Principles of analgesic use in the treatment of acute pain and cancer pain* (4th ed.). Glenview, IL: Author.

American Pain Society. (2002). *Chronic pain in America: Roadblocks to relief.* Summary of findings. [Available online: http://www.ampainsoc.org]. Accessed December 1, 2002.

American Society Consultant Pharmacists. (May 18, 1998). Obstacles to pain management. Symposia highlights.

American Society of Addiction Medicine. (1997). *Definitions related to the use of opioids in pain treatment.* [Available online: http://www.asam.org]. Accessed December 1, 2002.

Analgesic tolerance to opioids. (2001). *Pain Clinical Updates, 9*(5), 2.

Anderson, A. (2001). Cervicogenic processes: Results of injury to the cervical spine. *The Pain Practitioner, 11*(2), 9–11.

Andersson, G. (1991). The epidemiology of spinal disorders. In *The adult spine: Principles and practice* (pp. 107–146). New York: Raven Press, Ltd.

Aoki, K. (2001). Mechanisms of action of BTX-A. In: *Botulinum toxin type A for the prophylactic management of headache.* ACHS project 1509. Rancho Mirage, CA: Annenburg Center for Health Sciences, pp. 2–3.

Aronoff, G & Gallagher, R. (1999). Pharmacological management of chronic pain. In G. Aronoff (Ed.), *The evaluation and treatment of chronic pain* (3rd ed., pp. 433–453). Philadelphia: Lippincott, Williams, & Wilkins.

Arthritis Foundation. (1999). *Arthritis fact sheet.* [Available online: http://www.arthritis.org]. Accessed December 1, 2002.

Arthritis Foundation. (1998). *Rheumatoid arthritis* [brochure]. [Available online: http://www.arthritis.org/resource/brochures/pdf/Rheumatoid_Arthritis.pdf]. Accessed December 1, 2002.

Atchison, N., Osgood, P., Carr, D. & Szfelbein, S. (1991). Pain during burn dressing change in children: Relationship to burn area, depth and analgesic regimens. *Pain, 47,* 41–45.

Atlas, S. & Deyo, R. (2001). Evaluating and managing low back pain in the primary care setting. *Journal of General Internal Medicine, 16,* 120–131.

Aurora, S. (2000). Myths and misconceptions about migraine. In National CME/CE audio-confeence series, *Today's approach to migraine management.* Pragmaton: IL.

Barkin, R. (2002). Applying principles of science to the selection of a COX-2 non-steroidal anti-inflammatory drug. *The Pain Clinic, 4*(1), 41–47.

Barkwell, D. (1991). Ascribed meaning: A critical factor in coping and pain attenuation in patients with cancer-related pain. *Journal of Palliative Care, 7*(3), 5–14.

Barnett, E. (1999). Case marks big shift in pain policy. In *The Oregonian.* [Available online: http://www.oregonlive.com/news/99/09/st90201/html]. Accessed September 2, 1999.

Baumgartner, U., Magere, W., Klein, T., Hopf, H. & Treede, R. (2002). Neurogenic hyperalgesia versus painful hypoalgesia: Two distinct mechanisms of neuropathic pain. *Pain, 96,* 141–151.

Berg J., Dischler J., Wagner D., Raia, J. & Palmer-Shevlin, N. (1993). Medication compliance: A healthcare problem. *Annals of Pharmacotherapy, 27* (9 suppl), S1–S16.

Bernabei, R., Gambassi, G., Lapane, K., Landi, F., Gatsonsis, C. & Dunlop, R. (1998). Management of pain in elderly patients with cancer. SAGE study group. Systematic assessment of geriatric drug use via epidemiology. *JAMA, 279,* 1877–1882.

Beydoun, A. (1999). *New pharmacologic options for the treatment of neuropathic pain: A practical treatment guide.* New York: Dannemiller Educational Foundation and Intramed Educational Group.

Binder, W., Brin, M., Blitzer, A., Schoenrock, L. & Pogoda, J. (1999) Botulinum toxin type A (Botox) for treatment of migraine headaches: An open label study. *Otolaryngology-Head and Neck Surgery, 123*(6), 669–676.

Birse T. & Landers J. (1998). Prevalence of chronic pain. *Canadian Journal of Public Health, 8,* 129–131.

Blatman, H. (2002). Effective treatment of fibromyalgia and myofascial pain syndrome: A clinician's perspective. *American Journal of Pain Management, 12*(2), 67–68.

Blesch, K., Paice, J., Wickham, R., Harte, N., Schors, D., Purl, S. et al. (1991). Correlates of fatigue in people with breast or lung cancer. *Oncology Nursing Forum, 18*(1), 81–87.

Bonica, J. (1990). General considerations of chronic pain. In *The management of pain* (2nd ed., pp. 180–195). Philadelphia: Lea & Febiger.

Bonica, J. (1982). Postoperative pain: Parts 1 and 2. *Contemporary Surgery, 20,* Jan. and Feb.

Borodic, G. & Acquardo, M. (2002). The use of botulinum toxin for the treatment of chronic facial pain. *The Journal of Pain, 3*(1), 21–27.

Bostrom, M. (1996). Summary of the Mayday Fund Survey: Public attitudes about pain and analgesics. *Journal of Pain Symptom Management, 13,* 166–168.

Bowman, J. (1991). The meaning of chronic low back pain. *Journal of Occupational Health Nursing, 39*(8), 381–384.

Bowsher, D. (2001). Stroke and central post-stroke pain in an elderly population. *The Journal of Pain, 2*(5), 258–261.

Bragdon, E., Light, K., Costello, N., Sigurdsson, A., Bunting, S., Bhalang, K. et al. (2002). Group differences in pain modulation: Pain-free women compared to pain-free men and to women with TMD. *Pain, 96*(3), 227–237.

Brescia, F., Portenoy, R., Ryan, M., Krasnoff, L., Gray, G. (1992). Pain, opioid use, and survival in hospitalized patients with advanced cancer. *Journal of Clinical Oncology, 10*(1), 149–155.

Breuhl, S., Harden, R., Bradley, S., Galer, B., Salz, S., Backonja, M. & Stanton-Hicks, M. (2002). Complex regional pain syndrome: Are there distinct subtypes and sequential stages of the syndrome. *Pain, 95*(1-2), 119–124.

Brietbart, W., Rosenfeld, B., Passik, S., McDonald, M., Thaler, H. & Portnoy, R. (1996). The under-treatment of pain in ambulatory AIDS patients. *Pain, 65,* 243–249.

Brooten, D. & Naylor, M. (1995). Nurses' effect on changing patient outcomes. IMAGE: *Journal of Nursing Scholarship, 27*(2), 95–99.

Bruera, E., Schoeller, T. & Montejo, G. (1992). Organic hallucinosis in patients receiving high doses of opiates for cancer pain. *Pain, 48,* 397–399.

Burke, J. (2001). Psycho-neuroimmunology. *The Pain Practitioner, 11*(1), 5–7.

Cady, R. & Farmer-Cady, K. (2000). Migraine: Changing perspectives on pathophysiology & treatment. *Consultant, 40*(11) (Supplement), S13–S19.

Cahill, C. (1991). Managing postoperative pain. *Nursing 91, 21*(12), 42–45.

Cahill, C. & Bishop, J. (1992). A theoretical model for management of pain during the burn dressing change. *Abstract: American Pain Society 11th Scientific Meeting.* Skokie, IL: American Pain Society.

Cahill, C. & Burkett, P. (1999). *Beck depression inventory as a measure of treatment outcome.* Unpublished research.

Cahill, C. (1991). The effects of an educational intervention on the knowledge of nursing students in pain management principles. *Abstracts: American Pain Society Meeting.* Skokie, IL: American Pain Society.

Calkins, E. (1991). Arthritis in the elderly. *Bulletin on the Rheumatic Diseases, 40*(3), 1–9.

Cameron, T. & Elliott, S. (2002). Spinal cord stimulation. *Practical Pain Management, 2*(3), 13–15.

Cancer pain. (1990). In J. Bonica (Ed.), *The management of pain* (2nd ed., pp. 400–600). Philadelphia: Lea & Febiger.

Carr, D. (Ed.-in-chief). (2001). Analgesic tolerance to opioids. *Pain Clinical Updates, 9*(5), 1–4. Seattle: International Association for the Study of Pain.

Cassell, E. (1989). The relationship between pain and suffering. In C. Hill & W. Fields (Eds.), *Advances in Pain Research and Therapy* (Vol II, pp. 61–70). New York: Raven Press.

Cepeda, M., Africano, J., Manrique, A., Fragoso, W. & Carr, D. (2002). The combination of low-dose naloxone and morphine does not decrease opioid requirements in postoperative period. *Pain, 96,* 73–79.

Chapman, C. & Hill, H. (1989). Prolonged morphine self-administration and addiction liability: Evaluation of two theories in a bone marrow transplant unit. *Cancer, 63,* 1636–1644.

Cheville, A., Chen, A., Oster, G., McGarry, L. & Narcesian, E. (2001). A randomized trial of controlled-release oxycodone during inpatient rehabilitation following unilateral total knee arthroplasty. *Journal of Bone & Joint Surgery, 83-4* (4), 572–576.

Childers, K. (1999). *Use of botulnium toxin type A in pain management: A clinician's guide.* Liberty, MO: Academic Informations Systems.

Chibnall, J. & Tait, R. (2001). Pain assessment in cognitively impaired and unimpaired older adults: A comparison of four scales. *Pain, 92,* 173–186.

Christensen, D. (1998). *Docs prescribing pain medication deserve protection.* [Available online: http://www.medtrib.com/cgi-bin/medtrib/articles/record/record-569]. Accessed June 2000.

Cicune, D. & Just, N. (2001). Pain expectancy & work disability in patients with acute & chronic pain: A test of the fear-avoidance hypothesis. *The Journal of Pain, 2*(3), 181–194.

Clavier, N., Lombard, M. & Besson, J. (1992). Benzodiazepines and pain: Effects of midazolam on the activities of nociceptive non-specific dorsal horn neurons in the rat spinal cord. *Pain, 48,* 61–71.

Cleeland, C., Gonin, R., Hatfield, A., Edmonson, J., Blum, R., Stewart, J. & Pandya, K. (1994). Pain and its treatment in outpatients with metastatic cancer. *New England Journal of Medicine, 330*(9), 592–596.

Cleeland, C., Gonin, R., Baez, L., Loehrer, P., Pandya, K. Lipton, R., Stewart, W., Reed, M. & Diamond, S. (1997). Pain and treatment of pain in minority patients with cancer: The Eastern Cooperative Oncology Group Minority Outpatient Pain Study. *Annals of Internal Medicine, 127,* 813–816.

Cole, B. (2002). Mastering medications. *Practical Pain Management,* 27–31.

Collins, J. (1986). Prevalence of selected chronic conditions, United States 1979–1981. *Vital Heath Statistics, 10* (155), 31–66.

Committee on Opportunities in Drug Abuse Research. (1996). *Pathways of addiction: Opportunities in drug abuse research* (pp. 250–259). Washington: National Academy Press.

Cooper, J., Czechowicz, D., Peterson, R. & Molinari, S. (1992). Prescription drug diversion control and medical practice. *JAMA, 268,* 1306–1310.

Cummings, R., Kelsey, J. & Nevitt, M. (1990). Methodologic issues in the study of frequent and recurrent health problems. *Annals Epidemology, 1,* 49–56.

Curtis, C. (1997). *Partners Against Pain.* An audio-tape on pain management. Norwalk: Purdue Pharma.

Dahlof, C., Putnam, G., Mansbach, H., Scott, A. & O'Quinn, M. (2001). Sumatriptan tablets are effective for migraine attacks with onset any time: morning, day and night. *Abstract: International Headache Congress.* New York.

Dalessio, D. & Pouch, J. (1992). Trigeminal neuralgia: Neuroelectric measures of therapeutic efficacy. *National Headache Foundation Newsletter, 82,* 13.

Davis, G., Hiemenz, M. & White, T. (2002). Barriers to managing chronic pain of older adults with arthritis. *Image: Journal of Nursing Scholarship, 34*(2), 121–126.

Davis, K., Treede, R., Raja, S., Meyer, R. & Campbell, J. (1991). Topical application of clonidine relieves hyperalgesia in patients with sympathetically maintained pain. *Pain, 47,* 309–317.

DeConno, F., Caraceni, A., Martini, C., Spoldi, E., Salvetti, M. & Ventafridda, V. (1991). Hyperalgesia and myoclonus with intrathecal infusion of high-dose morphine. *Pain, 47,* 337–339.

Deering, C. & Jennings-Cody, D. (2002). Communicating with children and adolescents. *AJN, 102*(3), 34–42.

Devon, M. (2001). Obituary of Patrick Wall. *IASP Newsletter, 4,* 10–12.

Devor, M. (1999). Neurobiology of normal and pathophysiological pain. In G. Aronoff (Ed.), *The evaluation and treatment of chronic pain* (3rd ed., pp. 11–25). Philadelphia: Lippincott, Williams, & Wilkins.

Deyo, R. & Weinstein, J. (2001). Low back pain. *New England Journal of Medicine, 344,* 363–370.

Diamond, S. (2000). Migraine in women: Combating attacks during menses, pregnancy & lactation. *Consultant, 40*(4), (Supplement), S20–S24.

Diamond, S. & Winzel, R. (2001). Herbal headache remedies: What to tell your patient. *Consultant, 41,* 1618–1620.

Diamond, S. & Mallszewski, M. (1992). Headaches & posttraumatic stress disorder. *National Foundation Newsletter, 82,* 8–9.

Dickerson, E. (2001). Brief report: Global conversion models for methadone. *The Pain Clinic, 3*(4), 37–39.

Dodick, D. & Campbell, J. (2001). Cluster headache: Diagnosis, management, and treatment. In S. Silberstein, R. Lipton & D. Dalessio (Eds.), *Wolf's Headache and Other Head Pain* (7th ed., pp. 283–310). New York: Oxford Press.

Donaldson, C., Sella, G. & Mueller, H. (2001). The neural plasticity model of fibromyalgia. *Practical Pain Management,* 25–29.

DuPen, S. & Williams, A. (1995). Spinal and peripheral drug-delivery systems. *Pain Digest, 5,* 307–317.

Edmunds, J. (1995). Advances in migraine therapy: Focus on oral sumatriptan. *Neurology, 45*(6), (Supplement 7), S3–S9.

Edvinsson, L. (2001). Sensory nerves in man and their role in primary headaches. *Cephalia, 21,* 761–764.

Edwards, L., Pearce, S., Turner-Stokes, L. & Jones, A. (1992). The pain beliefs questionnaire: An investigation of beliefs in the causes and sonsequences of pain. *Pain, 92,* 267–272.

Egan, K., Ready, L., Nessly, M. & Greer, B. (1992). Self-administered midazolam for post-operative anxiety: A double blinded study. *Pain, 49,* 3–8.

Eidelberg, D., Sotrel, A., Vogel, H., Walker, P., Kleefield, J. & Crumpacker, C. (1986). Progressive polyradiculopathy in acquired immune deficiency syndrome. *Neurology, 36*(7), 912–916.

Ellison, N., Finley, R. & Paice, J. (Eds). (2002). Management of pain in patients with AIDS and HIV. *The Dannemiller Pain Report, 1*(4), 8–10.

Ellison, N., Lipman, A., Patt, R. & Portnoy, R. (1998). Opioid analgesia: An essential tool in chronic pain. *Patient Care,* 1–11.

Fanurik, D., Zeltzer, L., Roberts, M. & Blount, R. (1993). The relationship between children's coping styles and psychological interventions for cold pressor pain. *Pain, 53,* 213–222.

Ferrell, B., McCaffery, M. & Ropchan, R. (1992). Pain management as a clinical challenge for nursing administration. *Nursing Outlook, 40,* 263–268.

Ferrell, B., Taylor, E., Sattler, G., Fowler, M. & Cheyney, B. (1993). Searching for the Meaning of Pain. *Cancer Practice, 1*(3), 185–194.

Field, M. & Cassel, C. (Eds.). (1997). *Approaching death: Improving care at the end of life* (pp. 122–153). Washington: National Academy Press.

Fields, H. (Ed.). (1991). Low Back Pain. In *Core Curriculum on Professional Education in Pain.* Seattle: IASP, 61.

Fishbain, D. (1999). The association of chronic pain and suicide. *Seminars in Clinical Neuropsychiatry, 4,* 221–227.

Fogelholm, R., Robinson, L. & Murros, K. (1992). Tizanidine in chronic tension-type headaches: A placebo controlled double-blind cross-over study. *Headache, 32*(10), 509–513.

Follett, K., Hitchon, P., Piper, J., Kumar, V., Clamon, G. & Jones, M. (1992). Response of intractable pain to continuous intrathecal morphine: A retrospective study. *Pain, 49,* 21–25.

Foley, K. (1985). Treatment of cancer pain. *The New England Journal of Medicine, 313,* 84–95.

Fox, A., Sgarfman, M., Jones, J. & Fitzgerald, M. (2002). Migraine management in primary care: Focus on the triptans. *Clinician News Supplement,* 4–11.

Fox, C. (2002). Chronic opioid therapy: Another reappraisal. *APS Bulletin, 12*(1), 1, 8–10.

Freund, B. & Schwartz, M. (2000). Treatment of whiplash associated with neck pain with botulinum toxin-A: A pilot study. *The Journal of Rheumatology, 27*(2), 481–484.

Frich L. & Borgbjerg, F. (2000). Pain and pain treatment in AIDS patients: A longitudinal study. *Journal of Pain and Symptom Management, 18,* 253–262.

Frost, H., Lamb, S., Klaber Moffett, J., Fairbank, J. & Moser, J. (1998). A fitness programme for patients with chronic low back pain: 2 year follow-up of a randomized controlled trial. *Pain, 75,* 273–279.

Gamsa, A. & Vikis-Friebergs, V. (1991). Psychological events are both risk factors in, and consequences of, chronic pain. *Pain, 44,* 271–277.

Garfin, J. & Garfin, S. (2002). Low back pain: A quick guide to exercise as acute therapy. *Consultant, 4*(1), 350–353.

Gatchal, R., Polatin, P. & Mayer, T. (1995). The dominant role of psychosocial risk factors in the development of chronic low back pain disability. *Spine, 20*(24), 2702–2709.

Geisser, M., Roth, R. & Roberson, M. (1997). Assessing depression among persons with chronic pain using the center for epidemiological studies depression scale & the Beck depression inventory: A comparative analysis. *The Clinical Journal of Pain, 13,* 163–170.

Glare, P. & Walsh, T. (1991). Clinical pharmacokinetics of morphine. *The Drug Monitor, 13,* 1–23.

Glaser, J., Baltz, M., Neitart, P. & Bursen, C. (2001). Electrical muscle stimulation as an adjunct to exercise therapy in the treatment of non-acute low back pain: A randomized trial. *The Journal of Pain, 2*(5), 295–300.

Goldenberg, D. (1999). Controversies in fibromyalgia and myofascial pain syndromes. In G. Aronoff (Ed.), *The evaluation and treatment of chronic pain* (3rd ed., pp. 217–224). Philadelphia: Lippincott, Williams, & Wilkins.

Goldstein, L. (2001). TMJ repositioning. *Practical Pain Management, 2*(1), 20–21.

Goldstein, L. & Dabfm, D. (2002). Acupuncture for pain relief. *Practical Pain Management, 2*(3), 24–26.

Goulain, W., Kennedy, D. & Small, R. (2000). Methadone: History & use in analgesia. *APS Bulletin, 10*(5), 1, 8–9.

Green, J., Fralicker, D., Clewell, W., Horowitz, E., Lucey, T., Yannacone, V. & Haber, C. (2000). Infrared photon stimulation: A new form of chronic pain therapy. *American Journal of Pain Management, 10,* 113–120.

Grond, S., Zech, D. & Deifenbach, C. (1996). Assessment of cancer pain: A prospective evaluation in 2266 cancer pain patients referred to a pain service. *Pain, 64,* 107–114.

Harden, R. (2002). Chronic opioid therapy: Another reappraisal. In C. Fox (Ed.), *American Pain Society Bulletin, 12*(1), 8–12.

Hein, H. & Oci, T. (1993). Comparison of prostate cancer patients with and without pain, *Pain, 53,* 159–162.

Hendricks, M. (1999). Just give me something for the pain. *Johns Hopkins Magazine.* [Available online: http://www.jhu.edu/~jhu-mag/0699web/pain.html]. Accessed September 16, 2002.

Hicks, M. (1999). Complex Regional Pain Syndrome: A New Name for Reflex Sympathetic Dystrophy. In G. Aronoff (Ed.), *The evaluation and treatment of chronic pain* (3rd ed., pp. 191–199). Philadelphia: Lippincott, Williams, & Wilkins.

Hollister, L. (1989). Drugs of abuse. In B. Katsung (Ed.), *Basic and Clinical Pharmacology* (pp. 383–394). Norwalk, CT: Appelton & Lange.

Holmquist, G. (1999). The appropriate use of opioids in the management of chronic pain: A pharmacist's perspective. *Pharmacy Times, 29,* 3–11.

Holritz, K., Racolin, A. & Bookbinder, M. (1995). Nursing's changing role in cancer pain management. *Pain Digest, 5*(6), 318–324.

Holroyd, K., France, J., Nash, J. & Hursey, K. (1993). Pain state as artifact in the psychological assessment of recurrent headache sufferers. *Pain, 53,* 229–235.

Holroyd, K., Penzien, D. & Lipchik, G. (2001). Behavioral management of headache. In S. Silberstein, R. Lipton & D. Dalessio (Eds.), *Wolf's Headache and Other Head Pain* (7th ed., pp. 562–598). New York: Oxford University Press.

Holzemer, W. (2002). HIV and AIDS: The symptom experience. *AJN, 102*(4), 48–52.

International Headache Society. (2001). *Classification and diagnostic criteria for headache disorders, cranial neuralgias, and facial pain.* [Available online: www.i-h-s.org]. Accessed June 2001.

Jacobson, S. (July 21, 2002) The other face of botox. Reported in *The Tampa Tribune* Newspaper. Tampa, Fl.

Janig, W. (1992). Can reflex sympathetic dystrophy be reduced to an alpha-adrenoreceptor disease? *APS Journal, 1*(1), 16–22.

Janisse, T. (Ed.) (1991). *Pain management of AIDS patients.* Boston: Kluwer.

Jensen, M., Ehde, D., Hoffman, A., Patterson, D., Czerniecki, J. & Robinson, L. (2002). Cognitions, coping and social environment predict adjustment to phantom limb pain. *Pain, 95*(1–2), 133–142.

Jensen, M., Karoly, P. & Brauer, S. (1986). The measurement of clinical pain intensity: a comparison of six methods. *Pain, 27,* 117–126.

Jensen, M. & Royal, M. (2001). Is oxycarbazepine an effective treatment for migraine: Two case reports. *American Journal of Pain Management, 112,* 60–62.

Jensen, M., Smith, D., Ehde, D. & Robinson, L. (2001). Pain site and the effects of amputation pain: Further clarification of the meaning of mild, moderate, and severe pain. *Pain, 91,* 317–322.

Jensen, M. & Royal, M. (2001). Transdermal fentanyl in the treatment of pain in cystic fibrosis. *American Journal of Pain Management, 11*(3), 96–99.

Jensen, R. (2001). Mechanisms of tension-type headaches. *Cephalgia, 21,* 786–789.

Jensen, T. (2001). Recent advances in pain research: Implications in chronic headache. *Cephalgia, 21,* 765–769.

Johnson, M., Ashton, C. & Thompson, J. (1991). An in-depth study of long-term users of transcutaneous electrical nerve stimulation (TENS). Implications for clinical use of TENS. *Pain, 44,* 221–229.

Johnson-Umezulike, J. (1999). A comparison of pain perception of elderly African-Americans and Caucasians. *Nursing Connections, 12*(2), 5–10.

Johnston, C., Stevens, B., Craig, K. & Grunau, R. (1993). Developmental changes in pain expression in premature, full-term, two- and four-month-old infants. *Pain, 52,* 201–208.

Joint Commission of the Accreditation of Health Organizations (JACHO). (1999a). *Pain management standards.* [Available online: http://www.jcaho.org]. Accessed September 16, 2002.

Joint Commission of the Accreditation of Health Organizations (JACHO). (1999b). *Comprehensive Accreditation Manual for Hospitals: The Official Handbook.* [Available online: http/www.jcaho.org/standard/pm__hap.html]. Accessed September 19, 1999.

Joranson, D. (1995). Intractable pain treatment laws and regulations. *American Pain Society Bulletin, 5*(1–3), 15–17.

Jost, T. (2000). Medicare and Medicaid financing of pain management. *The Journal of Pain, 1*(3), 183–194.

Kaiko, R. (1988). Age and morphine analgesia in cancer patients with postoperative pain. *Clinical Pharmacological Therapeutics, 28,* 823–826.

Kaniecki, R. (2000). The impact of migraine: How this disorder affects us all. *Consultant (Supplement), 40*(11), S25–S28.

Keefe, F., Affleck, G., Lefenvre, J., Underwood, L., Caldwell, D. & Drew, J. (2001). Living with rheumatoid arthritis: The role of daily spirituality and daily religious and spiritual coping. *The Journal of Pain, 2*(2), 101–110.

Keefe, F. & Dunsmore, J. (1992). Pain behavior. Concepts and controversies. *APS Journal, 1*(2), 92–100.

Kelly, J. & Small, R. (2001). A review of cox 2 inhibitors. *American Journal of Pain Management, 11*(3), 77–89.

Klein, D. & Klein, P. (1991). Intermittent interpleural injection of bupivacaine and methylprednisolone for analgesia in metastatic thoracic neoplasm. *Clinical Journal of Pain, 7,* 232–236.

Kondamuri, S. (2001). The value of the pain score. *The Pain Clinic, 3*(6), 37–40.

Kornick, C., Santiago, T., Palma, J., Khojainova, N., Palmavera, L., Payne, R. et al. (2001). A safe and effective method for converting cancer patients from intravenous to transdermal fentanyl. *Cancer, 92,* 3056–3061.

Kudzma, E. (1992). Drug response: All bodies are not created equal. *American Journal of Nursing, 92,* 48–50.

Kulich, R. & Baker, W. (1999). A guide for psychological testing and evaluation for chronic pain. In G. Aronoff (Ed.), *The evaluation and treatment of chronic pain* (3rd ed., pp. 301–312). Philadelphia: Lippincott, Williams, & Wilkins.

Kunecki, R. (2000). The impact of migraine: How this disorder affects us all. *Consultant, 40*(11), (Supplement), S25–S28.

Kung, F., Gibson, S. & Helme, R. (2000). A community-based program that provides free choice of intervention for older people with chronic pain. *The Journal of Pain, 1*(4), 293–308.

Lander, J. & Fowler-Kerry, S. (1993). TENS for children's procedural pain. *Pain, 53,* 209–216.

Lang, A. (2000). A pilot study of botullinum toxin type a (Botox), administered using a novel injection technique for the treatment of myofascial pain. *American Journal of Pain Management, 10*(31), 108–112.

Lanzi, C., Zambrino, C., Ferrari-Ginevra, O., Termine, C., D'Arrigo, S., Vercelli et al. (2001). Personality traits in childhood and adolescent headache. *Cephalgia, 21,* 53–60.

Laskin, D. (1992). Headache and the aching jaw. *National Headache Foundation Newsletter, 82,* 10–12.

Leahy, S. & Sigler-Price, K. (1994). Clinical management of pain in children with cancer. *Cancer Practice, 2*(2), 37–45.

Leibskind, J. (1991). Pain can kill. *Pain, 44,* 3–4.

Levy, M. (1994). Pharmacologic management of cancer pain. *New England Journal of Medicine, 335,* 1124–1132.

Ligham, D., Saberski, L., Levin, S. & Martin, J. (2001). Effectiveness of magnetism for the treatment of chronic benign low back pain. *The Pain Clinic,* 37–41.

Ling, M. & Anderson, C. (2002). Managing pediatric pain. *Practical Pain Management,* 9–14.

Lipman, A. & Jackson, K. (2000). *Use of opioids in chronic non-cancer pain.* Purdue, CT: Power Pak CE, 1–10.

Lipton, R., Diamond, S., Reed, M. & Stewart, W. (2000). The burden of migraine: Counseling insight from the American migraine studies. *Consultant, 40*(11), (Supplement), 58–512.

Lipton, R. & Silberstein, S. (2001). The role of headache-related disability in migraine management: Implications for headache treatment guidelines. *Neurology, 56*(supplement 1), S35–S42.

Lipton, R., Stewart, W., Reed M., Deamond, M. & Stewart, M. (2001). Migraine's impact today. Burden of illness, patterns of care. *Postgraduate Medicine, 109,* 38–45.

Lines, C., Vandormael, K. & Malbeq, W. (2001). A comparison of visual analogue scale and categorical ratings of headache pain in a randomized controlled clinical trial with migraine patients. *Pain, 93,* 185–190.

Lonsberg, R., Schnudt, A. & Broenman, N. (1992). The relationship between spouse solicitousness & pain behavior: Searching for more experimental evidence. *Pain, 51,* 75–79.

Lowry, K., Kittle, D., Gaines, R. & Tobias, J. (2001). Postoperative pain control using epidural catheters following short segment posterior spinal fusion. *American Journal of Pain Management, 11*(2), 54–59.

Magni, G., Marchetti, M., Moreschi, C., Merskey, H. & Luchini, S. (1993). Chronic musculoskeletal pain and depressive symptoms in the national health and nutrition examination I. Epidemiologic follow-up study. *Pain, 53,* 163–168.

Manchikanti, L. (2000). The value and safety of steroids in neural blockade, part II. *American Journal of Pain Mangement, 10*(3), 121–133.

Mann, S., Jacobsen, P. & Redd, W. (1992). Assessment of acute pediatric pain: Do child self-report, parent ratings and nurse ratings measure the same phenomenon? *Pain, 48,* 45–52.

Manniche, C., Lundberg, E., Christensen, I., Bentzen, L. & Hesselsoe, G. (1991). Intensive dynamic back exercises for chronic low back pain: a clinical trial. *Pain, 47,* 55–63.

Mantyh, P. (2002). A mechanism based understanding of cancer pain. *Pain, 96,* 1–2.

Marchettini, P., Lacerenza, M., Marangoni, C., Pellagat, G., Sotgiu, M. & Smirne, S. (1992). Lidocaine test in neuralgia. *Pain, 48,* 377–382.

Marcus, D. (2000). Treatment of nonmalignant chronic pain. *American Family Physician, 61*(5), 1331–1338.

Mathew, N. (2002). Efficacy and tolerability of Almotriptan for the long-term management of migraine. *The Pain Clinic, 4*(1), 26–32.

Mathew, N. (1992). Cluster headache. *Neurology, 42*(3), (Supplement 2), 22–31.

McCaffery, M. (1996). The scientific method: Clinical practice guidelines to facilitate better care of patients with chronic pain. *Continuing Care,* March, 18–20.

McQuay, H., Tramer, M., Nye, B., Carroll, D., Witten, P. & Moore, R. (1996). A systemic review of antidepressants in neuropathic pain. *Pain, 68*(2–3), 217–227.

Medical Economics Company. (2000). *Physicians desk reference* (54th ed.). Montvale: Author.

Melzack, R. (1997). The short-form McGill pain questionnaire. *Pain, 30,* 191–197.

Melzack, R. & Wall, P. (1965). Pain mechanisms: A new theory. *Science, 150,* 971–979.

Mercadante, S. (1993). Celiac plexus block versus analgesics in pancreatic cancer pain. *Pain, 52,* 187–192.

Mersky, H. (1986). International Association for the Study of Pain, classifications of chronic pain: Descriptions of chronic pain syndromes and definitions of pain terms. *Pain*, (Supplement 3), S1–225.

Mersky, H. & Bogduk, N. (Eds.) (1994). *Classification of chronic pain—descriptions of chronic pain syndromes and definitions of pain terms* (2nd ed., pp. 40–43). Seattle: IASP Press.

Meyler WJ, de Jongste MJ, Rolf CA. "Clinical evaluation of pain treatment with electro stimulation: a study on TENS in patients with different pain syndromes." *Clinical Journal of Pain.* 10(1):22-7, 1994.

Minarik, P. (1993). Incorporating imagery in clinical practice. *Clinical Nurse Specialist, 7*(5), 234–240.

Mueller, L. (2002). Menstrual migraine: How mini-prophylaxis can work for your patient. *Consultant, 42*(6), 709–713.

Model guidelines for the use of controlled substances for the treatment of pain. (1998). Policy Document of the Federation of State Medical Boards of the United States, Inc.

Namey, T. (November/December 1990). Diagnosis and treatment of nondiscogenic low back pain and sciatica: Part II. *Pain Management,* 328–333.

Neal, P. (July/Aug. 1999). CARF Revises its Pain Standards. *APS Bulletin,* 16.

Ng, B., Dimsdale, J., Rollnik, J. & Shapiro, H. (1996). The effect of ethnicity on prescriptions for patient-controlled analgesia for post-operative pain. *Pain, 66,* 9–12.

Nicholas, M., Wilson, P. & Goyen, J. (1992). Comparison of cognitive-behavioral group treatment and an alternative non-psychological treatment for chronic low back pain. *Pain, 49,* 339–347.

Oaklander, A., Cohen, S. & Raju, S. (2002). Intractable post-herpetic itch and cutaneous deafferentation after facial shingles. *Pain, 96,* 9–12.

Ohlsson, L., Rydberg, T., Eden, T., Persson, Y. & Thulin, L. (2002). Cancer pain relief by continuous administration of epidural morphine in a hospital setting and at home. *Pain, 48,* 349–353.

Ong, K. & King, S. (2001). Neuropathic pain of the facial region. *American Journal of Pain Management, 11*(2), 12–52.

Paice, J. (1991). Unraveling the mystery of pain. *Oncology Nursing Forum, 18*(5), 843–847.

Pain and Disability: Clinical, Behavioral and Public Policy Perspectives. (1987). Copyright 1987, 2000. The National Academy of Sciences, all rights reserved. [Available online: http://print.nap.edu/pdf/0309037379/pdf_image/125.pdf]. Accessed April 28, 2003.

Pain assessment and management: An organizational approach. (2000). Oakbrook Terrace: Joint Commission on Accreditation of Healthcare Organizations.

Pain treatment in oncology patients is ineffective. (2002). *AJN, 102*(3), 243CCC.

Pappagallo, M. (1998). The concept of pseudotolerance to opioids. *Journal of Pharmaceutical Care Pain Symptom Control, 6,* 95–98.

Pasero, C. & McCaffery, M. (1996). Postoperative pain in the elderly. *American Journal of Nursing, 96,* 39–45.

Patient Centered Strategies for Effective Management of Migraine. (2000). Monograph published by the Primary Care Network.

Patt, R. & Burton, A. (1999). Pain associated with advanced malignancy, including adjuvant analgesic drugs in cancer pain management. In G. Aronoff (Ed.), *The evaluation and treatment of chronic pain* (3rd ed., pp. 337–375). Philadelphia: Lippincott, Williams, & Wilkins.

Payen, J., Bru, O., Bosson, J., Lagrasta, A., Novel, E., Deschaux, I., Lavagne, P. & Jacquot, C. (2001). Assessing pain in critically ill sedated patients by using a behavioral pain scale. *Critical Care Medicine, 29,* 2258–2263.

Payne, R. (1989). Cancer pain: Anatomy, physiology and pharmacology. *Cancer, 63*(11), 2266–2274.

Payne, R. (1999). Assessment and management of patients with sickle cell-related pain. In G. Aronoff (Ed.), *The evaluation and treatment of chronic pain* (3rd ed., pp. 405–419). Philadelphia: Lippincott, Williams, & Wilkins.

Pendergrass, S. (1999). Cancer pain management in the elderly. *Analgesia, 10*(1), 28–31.

Perkins, F. (2002). Coping with post-herpetic and painful diabetic peripheral neuropathy: Treatment similarities and differences. *Consultant, 42*(7), 936–942.

Perry, S. & Heidrich, G. (1982). Management of pain during debridement: A survey of U.S. burn units. *Pain, 13,* 267–280.

Pinzin, E. (March April 2001). Treating lumbar back pain. *Practical Pain Management,* 14–20.

Plaisance, L. & Ellis, A. (2002). Opioid-induced constipation. *AJN, 102*(3), 72–73.

Plummer, J., Cherry, D., Cousins, M., Gourlay, G., Onley, M. & Evans, K. (1991). Long-term administration of morphine in cancer and non-cancer pain: A retrospective study. *Pain, 44,* 215–220.

Portenoy, R. (1989). Epidemology & syndromes of cancer pain. *Cancer, 63*(11), 2298–2307.

Portenoy, R. (Ed.) (1998). Definitions and principles of assessment. In *Contemporary diagnosis and management of pain in oncologic and AIDS patients* (2nd ed., pp. 14–43). Newtown, PA: Handbooks in Health Care.

Portenoy, R. & Kanner, R. (1996). Opioid analgesics. In *Pain management: Theory and practice* (p. 259). Philadelphia: F.A. Davis Company.

Portenoy, R. & Lesage, P. (1999). Management of cancer pain. *Lancet, 353,* 1695–1700.

Porter, J. & Jick, H. (1980). Addiction rare in patients treated with narcotics. *New England Journal of Medicine, 302,* 123.

Poulson, L., Arendt-Nielsen, L., Brosen, K., Nielsen, K. Gram, L. & Sindrup, S. (1995). The hypoalgesic effect of imipramine in different human experimental pain models. *Pain, 60*(3), 287–293.

Primary Care Network. (2000). Impact based recognition of migraine. In *Patient-centered strategies for effective management of migraine.* Springfield, MD: Author.

Purdue Pharma. (2000). New horizons in pain management. *Symposium Spotlight,* 1–7. Connecticut: Author.

Purdue Pharma. (2001a). Ethical imperatives in the management of pain. *Symposium Spotlight,* 14–16. Connecticut: Author.

Purdue Pharma. (2001b). Myofascial release. *Symposium Spotlight, 2,*12–13. Connecticut: Author.

Purdue Pharma. (2001c). Opioid therapy: Critical issues and new directions. *Symposium Spotlight, 2,* 1.

Purdue Pharma. (2001d). Opioid therapy: Medico-legal issues. *Symposium Spotlight,* 11–12. Connecticut: Author.

Purdue Pharma. (2001e). Pain across the life span. *Symposium Spotlight, 3,* 3–5. Connecticut: Author.

Purdue Pharma. (2001f). Pain control: A challenge for the nurse practitioner. *Symposium Spotlight, 3,* 10–12.

Purdue Pharma. (2002a). Assessing chronic pediatric pain within a family context. *Symposium Spotlight, 5,* 9–11. Connecticut: Author.

Purdue Pharma. (2002b). Ethnic and cultural influences and health disparities in the management of chronic pain disorders. *Symposium Spotlight, 6,* 6–10. Connecticut: Author.

Purdue Pharma. (2002c). Preemptive analgesia in postoperative pain: The second round will need a change in tactics. *Symposium Spotlight, 6,* 4–5.

Purdue Pharma. (2002d). Sex, gender and pain: From bench top to clinic. *Symposium Spotlight, 5,* 5–7. Connecticut: Author.

Purdue Pharma. (2002e). Sickle cell-pains and gains. In *Partners against pain,* 6(4), 4. Connecticut: Author.

Purdue Pharma. (2002f). The future of cancer pain management skills: Development of a cancer pain objective structured clinical examination. *Partners Against Pain,* 6(5), 3–4. Stanford, CT: Author.

Purdue Pharma. (2002g). Treating the spectrum of pain: From postop to beyond. *Symposium Spotlight, 5,* 1–3. Connecticut: Author.

Raj, P. & Racz, G. (1998). Role of diagnostic and therapeutic nerve blocks in the management of pain. In G. Aronoff (Ed.), *The evaluation and treatment of chronic pain* (3rd ed., pp. 505–532). Philadelphia: Lippincott, Williams, & Wilkins.

Rappoport, A. (1992). The diagnosis of migraine and tension-type headaches, then and now. *Neurology, 42*(3), (Supplement 2), 11–15.

Rappaport, A., Sheftell, F. & Tepper, S. (2001a). Rebound headache. In *Conquering headache,* (3rd ed.). London: Empowering Press.

Rappaport, A., Sheftell, F. & Tepper, S. (2001b). Treatment with medication. In *Conquering headache* (3rd ed.). London: Empowering Press.

Rasmussen, B. (2001). Epidemiology of headache. *Cephalgia, 21,* 774–777.

Rawal, N. (2001). Acute pain management. *Analgesia, 12*(2), 2–8.

Raymond, I., Neilsen, T., Lavigne, G., Manzini, C. & Choiniere, M. (2001). Quality of sleep and its daily relationship to pain intensity in hospitalized adult burn patients. *Pain, 92,* 381–388.

Ready, B. & Edwards, W. (Eds.). (1992). *The management of acute pain: A practical guide.* Seattle: International Association for the Study of Pain.

Rederich, G., Rapoport, A., Cutler, N., Hazelrigg, R. & Jamerson, B. (1995). Oral sumatriptan in the long-term of migraine: Clinical findings. *Neurology, 45*(6), (Supplement 7), S15–S20.

Reyes-Gibby, C., Aday, L. & Cleeland, C. (2002). Impact of pain on self-reported health in community-dwelling older adults. *Pain, 95*(1–2), 75–82.

Richardson, J., McGurgen, P., Cheema, S., Prasad, R. & Gupta, S. (2001). Spinal endoscopy in chronic low back pain with radiculopathy: A prospective case series. *Anesthesia, 56,* 454–460.

Riley, J. & Gilbert, G. (2001). Sex differences in negative emotional responses to chronic pain. *The Journal of Pain, 2*(6), 354–359.

Riley, J. & Gilbert, G. (2001). Orofacial pain symptoms: An interaction between age and sex. *Pain, 90,* 245–256.

Riley, J., Robinson, M., Wade, J., Myers, C. & Price, D. (2001). Sex differences in negative emotional responses to chronic pain. *The Journal of Pain, 2*(6), 254–259.

Robinson, M., Riley, J., Myers, C., Papas, R., Wise, E. & Fillingim, R. (2001). Gender role expectations of pain: Relationship to sex differences in pain. *Journal of Pain, 2,* 252–257.

Rodriguez, C. (2001). Pain measurement in the elderly: A review. *Pain Management Nursing, 2*(2), 38–46.

Rosser, J., Goodwin, M., Gabriel, N. & Saberski, L. (2001). Patient-guided mini-laparoscopy: A new strategy for abdominal pain localization. *The Pain Clinic, 3*(6), 11–15.

Rothner, A. & Winner, P. (2001). Headaches in children and adolescents. In S. Silberstein, R. Lipton & D. Dalessio (Eds.), *Wolf's headache and other head pain* (7th ed., pp. 539–561). New York: Oxford University Press.

Rowlingston, J. & Keifer, R. (1998). Low back pain. In M. Ashburn & L. Rice (Eds.), *The management of pain* (pp. 261–274). New York: Churchhill Livingstone.

Saberski, L. (Ed.-in-Chief). (2001). Pain is a serious complication of mucositis. *The Pain Clinic, 4*(1), 33.

Saberski, L. (Ed.-in-Chief). (2002). Facts on back pain. *The Pain Clinic, 4*(1), 23.

Saberski, L. & Ramiro, R. (2000). The pharmacology of chronic pain management. *The Pain Clinic,* 35–46.

Saper, J., Hinner, P. & Lake, A. (2001). An open-label dose-titration study of the efficacy and tolerability of tizanidine hydrochloride tablets in the prophylaxis of chronic daily headache. *Headache, 41,* 357–368.

Saper, J. & Lake, A. (1999). Comprehensive/tertiary care for headache: A 6-month outcome study. *Headache,* April, 249–263.

Saper, J., Silberstein, S., Gordon, C., Hamel, R. & Swidan, S. (1999). Facial pain and the neuralgias. In *Handbook of headache management. A practical guide to diagnosis and treatment of head, neck and facial pain* (2nd ed., pp. 249–270). Philadelphia: Lippincott, Williams & Wilkins.

Saper, J., Silberstein, S., Gordon, C., Hamel, R. & Swidan, S. (1999). Medications used in the pharmacotherapy of headache. In *Handbook of headache management. A practical guide to diagnosis and treatment of head, neck and facial pain* (2nd ed., pp. 61–140). Philadelphia: Lippincott, Williams & Wilkins.

Sargent, J., Kuchner, J., Davis, R. & Kirkhart, B. (1995). Oral sumatriptan is effective and well tolerated for the acute treatment of migraine: A multicenter study. *Neurology, 45*(6), (Supplement 7), S10–S14.

Schecter, N., Birde, C. & Yaster, M. (1993). Opioid agonist-antagonists. In *Pain in infants, children & adolescents* (p. 147). Baltimore: Williams & Wilkins.

Schneider, J. (1998). Management of chronic non-cancer pain: A guide to appropriate use of opioids. *Journal of Care Management, 4,* 2-8.

Schwartz, R. (2001). Neuropathic pain: Which medication and why? *The Pain Clinic, 3*(4), 21–24.

Sengstaken, E. & King, S. (1993). The problems of pain and its detection among geriatric nursing home residents. *Journal of the American Geriatrics Society, 41,* 541–544.

Severson, J. (2000). Taking aim at shingles pain. *The Clinical Advisor,* 32–38. Shankland, W. (2000). Common causes of non-dental orofacial pain. *The Pain Practitioner, 10*(4), 4–8.

Shanti, B., Tan, G. & Saliva, S. (2001). Opioid rotation: Mechanisms, concepts and benefits. *Practical Pain Management,* 8–11.

Shulman, E. & Silberstein, S. (1992). Symptomatic and prophylactic treatment of Migraine tension-type headache. *Neurology, 42*(3), (Supplements), 16–21.

Silberstein, S. (1992). Advances in understanding the pathophysiology of headache. *Neurology,* (Supplement 2), 6 10.

Silberstein, S. (1992). The role of sex hormones in headache. *Neurology, 42*(3), (Supplement 2), 37–42.

Silberstein, S. (2002). Menstrually-related migraine treatments. *Practical Pain Management, 2*(3), 24–26.

Silberstein, S. & Lipton, R. (2001). Chronic daily headache, including transformed migraine, chronic tension-type headache and medication overuse. In S. Silberstein, R. Lipton & D. Dalessio (Eds.), *Wolf's headache and other head pain* (7th ed., pp. 247–282). New York: Oxford University Press.

Silberstein, S., Lipton, R. & Goadsby, P. (1998). *Headache in clinical practice* (pp. 19–30). Oxford, England: Isis Medical Media.

Silberstein, S., Lipton, R. & Goadsby, P. (2002a). Classification and diagnosis of headache. In *Headache in clinical practice* (2nd ed., pp. 11–20). London: Martin Dunitz.

Silberstein, S., Lipton, R. & Goadsby, P. (2002b). Epidemiology and impact of headache disorders. In *Headache in clinical practice* (2nd ed., pp. 28–29). London: Martin Dunitz.

Silberstein, S. & Silberstein, J. (1992). Chronic daily headache: Long-term prognosis following inpatient treatment with repetitive IV DHE. *Headache, 32,* 439–445.

Simone, D. & Ochoa, J. (1991). Early and late effects of prolonged topical capsaicin on cutaneous sensibility and neurogenic vasodilation in humans. *Pain, 47,* 285–294.

Sinatra, R. & Aratimos, N. (2001). The anatomy and physiology of acute pain. *The Pain Clinic, 3*(6), 28–35.

Sinchyshak, M. (2001). Treatment methods. *Practical Pain Management,* 21–23.

Sindrup, S., Madsen, C., Bach, F., Gram, L. & Jensen, T. (2001). St John's Wort has no effect on pain in polyneuropathy. *Pain, 91,* 361–365.

Smuts, J., Baker, M., Smuts, H., Stassen, J., Rossouw, E. & Barnard, P. (1999). Prophylactic treatment of chronic tension-type headache using botulinum toxin type A. *European Journal of Neurology, 6*(Supplement 4), S99–S102.

Solomon, G. (1992). Physician & patient attitudes on headache. *National Headache Foundation Newsletter, 82,* 1, 6.

Solomon, G., Skobieranda, F. & Gragg, L. (1993). Quality of life and well-being of headache patients: Measurement by the medical outcomes study instrument. *Headache, 33,* 351–358.

South, S. & Smith, M. (2001). Analgesic tolerance to opioids. *Pain Clinical Updates,* 1x(5).

Stack, B., Gregory, E., Gjerde, G., Hanssen, J. & Leivseth, G. (2002). Modified meniscoplasty for treatment of chronic disc displacement without reduction: 60 patients, 117 joints. *American Journal of Pain Management, 12*(2), 53–66.

Stephens, R. (1993). Imagery: A strategic intervention to empower clients. Part II—A practical guide. *Clinical Specialists, 7*(5), 235–240.

Stevens, B. & Johnston, C. (1994). Physiological responses of premature infants to a painful stimulus. *Nursing Research, 43,* 226–230.

Stewart, W., Linet, M., Celentano, D., VanNatta, M. & Ziegler, D. (1993). Age and sex-specific incidence rates of migraine with and without visual aura. *Am J Epidemiology, 34,* 1111–1120.

Stewart, W., Lipton, R. & Liberman, J. (1996). Variation in migraine prevalence by race. *Neurology, 47,* 52–59.

Stewart, W., Schechler, A. & Rasmussen, B. (1994). Migraine prevalence: A review of population based studies. *Neurology, 44* (6 supp. 4), 517–523.

Stoddard, F., Sheridan, R., Saxe, G., King, B.S., King, B.H., Chedekel, D. et al. (2002). Treatment of pain in acutely burned children. *Journal of Burn Care and Rehabilitation, 23*(2), 135–156.

Sullivan, M., Rodgers, W. & Kirsch, I. (2001). Catastrophizing, depression and expectancies for pain and emotional distress. *Pain, 91,* 147–154.

Summer, G. & Puntillo, K. (2002). Comparing burn pain and analgesic administration between inpatient and outpatient settings. *The Journal of Pain, 3*(2), suppl 1, p22, #686.

Sweeder, J. (2002). Educating clinicians on effective pain management. *The Pain Clinic, 4*(1), 11–19.

Swope, D. (2002). *Clinical practice perspectives: Botulinum neuro-toxins, where are we now?* New York: AlphaMedica.

Tasmuth, T., vonSmitten, K. & Kalso, E. (1996). Pain and other symptoms during the first year after radical and conservative surgery for breast cancer. *British Journal of Cancer, 74,* 2024–2031.

Tavola, T., Gala, C., Conte, G. & Invernizzi, G. (1992). Traditional Chinese acupuncture in tension-type headache: A controlled study. *Pain, 48,* 325–329.

Tearnan, B. (2001). Pain, disease and suicide. *The Pain Practitioner, 11*(2), 6–8.

Tennant, F., Liu, J. & Hermann, L. (2002). Intractable pain. *Practical Pain Management, 2*(3), 8–11.

Tepper, S. (2002). Migraine: How to use acute therapy most effectively. *Consultant, 42*(8), 977–981.

The assessment and management of acute pain in infants, children and adolescents. (1991). In *APS Bulletin, 11*(5), 3–7.

Therapeutic phases of migraine. (2000). In *Patient centered strategies for effective management of migraine.* Springfield, MO: Primary Care Network.

Thernstrom, M. (Dec 16, 2001). Pain, the disease. *N. Y. Times,* Section 6.

Turk, D. & Brady, M. (1992). What position do APS's physician members take in chronic opioid therapy? *APS Bulletin, 2*(2), 1–5.

Turk, D., Okifuji, A. & Scharf, L. (1995). Chronic pain and depression: Role of perceived impact and perceived control in different age cohorts. *Pain, 61,* 93–101.

Turner, D. (Jan-Feb 2001). Relieving pain with pharmaceuticals. *Practical Pain Management,* 36–38.

Twersky, R., Lebovitz, A., Williams, C. & Sexton, T. (1995). Ketorloac versus fentanyl for postoperative pain management in outpatients. *Clinical Journal of Pain, 11*(2), 127–133.

University of Kentucky Health Care. (1999). *Chronic pain: Statistics of chronic pain.* [Available online: http://111.ukhealthcare.uky.edu/disease/spine/chrostat.htm]. Accessed June 2000.

van Dijk, M., Bouwmeester, N., Duivenvoorden, H., Koot, H., Tibboel, D. & Passchier, J. et al. (2002). Efficacy of continuous versus intermittent morphine administration after major surgery in 0–3-year-old infants; a double-blind randomized controlled trial. *Pain, 98,* 305–313.

Vellemure, C. & Bushnell, M. (2002). Cognitive modulation of pain: How do attention and emotion influence painful procedures? *Pain, 95,* 185–199.

Vick, P. & Amer, T. (2001). Treatment of central post-stroke pain with oral ketamine. *Pain, 92,* 311–313.

Vioxx significantly reduced chronic low back pain in two new studies. (2001). *The Pain Clinic, 3*(6), 29.

Von Roenn, J., Cleeland, C., Gonin, R., Hatfield, A. & Pandya, K. (1993). Physician attitudes and practice in cancer pain management. A survey from the Eastern Cooperative Oncology Group. *Annals of Internal Medicine, 119,* 121–126.

Walker, M. & Wong, D. (1991). A battle plan for patients in pain. *American Journal of Nursing, 9* (6), 32–36.

Wall, P. & Melzack, R. (Eds.) (1994). *The textbook of pain* (pp. 337–351). Philadelphia: WB Saunders Co.

Warfield, C. & Kahn, C. (1995). Acute pain management. Programs in U.S. hospitals and experiences and attitudes among U.S. adults. *Anesthesiology, 83,* 1090–1094.

Watson, C., Chipman, M., Reed, K., Evans, R. & Birkett, N. (1992). Amitriptyline versus maprotiline in postherpetic neuralgia: A randomized, double-blind crossover trial. *Pain, 48,* 29–36.

Watson, C. & Evans, R. (1992). The post-mastectomy pain syndrome and topical capsaicin: A randomized trial. *Pain, 53,* 375–379.

Watson, K., Papageorgiou, A., Jones, G., Taylor, S., Symmons, D., Silmon, A. et al. (2002). Low back pain in schoolchildren: Occurrence and characteristics. *Pain, 97,* 87–92.

Way, W. & Way, E. (1989). Opioid analgesics and antagonists In B. Katzung (Ed.), *Basic and clinical pharmacology* (4th ed., pp. 368–382). Norwalk, CT: Appelton & Lange.

Weiner, R. (2002). JCAHO pain standards: How to prepare. *The Pain Practitioner,* p. 4.

Weiss, B. & Weiss, L. (2001). Getting off the pain roller coaster. *Practical Pain Management,* 22–24.

Wesselmann, U. (1999). Management of chronic pelvic pain. In G. Aronoff (Ed.), *The evaluation and treatment of chronic pain* (3rd ed., pp. 269–279). Philadelphia: Lippincott, Williams, & Wilkins.

Wilson, M. & Cahill, C. (2001). Headache treatment outcomes: A proposed paradigm for quantitative analysis. *Cephalgia, 21*(4), 338–339.

Wolfe, M., Lichtenstein, D. & Singh, G. (1999). Gastrointestinal toxicity of non-steroidal anti-inflammatory drugs. *New England Journal of Medicine, 340,* 1888–1889.

Won, A., Lapane, K. & Gambassi, G. (1999). Correlates and management of nonmalignant pain in the nursing home. *Journal of American Geriatric Society, 47,* 936–942.

Wong, D., Hockenberry-Eaton, M., Wilson, D., Winkelstein, M. & Schwartz, P. (2001). In *Wong's essentials of pediatric nursing* (6th ed., p. 1301). St. Louis: Mosby, Inc..

World Health Organization (WHO). (1990). Expert Committee. *Cancer pain and palliative care* (pp. 3–75). Geneva: Author.

World Health Organization (WHO). (1994).
Cancer pain and palliative care: Report of a
WHO expert committee. *Technical Report
Series 804.* Geneva: Author.

World Health Organization (WHO). (1996).
*Cancer pain relief: With a guide to opioid
availability* (2nd ed.). Geneva: Author.

Worldwide Intensivist. (2001). Pain physiology.
[Available online: www.anaesthetist.com].
Accessed May 28, 2001.

Worsham, S. & Ziegler, R. (2002). Effective
approaches. *Practical Pain Management,*
16–20.

Yorent, K. (2002). Head pains. *Practical Pain
Management,* 22–26.

Young, M., O'Young, B., Stiens, S., Hoffberg, H.,
Cassius, D. & Narrow, C. (2002). Terrorism's
effect on chronic pain perception. *Practical
Pain Management,* 9–12.

Yount, K. (2002). Head pains. In M. Young (Ed.),
Practical pain management (pp. 22–26). Glen
Mills, PA: PPM Communications, Inc.

Zakreska, J. & Patsalos, P. (2002). Long-term
cohort study comparing medical oxycarbazepine and surgical management of
intractable neuralgia. *Pain, 95,* 259–266.

ZeBranek, J., Kahan, B. & Marini, R. (2001).
Managing low back pain using injection ther-
apy and spinal manipulation, part II. *The Pain
Clinic, 3*(4), 11–16.

Zlotnick, S., Prince, T. & Frenchman, J. (1997).
Cost analysis of immediate-versus controlled
release medication administration in long-term
care. *Consultant Pharmacist, 11,* 689–692.

INDEX

A

AAAM (American Academy of Addiction Medicine), 186

AAPM (American Academy of Pain Management), 2, 14, 186

absorption opioid administration, 66

abstinence syndrome, 58, 93

Actiq, 72

acupuncture
    described, 85
    nursing interventions during, 85-86

Acute and Chronic Pain Assessment Tool, 24, 26*fig*, 59

acute pain
    cancer and, 145, 146-147*t*
    described, 4, 167
    migraine headache, 48, 173-180*fig*, 175*t*, 176*fig*, 177*fig*, 178*t*
    post-operative, 42, 167-172, 169*t*, 170*fig*, 171*fig*
    sickle cell disease, 173-174
    See also pain

acute pain analgesic ladder, 171*fig*

addiction
    behavioral differences between pain patient/addict, 59*t*
    defining, 15
    fear of, 15-16, 123
    opioids and, 58-59
    pseudoaddiction vs., 58-59

A-delta fibers, 32, 33, 34, 35

adjuvants. *See* analgesic adjuvant agents

adolescents. *See* pediatric patients

AEDs (anti-epileptic drugs)
    burn injury pain and, 124, 125
    cancer pain management and, 160-161
    described, 45
    indications for use, 46
    mechanism of action, 45-46
    neuropathic pain and, 103
    nursing implications for use of, 49-50

afferent neurons, 32

African Americans, 10-11

age/pain response link, 11-12

agonist-antagonist agents, 157

AHCPR (Agency for Health Care Policy and Research), 13-14, 161, 186

AIDS/HIV patients, 133-134

American Journal of Nursing, 156

American Medical Association House of Delegates, 185

American Migraine Study II, 2

American Society of Addiction Medicine, 58

amitriptyline (Elavil), 44

analgesia, 69

analgesic adjuvant agents
    acute pain analgesic ladder, 171*fig*
    antidepressants, 44-45, 46*t*, 160
    anti-epileptic drugs (AEDs), 45*t*-46, 103, 124, 125, 160-161
    antispasmodics, 47-48
    benzodiazepines, 46-47, 161
    botulinum toxin, 48-49
    cancer pain management using, 155, 160-161
    capsaicin, 47
    described, 42, 44
    herbal agents, 49
    lidocaine, 47, 161
    psychostimulants, 47, 161
    steroids, 47, 161

analgesic overuse headache, 179

antidepressants
    administration of, 45
    cancer pain management using, 160
    mechanism of action and indications for, 44
    nursing implications for use of, 49-51*t*
    primary effects and side effects of, 44-45
    selected pain management, 46*t*
    two primary classes of, 44

antispasmodics
    described, 47-48
    nursing implications for use of, 51

anxiety, 144

APS (American Pain Society)
    benzodiazepines recommendations by, 46-47
    cancer pain relief guidelines by, 3, 161
    chronic pain survey commissioned by, 2
    on "fifth vital sign" pain score, 23
    on healthcare professional pain management variables, 14

on psychological dependence, 58
undertreated pain guidelines for, 186
arachidonic acid cascade, 33
arthritis pain, 2
ASA (aspirin), 33, 39-40
assistive devices/orthoses, 79, 162

B

back pain
case study on chronic, 97-99
chronic, 95
NSAIDs used for, 42
prevalence of, 2
treatment of chronic, 97
types of chronic low, 95, 97
baclofen, 47-48, 51, 93
BDI (Beck Depression Inventory), 85
benzodiazepines, 46-47, 161
Bextra, 155
biofeedback instrumentation, 82*t*
biofeedback therapy, 78, 81-83, 92, 132*t*
Botox, 49
botulinum toxin
differences in serotypes of, 48*t*
documentation required for use of, 49
indications for, 48
injection of, 50*fig*
migraines/headache/chronic facial pain and, 48-49,
51
nursing implications for use of, 51
pharmacology of, 32, 48
bradykinin, 33
brain, 32-33
"breakthrough" pain, 64
bronchial side effects, NSAIDs, 42
bronchspasom, 42
"bulging discs," 95, 97
burn injuries
case presentation on, 123-125
factors impacting, 122-123
mechanisms/causes of, 122
specialized populations and, 121-125

C

C7–T1 Syndrome, 142
cancer pain
acute vs. chronic, 145
ameliorating/intensifying factors of, 145
APS guidelines for, 3
assessment of, 144
barriers to management of, 138-139
characteristics of, 140, 141*t*, 142-143
constant vs. intermittent, 145

due to cancer treatment, 143-146
elderly patients with, 126*t*
etiology of, 140
location, intensity, characteristics of, 145
mechanisms of, 139
NSAIDs used for, 42
nursing interventions/treatment considerations, 146-
149
postsurgical, 143*t*
psychological state due to, 144-145
scope of, 137
suffering due to, 144
types/causes of, 139-140
types of patients suffering from, 146, 147*t*
See also pain
cancer pain management
establishing goals, 145-146
non-pharmacological approaches to, 162-163
nursing interventions/treatment and, 146-149
pharmacological therapy used in, 155-161, 156*t*, 159*t*
relative potency of opioids for, 159*t*
role of nurse in, 153-154
team involved in, 154
WHO analgesic ladder/step-wise approach to, 154*fig*-
155
cancer pain syndromes
due to tumor involvement, 140, 142
leptomentingeal metastases, 143
overview of, 141*t*
pancreatic cancer pain, 143
peripheral nerve syndromes and, 142
plexopathies, 142
cancer patients
acute cancer-related pain of, 146-147*t*
chronic cancer-related pain and, 147*t*, 148
dying with cancer-related pain, 147*t*, 149
elderly, 126*t*
five types of, 146, 147*t*
history of drug abuse/cancer-related pain of, 147*t*,
148-149
pre-existing chronic pain/cancer-related pain of,
147*t*, 148
cancer treatment pain
chemotherapy, 143
postsurgical pain syndromes, 143*t*
radiation therapy, 143
capsaicin, 47
Carpal Tunnel Syndrome, 79
case managers, 191
case presentation
on burn pain in specialized populations, 123-125
on chronic lower back/leg pain, 97-99

on epidural nerve block/analgesia, 112

on herbal agents, 49

orthoses/assistive devices, 79

cayenne (Capsaicin), 49

ceiling effect, 66

celiac plexus blocks, 114-115, 161

cerebral palsy, 48

C fibers, 32, 33, 34, 35

chemotherapy, 143

children. *See* pediatric patients

choline magnesium trisalicylate (Trilisate), 155

chrondroitin, 49

chronic back pain

case study on, 97-99

described, 95

treatment of, 97

types of lower, 95, 97

chronic facial pain, 48-49

chronic pain

cancer and, 145

cost of, 3

described, 4, 89-90

gender differences in coping strategies for, 12

neuropathic, 89, 102-103, 104*fig*-105*fig*, 106

pathogenesis of, 90

RSD/CRPS (reflex sympathetic dystrophy syndrome), 47, 79, 99-102

See also pain

chronic pain syndromes

back pain, 95

case study on, 97-99

treatment of, 97

types of chronic low back pain, 95, 97

chronic pain treatment

approaches to, 90-91

components of, 91-92

intensity of, 92-93, 95

outcomes of, 90

philosophy of, 90

types of programs for, 91

CLBP (Chronic Low Back Pain), 89

clonazepam, 46, 161

Clostridium botulinum, 48

CNS (central nervous system) side effects

NSAIDs, 41-42

opioids and, 69

coagulation side effects, NSAIDs, 41

codeine (Tylenol #3), 72

cognitive-behavioral techniques, 84

cold and/or heat application, 79, 162

constipation, 73*t*, 157

continuous intravenous infusion, 159

continuum of care, 189

coping skills enhancement, 163

CRPS (Complex Regional Pain Syndrome), 99, 114

cryotherapy/diathermy, 79-80, 162

CSCI (continuous subcutaneous infusions), 158-159

cyclobenzaprine, 93

D

Darvocet-N, 72

Darvon, 72

DDD (degenerative disc disease), 95, 97

DEA number, 70

"Decade of Pain Control and Research" (Congressional mandate), 185

deep breathing, 82

Demerol, 72-73

dendrites, 31

dependence, 58

depression, 144

DHN (dorsal horn nucleus), 32

diabetes, 2

diathermy/cryotherapy, 79-80, 162

Dilaudid, 72

Dilaudid SR, 72

disease

pain associated with, 2

prevalence of pain in malignant, 2-3

distraction technique, 82

"doctor shopping," 58

"Dolocap," 68

Duragesic, 72

E

Eastern Cooperative Oncology Group (ECOG) Minority Outpatient Pain Study, 11, 12, 138

ECOG (Eastern Cooperative Oncology Group), 3, 14, 138

EDR (electrodermograph), 82*t*

Elavil, 44

EMG (electromyograph), 82*t*

epidural nerve blocks/analgesia, 66, 67*t*, 68, 110-114

epidural space, 159-160

ethical issues, 188

ethnicity variable, 10-11

exercise

cancer pain management and, 162

chronic back pain and, 95

flexion and extension based, 80*t*

headaches and, 80-81

F

FACES Pain Scale, 27, 129*fig*

facet disease, 95

families

Family Questionnaire, 96*fig*
    role in pediatric patient care, 132
fatigue/sleeplessness, 144-145
fear of addiction
    burn injuries and, 123
    clarification of terms, 15-16
    as impeding pain management, 15
    supportive studies regarding, 15
fentanyl (Duragesic, Actiq), 72
first order pain, 33

G
GABA (gamma-aminobutyric acid), 35, 46
gastrointestinal side effects, 40-41
Gate Control Theory, 35-36, 78
gender differences
    contributing variables to, 12
    pain interventions and, 12
    pain response and, 12
geriatric patients, 125-128, 126*t*
glucosamine, 49
GON (greater occipital nerve blocks), 110

H
Headache Inventory Test (HIT-6), 85
Headache Journal, 180*fig*
headache phase, 176
headaches
    acute pain from migraine, 48, 173-180*fig*, 175*t*,
        176*fig*, 177*fig*, 178*t*
    biofeedback program for treatment of, 83
    botulinum toxin for pain of, 48, 51
    tailored exercise treatment in case of, 80-81
healthcare professionals
    DEA number assigned to, 70
    fear of addiction by, 15-16, 123
    pain management variables of, 13-16
    See also nurses; physicians
health professional variables
    fear of addiction as, 15-16
    identification of, 13-14
    knowledge deficit as, 14
    regulatory barriers to adequate pain management as,
        14-15
heat and/or cold application, 79, 162
hepatotoxicity side effects, 41
herbal agents, 49
herniated disc, 95, 97
histamine, 33
HIT-6, 178
HIT-6 (Headache Inventory Test), 85
Hospice of Bluegrass in Lexington, 185
hospice/home care nurse, 191

hydrocodone (Lortab, Lorcet, Vicodin, Vicoprofen), 72
hydromorphone (Dilaudid, Dilaudid SR), 72
hypoalgesia, 102
hypotension, 113

I
IASP (International Association for the Study of Pain), 9,
    89
IHS (International Headache Society), 173-174, 175*t*
imagery technique, 81-82
implanted pump, 113
incomplete cross-tolerance, 57
informed consent, 49
infusion systems, 112-113
International Headache Consortium, 177-178
intraspinal opioid administration, 66, 67*t*, 68
IV protocols, 179

J
JCAHO (Joint Commission on Accreditation of
    Healthcare Organizations), 4, 186
JCAHO Standards Manual, 187
JCAHO Standards for Pain Management, 4, 186-188

K
Kadian, 70
Ketorolac, 155
knowledge deficit, 14
Korean pain response, 11

L
L1 Syndrome, 142
Laminae VI, 32
Laminae VII, 32
leptomentingeal metastases, 143
lidocaine, 47, 161
Lorcet, 72
Lortab, 72
LSB (lumbar sympathetic block), 114

M
M3G, 56
McGill Pain Questionnaire, 10, 24, 25*fig*, 27
MAO inhibitors, 50
massage, 35-36
Mayday Fund Survey, 139
meaning of pain, 12-13, 163
medications. *See* pain management medications
medulla, 32
Memorial Sloan Kettering Hospital study, 133-134
menstrual migraine, 175-176
Mepergan, 72-73
meperidine (Demerol, Mepergan), 72-73, 157
meperidinic acid, 57

methadone, 70, 72, 127-128

MIDAS, 178

midbrain, 32

migraine headaches

    evaluating, 177

    Headache Journal, 180*fig*

    IHS diagnosis/criteria on, 173-174, 175*t*

    impact based recognition of, 177*fig*

    incidence and prevalence of, 174

    menstrual, 175-176

    nursing role in management of, 179

    outcomes in management of, 179

    pathogenesis of, 174-176

    rebound, 179

    therapeutic phases of, 176*fig*

    treatment of, 48, 177-179, 178*t*

MMPI (Minnesota Multidimensional Personality
    Inventory), 85

modality oriented clinic, 91

Modrol Dose Pak, 47

Modulation process, 35-36

morphine (MS Contin, Oramorph, Kadian, MSIR), 70,
    113, 127

MSIR, 70

multidisciplinary program, 91

muscle re-education, 82

Myobloc, 49

N

naloxone (Narcan), 113-114, 160

National Cancer Policy Board, 186

nausea/vomiting, 69, 73*t*, 156-157

neonates, 131

nerve blocks

    cancer pain management using, 161

    mechanisms of, 32

    non-sympathetic, 110-114

    overview of major segmental procedures, 116*t*

    overview of, 109

    SCS (spinal cord stimulation), 115-117

    sympathetic, 114-115

Neuralgic Pain, 89, 140

neuroablative procedure, 161

neurons

    physiology of pain and, 31-32

    WDR (wide dynamic range), 99

neuropathic pain syndromes

    causes of, 140

    described, 89

    mechanisms of, 102

    pharmacologic options for, 104*fig*-105*fig*

    trigeminal and post-herpetic, 102-103, 106

neurotransmitters, 35

NFACS (neonatal facial action coding system), 130

NMDA (N-methyl-D-aspartate), 35

nociceptive pain, 139-140

non-cancer pain, 2

non-opioid analgesics/adjuvants

    NSAIDs, 33, 39-42, 41*t*, 43*t*

    nursing implications for, 49-51*t*

    selected list of, 43*t*

non-pharmacological pain management

    acupuncture, 85-86

    biofeedback therapy, 78, 81-83, 92, 132*t*

    cancer pain and, 162-163

    diathermy/cryotherapy, 79-80, 162

    exercise, 80*t*-81, 95, 162

    heat and/or cold application, 79, 162

    occupational therapy (OT), 78, 92, 98*fig*, 99

    orthoses/assistive devices, 79, 162

    overview of, 77

    physical therapy, 78, 92

    post-operative, 170-171

    psychological therapy, 83-85, 92, 132*t*

    relaxation therapy, 81-83, 92

    TENS units, 35-36, 78, 92, 101, 131, 162

non-sympathetic nerve blocks

    epidural nerve blocks/analgesia, 66, 67*t*, 68, 110-114

    greater occipital, 110

    trigger point injections, 110

normeperidine, 57

NSAIDs (nonsteroidal anti-inflammatory drugs)

    arachidonic acid cascade inhibited by, 33

    cancer pain management using, 155-156

    development of, 39-40

    indications for use, 42

    listed, 41*t*, 43*t*

    mechanism of action, 40

    post-operative pain management using, 170

    side effects of, 40-42

numeric pain scale, 23, 27

nurses

    cancer pain management role of, 153-154

    case managers and hospice/home care, 191

    migraine headaches management and role of, 179

    nursing practice guidelines for pain management by,
        190

    opioid pain treatment and role of, 59-60

    pain assessment and, 27-28

    pain education by, 189

    pain management professional roles by, 190-191

    patient advocate/communication/information roles
        of, 9

    See also healthcare professionals

nursing interventions
  acupuncture and, 85-86
  cancer pain management and, 146-149
  care of persons with pain and, 189
  considerations for elderly patients, 128
  epidural analgesia and implications for, 66, 67*t,* 68, 111-112
  greater occipital nerve blocks and, 110
  implications for non-opioid analgesics, 49-51*t*
  pain cocktails and implications for, 68-69, 93, 100*fig*
  patient compliance and, 13
  for patients using opioids, 73-74
  pediatric patients and, 131-133, 132*t*
  post-operative pain management and, 172
  SCS (spinal cord stimulation) and, 117
  sensory-reactive paradigm approach to, 4-5
  sickle cell disease pain and, 173
  specific opioid-related side effects with, 69, 73*t*
  sympathetic nerve blocks and, 115
  trigger point injections and, 110

O

occupational therapy (OT), 78, 92, 98*fig,* 99
opioid conversion chart, 71*t,* 157-158
opioid dosing
  ceiling effect and, 66
  pain cocktails, 68-69, 93, 100*fig*
  routes of administration, 63-64, 66, 67*t,* 68-69, 157-160
opioids
  action at receptors, 56*t*
  acute pain management using systemic, 65*t*
  addiction and, 58-59
  cancer pain management using, 155, 156-160, 159*t*
  chronic pain management using, 93, 95
  dependence on, 58
  diversion and, 58, 60*t*
  dosing with, 63-64, 66, 67*t,* 68-69
  elderly patients and, 127-128
  equivalents/conversion chart for, 71*t,* 157-158
  incomplete cross-tolerance of, 57
  legal requirements for use of, 70
  mechanism of action, 55-56
  metabolism of, 56-57
  most commonly used, 70, 72-73
  nerve blocks using, 32
  nursing interventions for patients using, 73-74
  organ system effects of, 69
  post-operative pain management using, 169-170
  primary treatment outcomes to be assessed, 60*t*
  pseudotolerance, 57-58
  role of nurse in treatment with, 59-60

specific side effects related to, 69, 73*t*
tolerance of, 57, 93
See also pharmacotherapeutics
oral opioid administration, 64, 157
Oramorph, 70
Oregon Board of Medical Examiners, 3-4
organizational issues
  assessment of persons with pain, 189
  care of persons with pain, 189
  continuum of care, 189
  education of persons with pain, 189
  implementation of rights/ethics, 188
  improving organizational performance, 189-190
  JCAHO Standards for Pain Management, 4, 186-188
  nursing practice in pain management, 190
  response to undertreated pain, 3-4, 185-186
orthoses/assistive devices, 79, 162
osteoporosis, 2
OT (occupational therapy), 78, 92, 98*fig,* 99
Outpatient Pain Needs Assessment Survey (ECOG), 3
oxycodone (Percocet, Percodan, Tylox, Oxycontin, Oxyir, Roxicodone), 72
Oxycontin, 13, 72
Oxyir, 72
OXY-IR (oxycodone without acetminophen), 124, 125

P

pain
  acute, 4, 167-179, 180*fig,* 181
  "breakthrough," 64
  defining, 4
  patient differences in meaning of, 12-13, 163
  physiology of, 31-36, 34*fig*
  post-operative, 42, 143*t,* 168-171*fig,* 170*fig*
  problem of, 1-3, 185-186
  subjective nature of, 9-10
  See also acute pain; cancer pain; chronic pain
pain assessment
  Acute and Chronic Pain Assessment Tool, 24, 26*fig,* 59
  of cancer pain, 144
  in children, 27, 129*fig*-130
  in the elderly, 127
  instruments for, 23
  JCAHO Whole Patient Assessment of, 189
  McGill Pain Questionnaire (MPQ) for, 10, 24, 25*fig,* 27
  nurses and, 27-28
  pain scales for, 23-24*fig,* 27
  process of the, 22-23
  special populations and, 24, 27
  three truths of, 22

unresponsive patients and, 27
Pain Cocktail Form, 100*fig*
pain cocktails, 68-69, 93
pain coping strategies
    enhancement of, 163
    gender differences in, 12
pain education
    nurse role in, 189
    patient compliance and, 13
pain management
    defining, 4
    fear of addiction and, 15-16
    gender differences in treatment and, 12
    JCAHO standards for, 4, 186-188
    myths of, 21
    non-pharmacological approaches to, 77-86, 162-163,
        170-171
    nursing practice guidelines for, 190
    patient rights and ethical issues of, 188
    protocols for psychology component of, 94*fig*
    sensory-reactive paradigm approach to, 4-5
    special populations and, 24, 27, 121-134
    team approach to, 4
    See also pharmacotherapeutics
pain management barriers
    AIDS/HIV patients and, 134
    cancer pain and, 138-139
    cost of chronic pain, 3
    geriatric patients and, 126
    litigation on under-treatment and, 3-4
    Outpatient Pain Needs Assessment Survey on, 3
    pediatric patients and, 128-129
    regulatory, 14-15
pain management muscle education, 83
pain reaction variables, 10-13
pain scales
    Acute and Chronic Pain Assessment Tool, 24, 26*fig,*
        59
    choosing a, 24
    FACES, 27, 129*fig*
    McGill Pain Questionnaire, 10, 24, 25*fig,* 27
    NFACS (neonatal facial action coding system), 130
    numeric, 23, 27
    PIPP (premature infant pain profile), 130
    types of, 23, 24*fig*
    variables of, 23-24
    VAS (Visual Analogue Scale), 23, 24*fig,* 27
pain variables
    assessment, 23-24
    health professional, 13-16
    patient, 11-13
pancreatic cancer pain, 143

parenteral opioid administration, 64, 66, 158-159
paroxysmal hemicrania, 42
PAR (post anesthesia recovery), 112
partial agonist agents, 157
Partners Against Pain newsletter, 172
patient compliance, 13
patient education
    compliance and, 13
    role of nurse in, 189
patients
    AIDS/HIV, 133-134
    behavioral differences between addict and pain, 59*t*
    cancer pain and types of, 126*t,* 146, 147*t*
    candidacy for non-sympathetic nerve blocks, 111
    continuum of care of, 189
    ethical issues and rights of, 188
    informed consent from, 49
    meaning of pain to, 12-13, 163
    opioids and diversion by, 58, 60*t*
    pain assessment of unresponsive, 27
    pain education of, 13, 189
    pain in geriatric, 125-128, 126*t*
    PCA (patient controlled analgesia), 64, 66
    PCEA (patient controlled epidural analgesia), 66
    pediatric, 128-133*fig,* 129*fig,* 132*t*
    positioning for comfort, 80
    "relief-seeking" behavior by, 58-59
    variables of pain reaction by, 10-13
patient variables
    age as, 11-12
    assessment and, 23-24
    compliance as, 13
    ethnicity as, 10-11
    gender as, 12-13
    listed, 10
PCA (patient controlled analgesia), 64, 66
PCEA (patient controlled epidural analgesia), 66
pediatric patients
    barriers to pain management for, 128-129
    biofeedback and psychological interventions for,
        132*t*
    children and adolescents, 131-132
    drawing of pediatric pain by, 133*fig*
    general treatment principles for, 132-133
    nonates, 131
    nursing guidelines for, 132
    pain assessment in, 27, 129*fig*-130
    pain-related research on, 132
    procedure-related pain in, 130-131
    selected interventions for, 131
    TENS units in, 131
Percocet, 72

Percodan, 72

peripheral nerve syndromes, 142

PGE 1 and 2, 40

phantom limb pain, 103, 106

pharmacotherapeutics
  analgesic adjuvant agents, 42, 44-49
  cancer pain management, 155-161, 156*t*, 159*t*
  chronic pain management using, 93, 95
  considerations for elderly patients, 127-128
  fear of addiction and, 15-16
  migraine headache, 178*t*-179
  non-opioid analgesics/adjuvants, 39-51, 43*t*
  post-operative pain and, 169-170
  See also opioids; pain management

physiatric cancer pain management, 162

physical dependence, 16

physical therapy
  chronic pain treatment using, 92
  for non-pharmacological pain management, 78

physicians
  DEA number assigned to, 70
  fear of addiction by, 15-16
  knowledge deficit of, 14
  litigation over under-treatment by, 3-4
  See also healthcare professionals

physiology of pain
  anatomy and, 33-36
  diagrammatic outline of, 34*fig*
  major structures involved in, 31-32
  modulation and, 35-36
  transduction and, 33
  transmission and, 33-35
  WIND-UP and, 35

PIPP (premature infant pain profile), 130

plexopathies, 142

pons, 32

posdrome phase, 176

positioning for comfort, 80

post-herpetic neuralgia, 103

post-operative pain
  ambulatory surgery and, 168-169
  described, 167-168
  effective management of, 169-172, 171*fig*
  factors influencing, 168
  intensity/duration of various types of, 169*t*
  NSAIDs used for, 42
  nursing interventions and, 172
  pathophysiological process of, 170*fig*
  physiology/pathophysiology of, 168
  preemptive analgesia and, 169

postsurgical pain syndromes, 143*t*

premonitory phase, 176

Prescription Controlled Substances Policy, 93

primary burn injury pain, 122

primary pain management care setting, 190

problem of pain
  diseases states associated with, 2
  organizational response to undertreated, 185-186
  prevalence in malignant disease, 2-3
  prevalence of non-cancer pain, 2
  widespread significance of, 1

professional pain management roles
  primary care settings, 190
  secondary care setting, 190-191
  tertiary care setting, 191

progressive muscle relaxation, 82

propoxyphene (Darvon, Darvocet-N), 72

prostaglandin, 33, 40, 42

pseudoaddiction, 58-59

pseudotolerance, 57-58

psycho-educational groups, 84

psychological dependence, 58

psychologic cancer pain management, 162-163

psychometric instruments, 84-85

psychostimulants, 47, 161

PT (psychological therapy)
  chronic pain treatment using, 92
  cognitive-behavioral techniques, 84
  pediatric patients and, 132*t*
  protocols for, 94*fig*
  psycho-educational groups, 84
  psychological approach to pain, 83-84
  psychometric instruments, 84-85

Q

QOL (quality of life), 85

R

radiation therapy, 143

rebound headache, 179

rectal opioid administration, 64, 158

reflex sympathetic dystrophy syndrome. *See* RSD/CRPS
  (reflex sympathetic dystrophy syndrome)

regulatory pain management barriers, 14-15

relaxation therapy, 81-83, 92

"relief-seeking" behavior, 58-59

respiratory depression, 69, 73*t*

rofecoxib (Vioxx), 42, 155

Roxicodone, 72

RSD/CRPS (reflex sympathetic dystrophy syndrome)
  baclofen as treatment for, 47
  described, 99, 101-102
  orthoses/assitive devices for, 79
  pathogenesis of, 99-100
  signs and symptoms of, 101

stages of, 100-101

treatment of, 101

S

St. John's Wort, 49

salicylic acid, 40

scheduled drugs, 70

SCS (spinal cord stimulation), 115-117

secondary burn injury pain, 122

secondary pain management care setting, 190-191

second order pain, 33

sedation, 69

sEMG (surface electromyography), 82

sensory-reactive paradigm, 4-5

sex-related hormones variable, 12

SGB (stellate ganglion block), 114, 115

sickle cell disease pain, 173-174

Skelaxin, 93

sleeplessness/fatigue, 144-145

SMP (sympathetically maintained pain), 99

sodium pump, 31

Soma, 51

special populations

case presentation on, 123-125

described, 121

pain assessment of, 24, 27

pain from burns and, 121-125

pain in geriatric patients, 125-128, 126*t*

pain in patients with AIDS/HIV, 133-134

pain in pediatric patients, 128-133*fig*, 129*fig*, 132*t*

spinal cord, 32

spinal route opioid administration, 159-160

spinal stenosis, 97

SSRIs (selective serotonin reuptake inhibitors), 44-45

steroids, 47, 161

subarachnoid space, 160

sustained-release opioids, 156*t*

sympathetic nerve blocks

celiac plexus blocks, 114-115

LSB (lumbar sympathetic block), 114

overview of, 114

SGB (stellate ganglion block), 114, 115

syndrome oriented clinic, 91

T

TCAs (tricyclics)

cancer pain management using, 160

described, 44-45

neuropathic pain and, 103

nursing implications for use of, 49-51

tips for common side effects of, 51*t*

TENS units, 35-36, 78, 92, 101, 131, 162

tertiary pain management care setting, 191

thalamus, 32

thermal feedback, 82*t*

TMD (temperomandibular joint disease), 80-81, 85

tolerance

defining, 16

incomplete cross-tolerance, 57

opioids and, 57, 93

pseudotolerance vs., 37-38

Tourette's syndrome, 48

tramadol (Ultram, Ultracet), 72

transdermal opioid administration, 158

transduction process, 33

transmission process, 33-35

trigeminal neuralgia (or tic doloreaux), 102-103

trigger point injections, 110

Trilsate, 155

tunneled epidural catheters, 113

Tylenol #3, 72

Tylox, 72

U

Ultracet, 72

Ultram, 72

undertreated pain

Oregon Board of Medical Examiners case on, 3-4

organizational response to problem of, 185-186

University of Kentucky College of Medicine, 185

uphoria, 69

V

VAS (Visual Analogue Scale), 23, 24*fig*, 27

Vicodin, 72

Vicoprofen, 72

Vioxx, 42, 155

vomiting/nausea, 69, 73*t*, 156-157

W

WDR (wide dynamic range) neurons, 99

WHO analgesic ladder, 154*fig*-155, 173

WHO cancer pain relief guidelines, 137

Whole Patient Assessment, 189

WHO (World Health Organization), 3, 137

WIND-UP process, 35

withdrawals, 58

women

pain interventions and, 12

pain response in, 12

Wong-Backer FACES Pain Rating Scale, 27, 129*fig*

Z

Zanaflex, 93

PRETEST KEY

Pain Management: Principles and Practice

1.	A	Chapter 1
2.	C	Chapter 1
3.	D	Chapter 2
4.	C	Chapter 3
5.	A	Chapter 3
6.	A	Chapter 4
7.	D	Chapter 6
8.	D.	Chapter 6
9.	A	Chapter 8
10.	A	Chapter 10
11.	C	Chapter 10
12.	C	Chapter 11
13.	C	Chapter 12
14.	B	Chapter 5
15.	B	Chapter 7
16.	A	Chapter 7
17.	C	Chapter 9
18.	C	Chapter 13
19.	B	Chapter 14
20.	A	Chapter 15

Notes

Notes

Notes

Western Schools® offers over 2,000 hours to suit all your interests – and requirements!

	Note
Advanced level courses are denoted by the letter **A**.	

Cardiovascular
Cardiovascular Nursing: A Comprehensive Overview ....32 hrs
Cardiovascular Pharmacology ....11 hrs
A The 12-Lead ECG in Acute Coronary Syndromes ....42 hrs

Clinical Conditions/Nursing Practice
A Advanced Assessment..35 hrs
Airway Management with a Tracheal Tube ....1 hr
Asthma: Nursing Care Across the Lifespan ....28 hrs
Auscultation Skills ....38 hrs
— Heart Sounds ....20 hrs
— Breath Sounds ....18 hrs
Chest Tube Management...2 hrs
Clinical Care of the Diabetic Foot ....8 hrs
A Complete Nurses Guide to Diabetes Care...............................37 hrs
Diabetes Essentials for Nurses ....30 hrs
Death, Dying & Bereavement ....30 hrs
Essentials of Patient Education ....30 hrs
Healing Nutrition ....24 hrs
Holistic & Complementary Therapies ....18 hrs
Home Health Nursing (2nd ed.) ....30 hrs
Humor in Healthcare: The Laughter Prescription ....20 hrs
Management of Systemic Lupus Erythematosus ....3 hrs
Orthopedic Nursing: Caring for Patients with
    Musculoskeletal Disorders ....30 hrs
Osteomyelitis..2 hrs
Pain & Symptom Management...1 hr
Pain Management: Principles and Practice ....30 hrs
A Palliative Practices: An Interdisciplinary Approach ....66 hrs
— Issues Specific to Palliative Care............................20 hrs
— Specific Disease States and Symptom
    Management ....24 hrs
— The Dying Process, Grief, and Bereavement. ....22 hrs
Pharmacologic Management of Asthma...1 hr
Seizures: A Basic Overview ....1 hr
The Neurological Exam ....1 hr
Wound Management and Healing..30 hrs

Critical Care/ER/OR
Basic Nursing of Head, Chest, Abdominal, Spine
    and Orthopedic Trauma..20 hrs
Cosmetic Breast Surgery ....1 hr
A Case Studies in Critical Care Nursing...................................46 hrs
Critical Care & Emergency Nursing ....30 hrs
Hemodynamic Monitoring ....18 hrs
Lung Transplantation ....3 hrs
A Nurse Anesthesia ....58 hrs
— Common Diseases ....20 hrs
— Common Procedures ....21 hrs
— Drugs ....17 hrs
A Practical Guide to Moderate Sedation/Analgesia ....31 hrs
Principles of Basic Trauma Nursing ....30 hrs
Traumatic Brain Injury ....3 hrs
Weight Loss Surgery: A Treatment for Morbid Obesity ....1 hr

Geriatrics
Alzheimer's Disease: A Complete Guide for Nurses ....25 hrs
Alzheimer's Disease and Related Disorders ....3 hrs
Nursing Care of the Older Adult (2nd ed.) ....25 hrs
Psychosocial Issues Affecting Older Adults ....16 hrs

Infectious Diseases/Bioterrorism
Avian Influenza...1 hr
Biological Weapons...5 hrs
Bioterrorism & the Nurse's Response to WMD ....5 hrs
Bioterrorism Readiness: The Nurse's Critical Role ....2 hrs
Hepatitis C: The Silent Killer (2nd ed.) ....3 hrs
HIV/AIDS ....1 or 2 hrs
Infection Control Training for Healthcare Workers ....4 hrs
Influenza: A Vaccine-Preventable Disease ....1 hr
MRSA ....1 hr
Pertussis: Diagnosis, Treatment, and Prevention ....3 hrs
Smallpox ....2 hrs
Tuberculosis Across the Lifespan ....3 hrs
West Nile Virus (2nd ed.) ....1 hr

Oncology
Cancer in Women ....30 hrs
Cancer Nursing (2nd ed.) ....36 hrs
Chemotherapy and Biotherapies ....10 hrs

Pediatrics/Maternal-Child/Women's Health
A Assessment and Care of the Well Newborn ....34 hrs
Birth Control Methods and Reproductive Choices ....4 hrs
Diabetes in Children ....30 hrs
End-of-Life Care for Children and Their Families ....2 hrs
Fetal and Neonatal Drug Exposure ....3 hrs
Induction of Labor..8 hrs
Manual of School Health ....30 hrs
Maternal-Newborn Nursing ....30 hrs
Menopause: Nursing Care for Women Throughout Mid-Life ......25 hrs
A Obstetric and Gynecologic Emergencies ....44 hrs
— Obstetric Emergencies...............................22 hrs
— Gynecologic Emergencies...............................22 hrs
Pediatric Health & Physical Assessment....................................15 hrs
Pediatric Nursing: Routine to Emergent Care............................30 hrs
Pediatric Pharmacology ....10 hrs
A Practice Guidelines for Pediatric Nurse Practitioners ....46 hrs
Respiratory Diseases in the Newborn ....3 hrs
Women's Health: Contemporary Advances and Trends (3rd ed.)..24 hrs

Professional Issues/Management/Law
Documentation for Nurses ....24 hrs
Medical Error Prevention: Patient Safety ....2 hrs
Management and Leadership in Nursing ....20 hrs
Ohio Nursing Law: How Practice is Regulated ....1 hr
Surviving and Thriving in Nursing ....30 hrs
Understanding Managed Care..30 hrs

Psychiatric/Mental Health
A ADHD in Children and Adults ....8 hrs
Attention Deficit Hyperactivity Disorders
    Throughout the Lifespan..30 hrs
Basic Psychopharmacology ....5 hrs
Behavioral Approaches to Treating Obesity ....13 hrs
A Bipolar Disorder ....10 hrs
A Child/Adolescent Clinical Psychopharmacology ....12 hrs
A Childhood Maltreatment ....10 hrs
A Clinical Psychopharmacology ....10 hrs
A Collaborative Therapy with Multi-stressed Families ....30 hrs
Depression: Prevention, Diagnosis, and Treatment.....................25 hrs
A Ethnicity and the Dementias ....25 hrs
A Evidence-Based Mental Health Practice....................................22 hrs
A Geropsychiatric and Mental Health Nursing.............................40 hrs
A Growing Up with Autism ....21 hrs
A Integrating Traditional Healing Practices into Counseling ....35 hrs
A Integrative Treatment for Borderline Personality Disorder ....21 hrs
IPV (Intimate Partner Violence) (2nd ed.)................................1 or 3 hrs
A Mental Disorders in Older Adults ....25 hrs
A Mindfulness and Psychotherapy ....25 hrs
A Multicultural Perspectives in Working with Families ....27 hrs
A Obsessive Compulsive Disorder ....9 hrs
A Problem and Pathological Gambling ....9 hrs
Psychiatric Nursing: Current Trends in Diagnosis ....30 hrs
Psychiatric Principles & Applications ....30 hrs
A Psychosocial Adjustment to Chronic Illness in
    Children and Adolescents ....8 hrs
A Schizophrenia ....5 hrs
Substance Abuse ....32 hrs
Suicide...21 hrs
A Trauma Therapy ....11 hrs
A Treating Explosive Kids ....14 hrs
A Treating Substance Use Problems in Psychotherapy Practice ......24 hrs
A Treating Victims of Mass Disaster and Terrorism.........................6 hrs

Visit us online at
westernschools.com
for additional CE offerings!

REV.1/9/09